WHAT DOES AN ANGEL LOOK LIKE?

Does it have wings? Is it male or female? Does it speak in your language? Was it once human, now returned to earth? Or is it an eternal heavenly creature?

Listen to the little girl who was yanked from in front of a speeding bus by her angel. Or to the soldier who was saved from a Vietcong ambush by his. Or the woman who prayed to her angel to keep her child from falling to certain death. Or to any of the other men and women who tell you what their angels looked like and what their angels did, in stories that may be hard to believe but are impossible to deny.

Besides these inspiring and extraordinary stories, this amazing book will share, step-by-step, its teachings on how you can meet your own guardian angel—an angel to be by your side to guide you and protect you on life's sometimes perilous path.

This is the book you have prayed for—and it will answer your prayers.

EMBRACED BY ANGELS

How to Get in Touch
with Your
Own Guardian Angel

William A. Burt

SIGNET VISIONS

SIGNET
Published by the Penguin Group
Penguin Books USA Inc., 375 Hudson Street,
New York, New York 10014, U.S.A.
Penguin Books Ltd, 27 Wrights Lane,
London W8 5TZ, England
Penguin Books Australia Ltd, Ringwood,
Victoria, Australia
Penguin Books Canada Ltd, 10 Alcorn Avenue,
Toronto, Ontario, Canada M4V 3B2
Penguin Books (N.Z.) Ltd, 182–190 Wairau Road,
Auckland 10, New Zealand

Penguin Books Ltd, Registered Offices:
Harmondsworth, Middlesex, England

First published by Signet, an imprint of Dutton Signet,
a division of Penguin Books USA Inc.

First Printing, March, 1997
10 9 8 7 6 5 4 3 2 1

Contents

Foreword   vii

1: Angels: The New Wave   9

2: Angels: What the Experts Say   28

3: Angels as Heavenly Protectors   47

4: Angels: The Great Comforters   68

5: Angels: When a Life Is at Stake   87

6: Flesh-and-Blood Angels   104

7: Angels: The Great Healers   121

8: Good Samaritans of the Highway   136

9: Angels: Suffer the Little Children   155

10: How to Make Contact with Your Angel   173

11: A History of Angels   193

12: Honky Tonk and Other Celebrity Angels   212

13: Angels and the Near-Death Experience   231

14: Angels to the Rescue
Dramatic Historical Cases   245

15: More Tips for Making Contact
and Other Angel Miscellany   264

Bibliography   283

Contents

Foreword

From the grim streets of New York Ciy to the sunny beaches of south Florida ... from Bartlesville, Oklahoma to Kaneohe, Hawaii ... angels are everywhere.

When I began this book of angel encounters, I wanted to concentrate on the more unusual stories from today's headlines, and thought I could come up with half a dozen or so really interesting yarns.

How wrong I was! In just one exhilarating six-month period I was receiving dramatic, funny, heartbreaking, but most of all inspiring stories from angel witnesses all over the country. Hundreds of them!

My research of local newspapers, magazines and other periodicals turned up some great material. But I found the real treasure trove of angel stories on the information superhighway, via computer in the Angel Encounters forum of Compuserve.

Warm thanks to all those forum members who shared their time, friendship, and thrilling stories with me, and for granting me permission to use their names. For others, I have respected their requests for anonymity.

Thanks again Augusto Angelo-Cuzzi, Washington, DC; Meryl Johnson, New York City; Mike Frederickson, Culver City, CA; Jennifer Munro, Peggy O'Connor, Buffalo, NY; Lawrence Gray, Chicago; Rudy Smith, Kaneohe, HI; Will Burns, Providence, RI; Anne Nigh, Glen Burnie, MD; Sandy Lawson, New Jersey; Michele Daly, Rutherford, NJ; Suenette Hunsberger, Silver Springs, MD; Antonia C. Palumbo, Cynthia M. Cornish-Band, Cathryn B., John T., Mandy, Steven F., Roger, George

C. Carmen, Chris W., Joe W., Debbie J., and Cal Winston, editor of *New Frontier* magazine.

To all those who telephoned and wrote I also extend sincerest thanks, especially Sandy Humphreys, Storrs CT, for the story about her son Sam; Judy Leary, Normal, IL, for the story about her son Daniel; Jean Hill Monroe, Houston, TX; Donald E. Styck, Leesburg, GA; Marvin Wingo, Abilene, TX; the Rev. Carl C. Williams, Bartlesville, OK; Jeanne Zentner, Algona, IA; Jan Zonyk, Michigan City, IN; and Clifton Keene, San Antonio, TX.

My apologies to anyone I may have omitted, or whose stories I was unable to use for space reasons. Maybe next time.

This book is dedicated to all these people—plus my wife Norma for her time and support and the kids Nicholas, Alexander, and Victoria for their patience.

—Bill Burt
Palm Beach, Spring 1995

CHAPTER ONE

Angels: The New Wave

I know angels exist—I've even met one.

As a reporter for a national newspaper for more years than I like to think about, I spent many years covering human tragedies, homicides, human interest stories, the truly bizarre and the often unexplained. So I like to think I've seen a fair slice of life.

Behind the skepticism and cynicism that often comes with a reporter's beat, I've managed to keep an open mind. Years later, I still think back on stories that have puzzled me, particularly stories involving mysterious strangers or unidentified Good Samaritans—unsung heroes who never seemed to stick around long enough to give their name or receive due credit for their heroics.

There are some remarkable tales like these that I've never managed to get out of my mind, or been able to come up with a good, earthly explanation for.

One otherwise quiet Sunday evening, almost thirty years ago, in the south London area, there was a horrendous train crash that killed about thirty people and injured hundreds more.

I was dispatched to the scene by my news desk shortly after the crash. It was a terrible scene, as you can imagine. Rescue workers were tending to scores of people they had extricated from mangled coaches, dangling perilously above a steep embankment. There were heart-rending screams of pain and anguish from less fortunate people obviously trapped inside the wreckage.

In addition to interviewing rescuers and survivors, I was called on to help escort the walking wounded down the embankment to a makeshift first-aid station. At the

top of the embankment, rescuers were shouting out for
volunteer doctors to help tend to trapped and injured
passengers.

On one of my trips down the embankment, I saw my
first angel. She was making her way to the wreckage,
crawling up the embankment on all fours. A lady doctor, obviously.

She was an elderly woman, probably in her late 60s,
wearing a light-colored raincoat and a distinctive black
beret. I knew she was a doctor because she was lugging
along a black leather bag, of the type doctors always
carried with them on calls in those days.

I was to see that little lady many times that awful
evening over a period of several hours. She seemed to
be everywhere. She was at the crash scene administering
to trapped passengers, dispensing at the first-aid station,
and talking gently to distraught relatives as they began
arriving at the scene.

At one stage, I approached her to ask her name. "Not
now," she gently admonished me. When I filed my story
with the newsroom, I paid tribute to the tireless rescue
volunteers, referring specifically to that "yet unidentified
lady doctor—just one hero in the night of heroes."

I would catch up with her later for a follow-up story.
Or so I thought. I spent the best part of the next day
trying to find the compassionate lady doctor in the black
beret. I spoke to rescue workers, police officers, ambulance workers, local hospital officials, and other doctors
who answered the call for volunteers.

None of them were able to help me find her. I spoke
to survivors and relatives I remember seeing at the
scene. Again, I drew a blank.

But the most baffling aspect of the story is that nobody remembered even seeing a lady doctor who answered her description. But she was there. I saw her, I
spoke to her, and I was awed by the tireless way she
worked.

My only explanation: I saw an angel at work.

Well, Halo Everybody!

From my experience researching this book, I am delighted to report that most angel believers cherish their encounters with their own special angels. But they don't consider themselves to be something special. Sure it's a personal, sometimes intimate experience, but it's also an important message that they are only too happy to pass on.

All the lucky people who had angel encounters whom I spoke to were only too glad to talk openly and frankly about it. They could not conceal the joy in their voices as they recounted their amazing experiences. I found their faith and enthusiasm both infectious and refreshing.

Just a few years ago, meeting and talking with an angel was considered by many to be a taboo subject. It was considered part of paranormal lore, occultish almost. But as more light has been shone on the subject, more and more Americans are coming forward with their wonderful stories and standing up to be counted.

It used to be just Christmastime and the first Sunday in October—when the Christian church celebrates the feast day of guardian angels—that angels crossed our minds.

It's a sad reflection on the society in which we live, but it seems that times have gotten so bad that guardian angels are turning up in individuals' lives with increasing frequency. People are more receptive to the heavenly beings than ever before, say leaders of angel-related organizations and businesses.

In the past year alone, guardian angel pins are popping up all over the place. At one time they could only be found in Catholic bookstores. Now you can find them at checkout counters in card shops, florists, and drugstores.

First Lady Hillary Clinton is seldom seen without her angel lapel pin. Celebrities wear them proudly—country rebel Willie Nelson for one. And all the family members of the ill-fated Nicole Brown Simpson could be seen wearing them as they attended the well-publicized O. J. Simpson murder trial.

But the White House didn't inspire the angel pin fashion trend (although Hillary's example could not have hurt sales). Actually, angel pins have been around for years, for sale at Christian outlets.

Angel pins used to be most commonly bought as gifts for people in the hospital, starting at about 99 cents and going up to about five dollars if they contain birthstones.

One customer at an angel "boutique", Jan Weddle in Duluth, Georgia, was asked why she was buying angel pins. It turns out she was buying them for her daughter and her daughter's roommate, both flight attendants for American Airlines. Who, Mrs. Weddle reasoned, would need them more than flight attendants?

At least five mail-order companies now specialize in angel-related goods; the Golden, Colorado-based Angel Collectors Club of America has seen its membership swell from only twenty members in the mid 1980s to sixteen hundred in the mid-1990s. Founded in 1975, the club's members pay twelve dollars annual dues and receive the club's quarterly newsletter, "Halo Everybody."

"Five years ago you couldn't find angels anywhere," says Blanche Thompson, past president of the club who lives in Tempe, Arizona. "Now everyone has jumped on the bandwagon." The club exchanges information on everything from angel cookie jars and postage stamps to—of course—angel-food cake recipes.

One of the earliest angel specialty stores on record is Heaven Scent Angels, a specialty gift kiosk in the Paradise Valley Mall in Scottsdale, Arizona, which features angels and "heavenly beings" in a variety of sizes and shapes.

Entrepreneur magazine in 1994 reported that angel specialty stores were among the fastest-growing segment of the retail market.

Angels On Wing, opened by former schoolteacher Sharon Courtier in Fort Lauderdale, offers angels of every kind, from craftsy angel dolls to elegant ceramic sculptures.

Courtier says, "I feel that we have made a world that is very frustrating to us. We have to stop and remember that angels are always there to help you. All you have to do is ask."

A large set of angel wings is the first item you see when you enter Sally Allen's Angels For All Seasons store in Denver. Inside the shop, customers can enjoy a total angel experience—you can eat angel food cake while relaxing in angel wing-backed wicker chairs, or you can look up to see cupids sitting in the skylights above.

Sally's store opened recently to phenomenal business. She did $150,000 the first four months, and now plans to open up other shops of angel collectibles in an airport and a mall.

She likes to think that she is selling hope rather than mere memorabilia. "Among our customers we have a lot of people who have lost children, or they themselves are dying," she said. "Basically, it's a gathering of people who are trying to get back to God."

"Anything that comes out with angels just sells," says Ken Churchill, of Churchill's Religious Goods and Gifts, whose angel trade has picked up noticeably in the past few years.

Churchill's store, in West Toledo, Ohio, carries angel mugs, stickers, boxes, pictures, plaques, puzzles, and rings, plus a sprinkling of angelic books, and a wide selection of celestial figures, flanked by an honor guard of saintly statues.

A visit to any gift shop these days reveals right away that trumpet-blowing, sword-wielding winged seraphims aren't just for Christmas anymore. You can find their images on wrapping paper, greeting cards, picture frames, jewelry, neckties, and cocktail napkins.

In addition, Harvard Divinity School has established a course on angels; Boston College has two. Even the largest book chains have had to establish special angel sections to meet customer demand.

As well as a proliferation of angel retreats, angel workshops, and angel seminar events in practically every state in the nation, you can let your fingers do the walking and make contact with fellow angel believers via your computer keyboard. There are hundreds of lively and active angel forums and conference centers available within the maze of Internet and other computer online services.

Understandably, today's angel subculture is pretty well organized. The AngelWatch Network in Mountainside, New Jersey—founded by angelogist and best-selling author Eileen Elias Freeman—monitors angelic comings and goings in its newsletter, which has eighteen hundred subscribers.

"The world is in a lot more trouble than it's ever been. People are recognizing their own sense of powerlessness." says Freeman. "We're not the only race of intelligent beings around. There is another race—and we call them angels."

Angels have become big business. Angel artifacts sell like hotcakes, particularly around Christmastime. As well as a whole library of angel books, there are angel calendars, diaries, dolls, pins, and watches, among other items.

At the fashionable Saks Fifth Avenue and Neiman-Marcus stores, they're selling a new "Angel" perfume from French clothing designer Thierry Mugler, who believes everyone has a guardian angel—or can at least smell like one.

More than thirty specialty stores and catalog houses devoted exclusively to angel products have sprouted up across the country.

Crystal Connection, an environmentally concerned store in Austin, Texas, sells icons of plant and river angels to encourage reverence for the planet.

"Our whole store is angels," says Debbie Tompkins, co-owner of Translations in Dallas, which offers angel napkin rings, plates, and thank-you notes.

Collecting angel memorabilia has become a thriving new hobby. The all-time champion of angel collectors has got to be sixty-two-year-old Joyce Berg, whose home in Beloit, Wisconsin, is crammed with 10,455 different artifacts. "They give you a good feeling," says Berg, who greets tourists in her wings, halo, and homemade silver angel dress.

Then there's Phoenix, psychic Carole Sheely, who performs "angel readings" using tarot and angel cards, with more than one hundred figurines and pictures in her collection.

A couple of years after the train disaster encounter, I was sent to the island of Arran in Scotland's Firth of Clyde to cover a missing climbers story, a frequent occurrence in that part of the country.

By the time I got there, the two missing climbers—schoolboys, part of a youth group on a hiking expedition—had turned up safe and sound.

As I still wanted to do a rescue story about their twenty-hour ordeal atop a mist-shrouded mountain, I spoke to both boys, who were none the worse for their experience.

"We followed the lady down the mountain," both told me. Apparently a slender young woman in a white frock had appeared to them out of the mist and beckoned the lost pair to follow her. No words were spoken, and they dutifully followed her to a safe trail down the craggy mountainside where they literally bumped into an anxious search party of experienced locals.

The lost pair were unable to shed any light on their rescuer. I asked the leader of the search party about their story. "That's what they say—but we didn't see any young lady in white," he told me.

As if reading my mind, the searcher smiled, and added, "Unless it was an angel."

He had read my mind correctly.

A Growing Belief

The angel phenomena shows no sign of leveling off. Belief is continually growing. Gallup polls have found that half of the nation, including nearly three-quarters of teenagers, believe in heavenly beings.

Angels are favorites among today's youngsters. Here's the breakdown of a 1990 Gallup poll of 506 American teens aged thirteen to seventeen who were asked which paranormal phenomena they most believed in:

Angels	74%
ESP	50%
Witchcraft	29%
Ghosts	22%
Loch Ness Monster	16%

In 1993, a *Time* magazine/CNN poll reported nearly 70 percent of Americans said they believed in Angels, and 46 percent said they believe they have a personal angel watching after them.

An incredible 75 percent of respondents in a more recent survey said they were convinced of the existence of angels. And an impressive 30 percent claimed they've actually had personal encounters with angels.

And what promoted this resurgence of interest in the nineties? While the current crop of angel chroniclers did not start flooding the market with their books until the late eighties, early angel acceptance was beginning to gain in popularity in 1975 when respected evangelist Billy Graham published his international best-seller *Angels: God's Secret Agents*. It has sold close to three million copies since then and was recently reissued by the publisher as simply *Angels*.

Dr. Graham's book naturally approaches the subject of angels from the Christian platform in a book replete with biblical backup and appropriate references. Angels number in the millions, he tells us, and they warrant mention almost three hundred times in the Jewish and Christian scriptures.

When Dr. Graham wrote his book he said it was time that people were reminded of the special power and blessings offered by angels. At the time, he predicted that angels would be a comfort in a coming period of world crisis.

Twenty years later, with the selfish seventies and the greed-ridden eighties behind us, his message has taken root in the spiritually-aware nineties, with an even larger, eager audience.

God's Secret Agents got people talking about their angel experiences. Dr. Graham's seal of approval brought many believers out of the closet to talk openly about their personal angelic encounters.

As a magazine editor, over the last two decades I have published hundreds of articles, tailored for tabloid readership, about fascinating angel encounters—eyewitness accounts of angel sightings by earthlings.

Guideposts, a popular inspirational magazine founded by the late Norman Vincent Peale, has always been in the forefront with stories of angel encounters, long before the Billy Graham book.

People have always loved angel stories, acknowledges Rick Hamlin, a senior editor of *Guideposts,* because in them, "God does all the work. We all love mystery and we're fascinated with sort of a glimpse of the beyond."

Long before the current angel rage, *Guideposts* had provided a regular forum for angel stories, many of which are published in a collection called *Angels Among Us.*

Hamlin says angel stories remain among the magazine's most popular. In fact, he says, the publication's single most requested story is about an angel encounter entitled "The Host of Heaven," first published in December 1963.

This story, reprinted in numerous inspirational magazines since its publication in *Guideposts,* tells how the author, Dr. S. Ralph Harlow, a former professor of religion and philosophy at Smith College, along with his wife Marion, were walking through the woods near their home in Ballardville, Massachusetts one spring morning when they heard the murmur of muted voices in the distance. The voices seemed to be coming close at a

faster pace than the Harlows were walking. But no one
appeared to be around them.

"I said to Marion, 'We have company in the woods
this morning'," writes Dr. Harlow.

When the Harlows looked upward they saw a group
of six beautiful young women in flowing white garments
hovering about ten feet over their heads. The angelic
group were engaged in earnest conversation.

We saw ... a floating group of spirits—of angels,
glorious beautiful creatures that glowed with a spiritual aura," marveled Dr. Harlow. "We stopped and
stared as they passed over us. Their faces were perfectly clear to us. They seemed to float past us.

As they passed, their conversation grew fainter and
fainter until it faded out entirely. We stood transfixed
on the spot, still holding hands and still with the vision
before our eyes. For those split seconds, the veil between our world and the spirit world was lifted.

Afterward, comparing notes with his wife, Dr. Harlow
noted the two had seen exactly the same thing, down
to the most minute details. Although he had previously
considered angels to be largely symbolic, after that experience he was no longer a skeptic and became a devout
advocate of the existence of angels.

Guideposts always checks all stories it receives for
credibility and biblical soundness, and always tries to
ensure they are grounded in reality, says Hamlin.

The Harlows' encounter, he says, was considered a
good one because of the presence of two eyewitnesses,
and the credibility of Dr. Harlow himself, who was a
college professor with degrees from Harvard and Colum-
bia Universities, as well as Hartford Theological
Seminary.

After reading countless manuscripts about angel encounters, Hamlin has found a number of common threads in
the stories, one of which is angels who come to the rescue of stranded or distressed motorists on the highway.

They seem always to be wearing blue jeans and T-shirts. They fix the car, and when the motorist turns around to thank them they are no longer there," he says. "And a lot of the stories we get are protection stories, as one of the angel's traditional roles in life is that of protector.

The current proliferation of angel stories, says Hamlin, has come about as a popular reaction against modern-day religion's tendency to play down the transcendental, mystical side of true faith. Angel encounters are a reminder that such experiences are an important part of faith.

One other experience still itches in my memory.

This was also in the west coast of Scotland, in the fishing town of Campbelltown on the remote Mull of Kintyre.

I was dispatched there after a report about a fishing boat being lost at sea. This wasn't a regular commercial fishing boat. It was more like a social club fishing trip, with about twenty to thirty souls on board—fathers, sons, uncles, grandfathers.

Anyway, the boat was long overdue. It was a stinking, howling night. Around eleven o'clock, townspeople gathered anxiously at the pier, staring beyond the sheltered harbor toward the treacherous black storm-tossed Atlantic.

Suddenly the lost boat appeared at the entrance to the tiny harbor. It was battered, crippled, its engine barely sputtering. And tragically three locals had been lost at sea, swept overboard at the height of the storm that popped up from nowhere.

I interviewed most of the people on board about their experience. They had been drifting aimlessly at the mercy of the storm for hours. Their equipment on board wasn't functioning. They tried to hug the shore, but were in constant danger of being thrown against the rocks on the craggy coastline.

Out of the pitch blackness, the desperate fishermen

saw a series of sparks. "It was as if someone was flicking a huge cigarette lighter," one of the survivors told me.

As they neared the constant flickering lights, they saw that the signals were coming from hands belonging to a mysterious figure perched precariously on a rock. Despite being lashed by wind and rain, the figure steadfastly stood his or her ground as it continued to send out a series of sparks.

Yes, the figure on the rock guided the boat to the harbor entrance—and to safety. Yet no one waiting at the pier saw the series of sparks that led the boat in.

Townspeople had set off flares at the pierside as a signal to the lost boat, but none of the survivors had seen them. All they remembered was the flickering series of sparks coming from a craggy, almost inaccessible promontory almost half a mile away.

As you'll have gathered by now, no one was ever able to come up with a satisfactory explanation for the figure on the rock, or for how on earth he or she managed to produce a continual series of bright sparks on a miserable night.

I'm convinced that's because there is no earthly reason. A whole town is convinced that angels were at work that sad night.

We Can All Share

In times of trouble, particularly where there is personal anguish and suffering, you can be sure loving and compassionate guardian angels will be there.

I'm convinced they are with us right now, even as you read these words.

As you read the inspirational and moving stories in the pages of this book, don't despair if you don't number among the many thousands of Americans who have had close and life-changing encounters with their personal guardian angels.

You too can share in the miraculous angel experience.

As you read these thrilling firsthand stories shared by those whose lives have been wonderfully transformed by making contact, you will also begin to learn the secrets of how you too can recognize the existence of your own guardian angel, make contact, and begin a lifelong dialogue that will change your life.

Angels have been with us from time immemorial. But it is only in recent years that they have become imbedded in the public consciousness. And all around the world fervent angelogists—as they are now calling themselves—are fanning the flames and keeping the angel phenomenon very much alive.

Angel belief is probably at its highest level in three hundred years, since the eighteenth century Age of Enlightenment when an era of scientific discovery cast doubt on all things paranormal and supernatural.

Belief in angels was one of the casualties of this so-called period of logical thinking, although angels did show up in various commercial forms around Christmas (usually as a tree decoration) and in movies (more often than not, as fantasy fun figures).

Today, angels have returned with a vengeance (in the benign sense of the word, of course). And they have crossed denominational lines. From the devoutly religious to earnest New Agers, angels are in.

Although most angel believers cherish their encounters with their own special angels, they do not consider themselves to be something special.

Sure it can be a personal, intimate experience, but all the lucky people I spoke to who have had angel encounters were only too glad to talk openly and frankly about them. They could not conceal the joy in their voices as they recounted their amazing experiences.

A few years ago, meeting and talking with an angel was considered by many to be a taboo subject—paranormal or even occult. But as more light has been shed on the subject, more and more Americans are coming forward with their wonderful stories and standing up to be counted.

While some have preferred to have their names and

locations disguised for obvious personal reasons, most of the angel believers I interviewed were only too glad to give me their real names, plus a little background about themselves.

They don't consider themselves custodians of some sacred trust. They want everyone to get a piece of the excitement, happiness, and wonderment their angels have brought them.

The advice and encouragement of these eyewitnesses—along with encouraging words from other experts in the field of angelology—will encourage you to go ahead and make contact with your own angel right now.

And once you have mastered the secrets of making angel contact, this book will also detail the wonderful ways your angel can nurture and guide you through life's most critical emotional and physical crises.

Once you have learned to enjoy the thrill of being embraced by your own angel, you'll begin an enlightening journey that could even save your life, as thousands have found out to their eternal gratitude.

As people from all walks of life are finding all sorts of reasons to seek answers about angels for the first time, they are asking all kinds of questions about angels.

What is their nature? Why do they appear to some people and not to others? Do people turn into angels when they die? What role do they play in heaven and on earth? You will find the answers to these questions here.

What Does Mainstream America Think?

America's biggest-selling tabloid newspaper, *The National Enquirer*, often has, like it or not, a better feel for the pulse of the everyday man than most of its mainstream counterparts.

For forty-plus years it has faithfully been documenting stories of angel encounters and experiences, long before angels became popular among more elitist groups. The paper's 1994 nationwide man-in-the-street poll made interesting reading.

Do you believe in angels? was the question the paper asked. A surprising eight out of every ten people who were asked that question in the survey said they were convinced angels are real. Eighty percent, as opposed to the more often quoted sixty-nine percent in the 1993 *Time* magazine/CNN poll, believe in angels.

One hundred people in five cities across the United States were surveyed and here's what they said:

"I believe in angels," declared Peggy Clenney of Dallas. "Several years ago, I had a bad car wreck. I was scared and upset. But a lady came to the car window and as soon as she appeared, I felt an unusual peace."

"When I need angels, they seem to be around for me," said Joanne Santoro of Chicago.

John Yoon of Los Angeles explained, "Angels are messengers from God. They also help determine our future by intervening in our lives."

Slightly more women than men believe in angels. And the survey city where people are most likely to believe is Orlando, Florida, where 95 percent told us the heavenly spirits are real.

In Chicago, 80 percent said they believe in angels. And in Los Angeles, Philadelphia, and Dallas, 75 percent are believers.

"I believe in angels," said Susan Dahlin of Orlando. "I have an eighteen-month-old daughter who had open-heart surgery when she was only eight months old. She survived—and I feel a guardian angel was by her side."

In another nonscientific poll by the *Arizona Republic* newspaper, Carol Neumann, who is working toward a master's degree in interior design at Arizona State University, said she has never seen the glow of a halo, heard a heavenly voice, or felt the divine rush of wings, yet her faith in angels is undiminished. "Maybe I'm naive, or maybe it's wishful thinking, but as the world gets worse, I choose to believe in them more. I think the world would be a better place if everyone believed in angels."

Angels: Stars of the Silver Screen

As well as a whole slew of angel-themed books and magazines, television and movies appear to be held aloft by angels these days. The public's appetite for angel-oriented shows was whetted in the 1980s by the late Michael Landon's "Highway to Heaven" television series—a precursor of the later "Touched by an Angel" series, which stars Roma Downey as an angel-in-training and Della Reese as her training officer.

"The concept of angels is testing through the roof," says program researcher David Poltrack of CBS, the network behind "Touched by an Angel."

All the major networks have aired angel specials, among them NBC's two-hour special, "Angels: The Mysterious Messengers," and a PBS program in the works, based loosely on David Connolly's book, *In Search of Angels.* Fox network's "Encounters" has had a special angel segment.

ABC, at the time of writing, was prepping another angel series, "Heavens to Betsy," starring Dolly Parton. And Aaron Spelling launched "Heaven Help Us," an angel series starring John Schneider and Ricardo Montalban.

Oprah, Geraldo, Sally Jessy, and Donahue, to name just a few, along with all the TV talk shows and tabloid news magazine shows, have featured segments with angelogists.

Movies featuring angels have always done well at the box office—the best-loved one of all time is *It's a Wonderful Life*, the Jimmy Stewart classic shown repeatedly at Christmastime.

Stewart's character, George Bailey, is saved from suicide by his guardian angel Clarence. And who could ever forget that sappy, happy ending when a tinkling Christmas tree bell ornament signals that Clarence, the bumbling angel in training, has at last earned his wings.

In the film *Grand Canyon*, Kevin Kline plays a Los Angeles businessman on his way to a meeting when he steps off a curb directly into the path of a speeding bus. Suddenly, a hand grabs him and yanks him back to safety. His savior is a young woman wearing a Pittsburgh Pirates baseball cap. "Was that a real person?" he ponders. "Or was that something else—you know, sent from somewhere else?" Angels at work again in Hollywood.

The hit movie *Field of Dreams* never actually addresses the subject of angels directly, but moviegoers are in little doubt that the disembodied voice that told Kevin Costner, "If you build it, he will come," is the voice of an angel on earth to heal emotional hurts in the father–son relationship between Costner's character and his deceased father.

And in *Heaven Can Wait*—a remake of the 1940s angel movie *Here Comes Mr. Jordan*—Buck Henry is the mischievous angel whose job is to take care of unfinished business after the premature death of an irresponsible football star, played by Warren Beatty.

Audiences were both thrilled and puzzled by *Wings of Desire*, a 1988 German film about a hero angel called Cassiel hovering above the skies of West Berlin. It was so well received by critics that the Germans made a sequel in 1994—*Faraway, So Close* in which hero angel Cassiel was still hovering over Berlin, offering us mere mortals hope for a saner and better future.

More recently, *Angels in the Outfield* is one of several angel-oriented theatrical releases that have done well at the box office. More are in the planning stages, since Hollywood has achieved considerable success with other heavenly offerings, from golden oldies *I Married an Angel*, *It's a Wonderful Life*, and *Heaven Knows Mr. Jordan* to the more recent *Heaven Can Wait*.

Angels have even invaded Broadway, and not just as financial backers. Tony Kushner's Pulitzer prize-winning *Angels in America*, the story of a divine messenger who ministers to a man with AIDS, closed recently, although a movie version is now in the works.

"So Where Do I Fit In?"

Although there's been much said, written, and televised about angels in recent years, all too often what has not been addressed is the reader's most frequent question: What about me?

Sadly, most of us are left a trifle frustrated, not realizing that we too can enjoy and share in the companionship of these warm, compassionate beings who are continually watching over us.

I hope that in these pages the reader will discover and appreciate, perhaps for the first time, the fact that it's not a terribly difficult leap for all of us to make contact with a loving spirit who will remain our most trusted and closest friend for life.

Angel believers, including many respected academics and scholars, will also tell how making angel contact:

- Eases the fear of death or dying by providing reassuring glimpses into what awaits on the other side.
- Ensures you will always have someone to talk to in your darkest moments.
- Helps you cope with illness, bereavement, and other types of anguish.
- Banishes loneliness forever by offering a comfortable shoulder to cry on twenty-four hours a day.
- Convinces even the most skeptical among us that the solutions to the most difficult of life's problems are only as far away as that angel on their shoulder.

It is no accident that angel interest is at a peak today—probably more than at any other time in history.

Why? Experts offer a variety of logical explanations (none of them, fortunately, in "The End of the World Is Nigh" category). They are:

- Angels exemplify love—the driving force of the 1990s, as opposed to the materialism and greed that were rampant in the 1980s.
- Angels are the ultimate companions. Loneliness is one of the biggest scourges in today's society; everyone yearns for companionship.
- Angels symbolize trust. In a society in which truth and honesty are often at a premium, it's comforting to know there are people you can trust with your life.
- Angels extend hope. They are beacons of hope for a secure and contented life, as well as the promise of a wonderful life hereafter.

In this book, you will read and enjoy stories of angels who bear the gift of comfort. And comfort is a powerful theme in angel stories. Whether they're encountered on a battlefield or in a hospital ward at the bedside of the dying, angels are comforting presences bearing souls away to heaven.

Angels play an especially important role as transistors to the hereafter. They reassure both the patients and those they love that whatever will come next is not to be dreaded.

Assures evangelist Billy Graham in his book, *Angels* (Word Publishing): "When we die, an angel will be there to comfort us, to give us peace and joy even at that most critical hour. I am convinced angels are helping us every day, comforting us in times of sorrow, and rescuing us when we are faced with adversity."

CHAPTER TWO

Angels: What the Experts Say

Angels appear in all shapes and forms, and have been described in various ways by many—some with very well-known names—from all walks of life.

Some have seen angels in the classical sense—glowing figures clad in white. Others have seen angels as children, some as men dressed in black, some as black men dressed in white—even some in the guise of a warning pet or other animal.

They exist for all of us, albeit in different forms. Down through the ages, witnesses both famous and ordinary have reported experiencing the grace and uplifting power of angels.

In the Middle Ages, Joan of Arc, the sixteen-year-old farm girl who led an army that defeated the English and saved the French throne, said she was inspired by the voices of the two archangels, Michael and Gabriel.

And the father of our country, George Washington, often spoke of being supported by the presence of his guardian angel. Washington even credits his success at Valley Forge to an inspiring visit from his angel, who appeared to him during that terrible winter when he was at a low emotional ebb and gave him the faith that assured him of victory.

Another famous president, Abraham Lincoln, revealed that he too sought the wisdom and counsel of his guardian angel while in the White House, as he agonized over how best to unite his troubled nation during that dark period of bloodshed and dissent. Lincoln even mentioned angels in one of his famous speeches when he called upon "the better angels of our nature" to help heal our nation.

Great heroes and adventurers of history even called on angels to assist them during bleak moments. South Pole explorer Sir Ernest Shackleton told how he and his expedition were always aware of "one more" in their midst as they made dangerous treks across treacherous ice.

And when famous mountaineer Francis Sydney Smythe set out to scale Mount Everest in the 1930s, he claimed there was "a friendly presence" climbing at his side throughout the hazardous expedition. This friendly presence was so real to him and made him feel so safe in the jaws of great danger that, at one point, reported Smythe, he even divided his meager ration of chocolate to share with it. "In its company," he recalled, "I could not feel lonely, neither could I come to any harm. It was always there to sustain me on my solitary climb."

While making his celebrated transatlantic flight, air pioneer Charles Lindbergh talked about the "presence" that was in the cockpit with him as he flew across the Atlantic, watching over him when he accidentally dozed off.

Another flying ace, Captain Eddie Rickenbacker, is convinced God sent an angel to rescue him and his flying crew as they faced certain death after crash-landing in the South Pacific during World War II.

After Captain Rickenbacker and his crew were forced to ditch their B-1 in the treacherous ocean, nothing was heard from them for weeks and they were given up for dead. Back home, a nation prayed for a miracle.

Later, when he was safely returned stateside, Rickenbacker recounted a remarkable story of how he and his companions survived. They were adrift in a rubber raft with no food, perilously close to death, when a miracle happened.

"A gull came out of nowhere and lighted on my head," recalled Rickenbacker. "I killed him and we divided him equally among us. We ate every bit. Nothing ever tasted as good." That was a profound and meaningful experience for war hero Rickenbacker. It totally changed his life in postwar years.

The great composer, George Handel, experienced a celestial encounter while completing *The Messiah.* When he finished composing the "Hallelujah Chorus," a servant found him sitting alone with tears streaming down his face. "I did think I did see all heaven open before me!" Handel exclaimed.

Images of Angels

Just as the role of angels has evolved through the ages, so has their look.

For thousands of years, in ancient Near East cultures from Mesopotamia to Israel, angels wore no wings. They didn't need them—the biblical account of Joshua's dream, for example, has angels climbing between heaven and earth on a ladder.

During the rise of Christianity, angels went through a major makeover. In the Greek philosophy of the time, angels, like humans were believed to have souls. "Psuche" or "psyche," the Greek word for soul, came to be represented by butterfly wings and Cupid-like infant figures fluttering in the air. From that point on, angels sprouted wings in Jewish, Christian, and, later, Islamic imagery.

Modern-day witnesses have reported angels in the form of old men, old women, departed relatives, strangers in white, young women in white, black men driving white Cadillacs, unseen hands and arms, unseen forces, clouds of white light—even friendly animals or birds.

Certainly no one in my research reported seeing a fierce multiheaded creature brandishing a sword. The closest report to that was the vision of the Archangel Michael astride a white horse, sword upraised, who came to the aid of Allied soldiers during a World War I engagement.

In other, less ponderous literature, angels and what form they take are discussed in gentler terms. Traditionally, angels were said to assume bodies only as needed to carry out a task. This meant that they had no gender, despite the sentimental Victorian image of the pale, gentle-eyed virgin with wings.

One particularly fascinating case history I came across—described by two different families in different parts of the country—is of an angel who appeared to them as "a black man driving a white Cadillac."

Other witnesses report their angels as pretty girls; some describe elderly men with long white beards. In some instances, angels have been merely a disembodied warning voice or a strong invisible hand.

While witnesses and researchers might differ as to what form an angel takes, all are agreed on one thing: The encounter is a thrilling emotional high. And you will be left in no doubt that you are making contact with the real thing when your angel appears to you—regardless of its race, shape, gender, or form.

Billy Graham's Angels

Despite the subject's checkered history that spans the centuries, few mainstream theologians have cared to address the subject. The first in modern times was probably the celebrated evangelist Billy Graham who, with his immensely successful 1975 book, *Angels: God's Secret Agents*, fanned the flames of belief again and sold a staggering 2.6 million copies.

Two decades ago, when he first published his book, Dr. Graham wrote that he was convinced angels exist to provide unseen aid on our behalf. But he admitted, "I do not believe in angels because I have ever seen one—because I haven't. I believe in angels because I have sensed their presence in my life on special occasions."

Since then, however, the famed evangelist has experienced a profound and personal experience with a guardian angel.

At the age of seventy-four, he was diagnosed as having

Parkinson's disease along with a few other debilitating ailments normally associated with advancing years.

Understandably exhausted after half a century of spreading the gospel around the world, Dr. Graham admits that he came close to asking God to take him home—only to experience an incredible encounter with his guardian angel, who revealed to him that his work on earth was not yet complete.

Reassured and reinvigorated after the encounter, Dr. Graham later announced to his associates that his ministry was far from finished. "Like Jacob, who wrestled all night with God, I fought with my guardian angel when he told me I could not enjoy the bliss of heaven until my work on earth was done," Dr. Graham confided.

"Unlike Jacob, I didn't win," Graham admitted. "Once I realized that I was resisting God's will—and not my guardian angel's—I accepted it, as I always have. The angel convinced me, I must continue my work on Earth. He saved my life!"

Said a ministry colleague: "Billy's never made a secret of his yearning to lay down his burdens in this life and move on to the glories of the next, but he's always been content to await God's call."

That was before he had his angel experience, followed by a series of other encounters, during one of which he was even given a glimpse of heaven. Said another colleague, "Billy has told his family and close friends of a spectacular celestial experience in which he glimpsed heaven, and he says that words alone can't convey to the world the splendors of what he saw.

The glimpse of heaven came after his most recent angelic visit. "His guardian angel appeared to him as a winged warrior dressed in radiant white garments. The angel spoke to him but not in any language he recognized ... although he understood every word the angel spoke," revealed the preacher's friend. The angel told him he had been looking after him all his life.

Dr. Graham's friend recounts the glimpse of heaven revealed to the evangelist by the angel:

Its awesome beauty was so inspiring, Billy could not describe it, other than to say it was the most wonderful experience of his life.

Billy said his guardian angel whispered that God himself would welcome Billy when he finally came before him. The angel's message was that God wasn't ready to call Billy home, and that he must continue to spread God's word as long as the Lord wants him to.

Now he has a good explanation for why he's working so hard," added the friend. "He has direct orders from his guardian angel, and even if he doesn't relish it, he's determined to obey. Billy has accepted God's will that he remain here a while longer and continue his work. He's acting like a new man.

Thanks to his recent experiences, Billy Graham is one of the lucky few who have not only met their special angels, but who know exactly how their angels look. Others are less fortunate and can go a lifetime conversing with their angels without actually enjoying any kind of vision or physical confrontation.

So What Can We Expect?

Why should we believe angels exist? And what can we expect to see behind their voices? It depends on who you ask. Here's a roundup of expert opinions:

Poet Margaret Gibson of Preston, Connecticut, admits she doesn't know exactly who her angels are or what they might look like, but she has had dreams of angels that crop up all the time in her writing. She is working on a novel-length poem in which one character has visions of angels.

Angels, she says, are invaluable because they get us talking about parts of our inner selves we normally would not discuss. And there's no harm in imagining what they might look like.

"The ability to imagine is very vivid. It's hard to discriminate between the images we create and those that come from other sources," Gibson says, adding with a laugh, "So I've managed to get them delightfully mixed up."

Regina Plunkett Dowling, chaplain at St. Joseph College in West Hartford, Connecticut, says her idea of angels is "something more concrete than vague divine energy." Says Rev. Dowling, "In situations where I had gotten myself into some difficulty, I felt I was not alone."

For the Rev. Marc Neal of the Jerusalem Missionary Baptist Church in Akron, Ohio, "Angels are real." Like most clerics, he points to the Bible as proof:

> Psalms 14:8 declares that God created the angels. I believe in guardian angels as well. Psalms 34:7 says, "The angel of the Lord encampeth around about them who fear Him." So God does have angels watching over those who reverence Him.
>
> Also, Matthew 18:10 says, "In heaven their angels do behold," personalizing it, meaning each child has an angel. And some have come in contact with angels and not even known it, based on Hebrews 13:2, "Some have entertained angels unaware."

Since there are almost three-hundred biblical references to angels, it is impossible for clergy, theologians, and academics to ignore them. More experts than ever before acknowledge the reality of angels and the role they play in everyday life.

Reverend Robert Haas, pastor of Toledo, Ohio's Good Shepherd parish and a lifelong angel believer, agrees: "People want something beyond to give meaning to life, to reach God. But God is so vastly superior to us. Angels are above us, but they're kind of more on our level."

Reverend Edward O'Connor, who taught theology for forty-one years at the University of Notre Dame, said he thinks the revival of interest in angels follows a period in which they were neglected: "Intellectuals in the church by and large don't believe in them and brush them off, so they disappeared from currency until people realized they lost something important."

The Rev. Maurice Roy, pastor of Holy Angels Church in St. Albans, Vermont, said for some religions, angels are an informal tradition. "There has been kind of a tradition in the Catholic church of each person having a guardian angel watching over them," he explains.

Angels have always been a part of the scriptures of Judaism, Christianity, and Islam. Today they are also a part of New Age teachings, in which they are looked on as spiritual resources that can be tapped for personal well-being and self-improvement.

The more orthodox view of angels, drawn from the more religious Judeo–Christian tradition, is that they are spiritual beings created by God to serve God and to aid humanity. Although they possess understanding and free will, they are considered superior to humans. Many believe angels have the ability to take on human form to deliver messages.

And, as depicted in popular film portrayals, they also have the ability to reveal themselves as departed relatives and other humans who have died and gone to heaven— although that is not supported by all religious viewpoints.

Belief in angels has been a part of Catholic doctrine since 1215 A.D., said the Rev. Warren Murphy, pastor of St. Andrew's Catholic Church in Fort Worth. But teaching about guardian angels is no longer emphasized. Still, says Father Murphy, there are ample angel references in the New Testament for those who choose to believe, and he cites Matthew 18:10, in which Jesus said, "Take heed that ye despise not one of these little ones: for I say unto you that in heaven their angels do always behold the face of my Father which is in heaven."

Angels have emerged as one way of explaining how God relates to the world, says Nadia Lahutsky, associate professor of religion at Texas Christian University: "I think there is a kind of a renewed interest in religious matters in general, and this could be the root of this new interest in angels."

Kimberly Patton, a comparative and historical religion professor at Harvard University, says the reason for the resurgence of angel belief is simple: "Angel figures appear during times of great anxiety and fear about the possibility of a people's future existence. I think that is why they are so popular right now. People are unsure of their personal place in the world and they like to think that something is watching over them."

William S. Babcock, professor of church history at Southern Methodist University's Perkins School of Theology and author of the chapter on angels for the 1991 tome, *Encyclopedia of the Early Church*," speaks for many clerics when he describes current interest in angels as "faddish" and says, "I think for most contemporary Christians, angels are not a functioning part of their religion. We are not for or against them. We just don't think about the subject."

Nevertheless, angels play a persistent role in religious history, said Babcock, who points out: "We still have angels' names everywhere. For instance, we have a St. Michael and All Angels Episcopal Church in Dallas, and Michael is an archangel."

On the other hand, committed believer Father Donald Fisher, pastor of a Catholic parish in Dallas, asserts that angels are making a legitimate comeback: "It's not a fad or a trend. It's just happening. We are more in need of support from beings more intelligent and more attuned to the spiritual world than we are. I definitely feel that I have been in the presence of angels. I just feel I have a very strong contact with a figure who is my guardian angel. I pray with this person and seek his guidance." Or *her* guidance, perhaps?

Why this upsurge in belief? The belief in angels implies that we are not alone in the universe, that someone up there likes me. "It's a New Age answer to the homelessness of secularity," says theologian Ted Peters, of Pacific Lutheran Theological Seminary in Berkeley, California.

"Most people think of angels as benign, pleasant, and helping," observes University of Wisconsin psychiatrist Richard Thurrell. "And it's nice to have comfort in a cruel world."

"Angels are a direct line to heaven," opines the Rev. Karl Chimiak, a Silver Springs, Maryland, priest who credits angel awareness with boosting church attendance. That's why he now holds an annual two-day seminar devoted exclusively to the Catholic Church's teachings on angels. After all, he points out, Pope John XXIII is on record as urging parents to teach their children about guardian angels.

New Ager Murray Steinman, a spokesman for the Church Universal and Triumphant in San Francisco, is just as quick to speak up for angels. It was a guardian angel, he claims, who saved him from street muggers just recently.

"I made some quick, silent prayers to the Archangel Michael, and it just turned things around. The muggers retreated," says Steinman. Angel intervention transcends all recognized religious boundaries, he adds. Communication with angels starts "if you just suspend belief and just recognize they are there. Everyone I know has a working relationship and a living relationship with angels. It's a constant daily interaction. It's like what you'd have with your wife and kids."

"When I die," says Lawrence S. Cunningham, chairman of the University of Notre Dame's theology department, "I'll be very disappointed if I don't meet any angels."

"Angels represent God's personal care for each one of us," says Father Andrew Greeley, the famous Chicago-based sociologist-novelist.

Reverend Robert C. Wolf, of Guardian Angels Catholic Church, Copley Township, Ohio, refers us to the Book of Exodus where God says, "See, I am sending an angel before you to guide you on your way."

The Bible provides proof of the existence of angels, says Father Wolf. "They were made by God before human beings. They serve as messengers to inform, guide, warn, and protect people. Some are called 'guardian angels.' Tobit was assisted by the guardian angel Raphael. An unnamed angel stood by Jesus in the Garden. We have many 'guardian angels' besides our invisible, spiritual friends. They are people who help, guide, and protect others. We are grateful to have the heavenly spirits protect us, and we also need to be human guardian angels to each other [see Chapter Six]."

Rabbi Zushe Greenberg of the Chabad Jewish Center of Solon, Ohio, agrees. He says;

> Judaism emphasizes that the most important point in the universe is the person. Better to improve this world than to search for what is going on in the world above us. So angels are not a central issue, but they are real. In many places in the Bible, they are mentioned. But the angels are like robots, only messengers from God. Many people think they can pray for an angel to help them. An angel cannot help them; God can. For every good deed, you create a good angel. From a bad deed comes a bad angel. Only humans are created in the image of God—with free will. Angels do not have it. That is why Judaism is about people, not angels.

But the Reverend Julia Johnson-Topa of the Unity Chapel of Light in Tallmadge, Ohio, not only accepts a more realistic viewpoint about angels, she has had a personal experience to prove it. "Angels are a present reality for me, because the Bible says, 'For He will give his angels charge of you' [Psalm 91]. Angels ministered to Jesus and, if we live in an awareness of their presence, will minister to us too. Sometimes they will come as divine ideas that give us guidance, and sometimes they will appear as persons," she says.

"Once, lost and frightened on a dark road, I prayed for help. Out of nowhere, a policeman appeared, who showed me the way out. I thanked him and said, 'You are an angel.' He replied, 'Yes, I am.' Then he disappeared. There is no doubt in my mind that I entertained an angel in disguise that night."

"Every man has a guardian angel, from the beginning of their existence," declares Monsignor Alessandro Maggiolini, one of the Vatican's top theologians. "Guardian angels aren't the stuff of fables. They're spiritual beings who work hard for our benefit."

What theologians are somewhat reluctant to address is exactly what angels are supposed to look like. And when they do, their impressions are often at odds. For example, one Vatican theologian, Monsignor Giuseppe Del Ton, who has researched the subject, describes angels thus:

> They have eyes which see, ears that hear, hands that touch, and hearts that love. They are extremely clever and each has his own personality. Each human being has his own guardian angel, assigned to him from the very first day of his life. This angel has the precise task of taking care of his protégé and is responsible for him.

Canadian anthropologist Ian Currie is convinced that angels are indeed entities with a special mission to help us, but he leans towards the belief that angels are entities without bodies.

"They often coach us, or offer intense emotional support, or give us advice without us even knowing it. In some cases, they have saved their charges from harm, or even death," says Professor Currie, who has regressed subjects hypnotically and had them describe their guardian angels in detail to him. "Their descriptions tend to be classical—people in robes with bright light surrounding them."

In the face of much skepticism, human belief in angels has withstood the test of time as evidenced today with more and more people coming forward to share their intimate stories of heavenly visitations.

Angels are all around us. They are more popular— and more visible—today than ever before. And while angels have always been with us, it's as if we have just discovered them.

Tens of thousands of people from all walks of life have been helped, guided, saved, or comforted by their guardian angels and are eager to reveal their close encounters with these heavenly beings.

"With angels around, people feel they don't have to bother an Almighty God in order to get help," says Professor Robert Ellwood, a specialist in unorthodox religions at the University of Southern California.

At his First Church of the Angels in Carmel, California, the Rev. Andre D'Angelo has no hesitation in calling on angel power to help parishioners work out "unresolved traumas." Rev. D'Angelo likes to compare God to the chief executive officer of a large corporation. "You can't always get through, but you can always reach a good executive secretary," he reasons. "An angel is like a good executive secretary."

New Age believers see angels through crystal-clear images—like Lori Jean Flory, thirty-six, of Aurora, Colorado, who has been experiencing angel encounters since the age of three. Usually they appear to her as light in motion with a vaguely human shape, and the message is always the same. She says, "They want us to know our pure essence is pure light and pure love."

Reverend Thomas Thompson, director of the Marian Library at the University of Dayton in Ohio, says he would never put down belief in angels. "It's quite possible people have these encounters," he says. "It's nothing new that people claim an absolute stranger told them to do something and they did it and averted disaster."

New Age minister Larry E. Young, from Miami Township, near Dayton, Ohio, says angels came to him a few years ago after he was hurt in a car accident. They offered him the option of going to heaven or returning to life on earth.

"When I tell people, they either think I'm crazy or they want to hear more," says the minister. "But I don't really care what people think. I had the experience."

The UFO Angels Theory

Here's another entertaining thought on angels: Could space aliens be heavenly messengers sent by God to help keep us on the straight and narrow?

This is the other-worldly theory suggested by Methodist minister Milton Nothdurft of Prescott Valley, Arizona, who has been studying reported UFO visitations for half a century. Pastor Nothdurft's highly original proposition is not accepted by all angel believers. But it certainly puts a spiritual slant on the centuries-old UFO controversy.

He's not alone in his other-worldly theory. Dr. Billy Graham, in his best-selling angel book, brings up the UFO phenomenon. He writes:

> Some reputable scientists deny and others assert that UFOs do appear to people from time to time. Some scientists have reached the place where they think they can prove that these are possibly visitors from outer space.
>
> Some Christian writers have speculated that UFOs could very well be a part of God's angelic host who preside over the physical affairs of universal creation. While we cannot assert such a view with certainty, many people are now seeking some type of supernatural explanation for these phenomena.
>
> "Nothing can hide the fact, however, that these unexplained events are occurring with greater frequency around the entire world and in unexpected places.

Did a squadron of celestial angels in heavenly chariots invade Japan on January 15, 1975? Dr. Graham cites what is now considered one of the most telling UFO sightings of modern times.

Fifteen to twenty glowing objects soared silently through the evening skies over half the length of Japan, causing widespread consternation as sightings were reported in cities seven hundred miles apart in the space of one hour.

Police stations and government offices were swamped with hundreds of phone calls as the spectacular squadron in the skies soared south. Yet no signal ever showed up on military radar.

After watching the dazzling display from the Control Room of Tokyo's Meteorological Bureau station, Professor Masatoshi Kitamura admitted, "I was totally mystified. Nothing showed up on my radar. I reported my sighting to the airport control tower and they told me nothing showed on their radar either."

If you find that hard to swallow, listen to Endwell, New York, Presbyterian pastor Barry H. Downing, who is also convinced that UFOs are not only real but have deep religious significance. In fact, Rev. Downing feels that recognizing the existence of these unidentified flying objects could do much to strengthen faith and renew confidence in biblical accounts.

"It would establish scientific plausibility for the whole biblical field," he says. "It would reinforce faith and make it possible in a scientific context."

Rev. Downing says skepticism over the UFO phenomenon has been reinforced by waffling and equivocation by government sources over the years. He's used to people scoffing at his views and he takes the criticisms in good humor. "I can't prove I'm right, but there's lots of evidence for it, and until it wins out, some people are just going to have to laugh," he says.

He theorizes that activities of UFO-borne "higher beings" or "angels" are likely from another dimension rather than from other planets. This type of phenomenon, he postulates, is very similar to documented biblical events, from the guidance of the Israelites out of Egypt to the ascension of Christ.

Accepting this possibility, says Rev. Downing, could bridge the gap between fundamentalist literalism and liberal theology's "demythologizing" of supernatural events as only symbolic. "It would cut down the distance between liberals and fundamentalists and serve as a mediating force between the two extremes," he argues. "The mythological concepts would have to be reexamined, which would be important for the liberal wing. The conservative wing, which stresses certainty and wants everything locked up tight, also would be impacted. This would mean unlocking things."

The fifty-year-old minister is far from being a flake. He received a bachelor's degree in physics and, after completing work at Princeton Theological Seminary, earned a doctorate at the University of Edinburgh in Scotland in the field of interrelations of science and religion.

A minister for over twenty years at Endwell's Northminster Presbyterian Church, Pastor Downing is also theological consultant to the Mutual UFO network, based in Seguin, Texas, and to the Fund for UFO Research, based in Washington, D.C.

His ideas about UFOs and about eternity as a coexisting universe are based on Einstein's relativity theory, and he has written about them in a book, *The Bible and Flying Saucers.* "What is clear from the Bible is that God's will for the Jews, and eventually for all mankind, was 'revealed' by beings from another world," he writes. "Usually these beings looked very much like ordinary human beings (they almost never have wings)."

Pastor Downing says it was "a hovering, UFO-like cloud" by day and a glowing "pillar of fire" by night that guided the Israelites out of Egypt, projecting some force that parted the Red Sea and leading them for years across the desert. Other UFO-related events from the Bible include:

- The firelike phenomenon on Mount Sinai in which Moses received the Ten Commandments
- The Prophet Elijah being taken to heaven in a fiery chariot
- The star of Bethlehem
- The engulfing light of Jesus' transfiguration
- Jesus' being "lifted up" at his ascension
- The blinding visitation of Paul on the road to Damascus

"All these were UFO types of reports," Downing claims. He says that a 1969 government commission finding that Air Force observations offered "insufficient evidence" to substantiate UFOs was a government "coverup" and that the full report never was released. He refers to a 1975 letter from then-Senator Barry Goldwater (R-AZ) which alleged that the true findings of the commission were being withheld as "above Top Secret."

"If the government weren't lying in denying UFOs exist, we'd have had a religious revolution starting forty years ago," argues the pastor. "It would not mean undermining biblical faith, but rather reinterpreting it in light of UFO phenomena."

However, Rev. Downing rarely brings his controversial theories with him to the pulpit, although his church members are aware of his interest in the subject and "three or four have said they've had UFO experiences," he adds.

How Will I Recognize My Angel?

So what *do* they look like? Suffice to say the appearance of the angel is in the eye of the beholder.

What form do angels take? Well, we've heard about them looking like the guy next door, a child, even a dog. We've been told of angels manifesting themselves as gentle nudges, caresses, comforting hands, a soft voice. You have to take your pick. The gentle-faced, winged persons we remember from old prints and books aren't likely to be on the agenda.

Since spiritual form is kind of hard to define, the great artists of the fourth century decided in their wisdom to give them those wings and halos so they wouldn't be confused with common mortals. And as for the little rosy-cheeked, dimply guys, they were the creations of such master painters as Rembrandt and Botticelli.

But why is it some people can "see" angels while others cannot? The Rev. John Westerhoff, a pastoral theologian at Duke University's Divinity School, probably answers that best with this explanation:

"Angels exist through the eyes of faith, and faith is perception," he observes "Only if you can perceive it can you experience it. For some, their faith doesn't have room for such creatures. That's not to demean their faith. That's just the way they are; they can't believe things that aren't literal, that are outside the five senses."

From my many interviews with angel witnesses, I have to agree with angel expert–author Sophy Burnham who says angels disguise themselves—as a dream, a comforting presence, a pulse of energy, a person, a nudge, a coincidence, whatever it takes to get the message across—rather than appearing in a more dramatic form. That way, she reasons, the more skeptical among us are able to explain the encounter away as coincidence or an everyday happening. "It is not that skeptics do not experience the mysterious and divine," she explains, "but rather that the mysteries are presented to them in such a flat and factual, everyday, reasonable way so as not to disturb."

The general rule, she says, is that people receive only as much information as they can bear, in the form they can stand to hear it.

That's why you should be looking for your angels in more familiar forms. They can sometimes appear in the physical bodies of loved ones who have passed away, believes famed evangelist Graham, who has recounted many cases where a loved one has returned from beyond the grave to help out in times of need or peril.

"A few years ago, the idea of angels helping would have been scorned by most educated people . . . all this has changed. The time has come for us to focus on the positives of faith—and the existence of angels is one of them," says Dr. Graham.

Angel expert Eileen Freeman, who publishes a newsletter "AngelWatch," has her own idea of how angels might appear to us. She says, "The way angels tend to be portrayed as recycled human beings is not traditionally believed to be true."

In short: Appearances mean nothing. And—whatever their form—you can be sure you will know and recognize your personal angels when they make themselves known to you.

And when are we most likely to encounter our angels? Not too long ago, it probably would have been difficult to answer this question. People who believed they had encounters were reluctant to talk publicly about them. This has all changed dramatically in these enlightened times. We've learned a lot from the firsthand experiences of these on-the-record angel believers.

Two things hold true. The more desperate the situation, the more dramatic the encounter is likely to be. And, as with near-death experiences, with their recurring accounts of long tunnels and visions of light, angel encounter stories are uncannily similar and told with impressive emotional conviction.

The really dramatic angel encounters seem to occur most when our awareness is most acute, usually when we are confronted with intense fear, or when everyday problems have become overwhelming and hopelessness and despair rear their ugly heads.

At best, our intervening guardians can rescue us from dangerous situations or make our problems go away. At worst, they can reduce our fears and make coping a cinch.

Often an angel encounter seems so logical an intervention that we initially fail to recognize it for what it is. You know the kind of thing—you're stuck in the snow or in a muddy ditch and a Good Samaritan comes to the rescue ... you're piloting a small plane with engine trouble and the reassuring guidance of a traffic controller guides you to earth ... you're in deep waters and a strong lifeguard cradles you to safety.

It's only later that you notice that there are no tire tracks in the snow or mud ... there never was a controller in the airport tower ... and that that particular beach does not have a lifeguard. In retrospect, when you find this out, the logical becomes the miraculous. And another amazing angel encounter story is born.

CHAPTER THREE

Angels as Heavenly Protectors

Angels make their protective presence known in all kinds of ways. They can be that inner voice you hear urging you not to go on a perilous journey, or warning you not to enter a building or travel down a hazardous road where danger lurks.

When future events prove that we've made the right last-minute choice, many of us pat ourselves on the back, congratulating ourselves on our terrific intuition or psychic ability. Perhaps we should instead be offering up a silent prayer for the wise counsel of our protecting angel.

When she was a child, Donna C. had always felt she had a "benevolent protector" looking out for her, too. Here's what happened to her when she was on her honeymoon a few years ago:

"We were in the Carolinas and had planned to do some white-water rafting the next day. We were really excited about it because neither of us had ever been rafting before. That night, while I was sleeping (it wasn't a dream), a female voice said twice, 'Don't go in the water.'

"This freaked me out for some reason, and my understanding husband agreed to drop the plans to go. When we got home from our honeymoon, there was an article in the paper about a young woman who was lost overboard and drowned in the very same river we had planned to raft.

"It may just have been a coincidence, but I don't believe that. Just writing about this today gives me goosebumps!"

Childhood Memories

Augusto Angulo-Cuzzi, a native of Lima, Peru, now married thirteen years, lives in the Washington, D.C. area with his wife, a former nurse, and his two daughters, aged twelve years and one month. Augusto is convinced that angels have been following him all his life.

He was brought up in a strong Catholic family with a comprehensive religious education—Augusto attended the Catholic University in Lima, where he obtained degrees in engineering and accounting. He went on to obtain his master's degree in information management at George Washington University, and today works for an international organization based in D.C. He is currently studying for his Ph.D. in finance or economics.

Angel encounters as a schoolboy and later as a college student are still imbedded strongly in his memory. Here is Augusto's story:

These things happen all over the world. Angels have saved me in at least four opportunities that I can vividly remember. They all happened in Lima, Peru, where I am originally from.

When I was about six or seven years old, I began to run after a ball that was rolling across the street. When I was still on the sidewalk, about four feet from the roadway, some kind of invisible force seemed to grab hold of me. It was so strong that it made me fall to the ground. That invisible force saved my life—as I fell I saw a big old car speeding by on the roadway at that very moment.

Then, when I was about nine or ten years old, walking home from school one day, I turned a corner and was faced with a huge Great Dane. I was familiar with the animal, which used to always bark ferociously from behind the locked wooden gate of his home. But today he was loose—and coming directly at me!

He leapt on me, placing his two front paws on my shoulders. His large jaw was opening and shutting menacingly just a couple of inches from my face. I was petrified.

Suddenly, someone called his name. Immediately, he jumped, leaving me alone, and obediently scampered back into his house. I looked around but there was no one else there. Yet I know someone very near at hand had called the animal off.

The most dramatic childhood incident was still to come. I was fifteen years old, and used to travel to school by bus. One day I was entering the bus through its rear door—which was normal on these buses because they had a driver and a collector on board.

I never did manage to get on the bus that day. As I was boarding the bus, the driver did not see me and accidentally closed the door prematurely. There I was, still on the outside—with my right foot jammed firmly in the closed door. The driver or collector did not see me and, to my horror, the bus started moving off with me trapped on the outside!

Desperately I tried to keep up with the bus by hopping on my left leg. It was a useless exercise as the bus began gaining speed. I eventually fell over.

There I was, being dragged along by the bus. As it gained momentum, I could hear the wind whooshing over my body as the rear tires began to get dangerously close to my head. The rest of my body was under the bus.

After being dragged for about half a block like this, the door suddenly opened, releasing my trapped right foot. An unseen force pushed me to the right to safety so that I escaped the rear wheels of the bus.

That bus never did stop. To this day, I believe the driver did not see me. If someone else had not been watching over me, I believe that bus would have cut me in half.

I was lucky to escape without injuries—only a slightly bruised left foot from where it had scraped along the ground. My left shoe, of course, was all torn up from the scraping.

Amazingly, I had no broken bones or cuts. I remember limping back to the bus stop after the incident to pick up my missing right shoe and my school books and papers, which were strewn all over the road.

To tell the truth, I was feeling more embarrassed than anything else. Two schoolgirls I knew had witnessed the entire incident, so I guess my ego was bruised more than my body.

I'm not the only one in my family who has been extricated from dangerous situations by their angels. Relatives have told me of being protected from danger by tall, strong strangers who have actually escorted them through tough, gang-infested neighborhoods—but all the time, to other witnesses, they were actually walking alone!

On several occasions, I too have found myself in a threatening situation and been rescued by the reassuring presence of an unseen entity.

One time, when I was about sixteen or seventeen, I was walking downtown with some friends in the early hours after a New Year's Eve party when we were confronted by a gang of about six or seven older, tough guys.

They threatened us and we ran for our lives. But they caught up and grabbed hold of two of us, myself included. Two of them took out knives.

One of them grabbed hold of me roughly, snatched my watch, and began running off. Then one of the ruffians behaved very strangely.

With no reason or explanation, he chased after the other, recovered my watch, which he handed back to me, then calmly persuaded his fellow gang members to leave us alone. They all left quietly.

I couldn't understand why at the time, although it reminded me of the time when the Great Dane was mysteriously called off. I'm sure my angel was at work again.

When I was around twenty-two years old, I was driving to college one day and stopped at an intersection where a policeman was directing traffic.

The policeman, who was facing me, stopped crossing traffic and gave me a signal to go ahead and cross the intersection. But I was frozen at the controls. I simply couldn't move. For several inexplicable seconds, I sat staring at the policeman as he kept urgently signaling me to proceed.

As this gesturing was going on, a car suddenly zoomed directly across my path from out of nowhere. If I had obeyed the signal to proceed, I would have been in a collision that would surely have killed me.

I became unfrozen and was able to proceed. As I passed the astonished policeman, our eyes met. The expression on my face was telling him, "You see."

An Unusual Intervention

New Yorker Meryl Johnson has known angels as her protectors all her life. When she was a little child her mother used to paste angel pictures on her bedpost to watch over her as she slept.

"It seemed a charming idea to my mother at the time," remembers Meryl. "My parents thought it cute that I had an angel as an imaginary friend when I began talking to my protector, whom I called Angel. If they'd only known then that my angel was talking back to me!"

Growing up, Meryl is convinced her angel was at her side to watch over her and help her make some of life's most difficult choices. A really unusual and dramatic angel intervention she recalls was when she was seventeen, an impressionable young lass who had left home to attend college in a major city.

She felt for the first time she was truly on her own, having taken a part-time job at the university bookstore and living in her very own apartment not far from the campus. But she was to have her innocence tested:

I know this doesn't sound like what you'd expect an angel encounter to be. It sounds more like something that would fall into the 'signs and omens' category. But to me it was a very true and real experience with my protecting angel.

I had begun to make friends at school and I made no secret of the fact that I had psychic gifts, a confession that no doubt made me a sitting duck for someone who wanted to take advantage of my interest.

A very charming, well-dressed professor made friends with me, often 'accidentally' running into me in a little restaurant where all the younger students used to eat because the food was good and cheap.

He was very polite and cautious at first, but one day he gradually brought up the fact that he belonged to a Satanic cult! I'd like it and I'd like its members, he tried to reassure me, adding that I was just the kind of member they were looking for.

As he talked, we took a walk across the campus in the shade of the trees. It was late afternoon, just before sunset, a beautiful, clear day. He was very personable as he described his group, but slightly nervous, as if he was not quite sure how I was going to react.

I gradually realized we were being followed—by a large flock of birds. The birds seemed to be screeching at us, moving from tree to tree overhead. And all the time, they were dropping juicy grey and white deposits on the professor's immaculate new jacket—which I'm sure he had worn to further impress me. Strangely, none of them were dropping anything on me!

I asked him what was going on. Did this happen often? Was nature turning against him? He was becoming quite flustered and upset. And for good reason.

Wiping the mess from his ruined jacket, he said that nothing like this had ever happened before. He kept on talking, and I kept nodding. But by this time I was paying more attention to the remarkable behavior of the birds.

I was no longer interested in hearing about the activities of him or his cult friends. I wasn't the least impressed by his talk of black masses or the prospect of being one of the virgins on his altar. Politely and firmly, I told that professor I was in no way interested in his offer.

The birds sure did get the message across—a message

I am convinced to this day that came from my guardian angel.

But looking back on that incident today, I was young and gullible—and I might have at least tried out for the group if it hadn't been for the strange and dramatic behavior of the birds.

Cathryn B. was also under the protection of her guardian angel when she was an impressionable young college student at San Francisco State University. As she tells the story:

My first weekend away from home at San Francisco State University, I stupidly went walking on Ocean Beach alone at dawn. (Now, thank goodness, there's a levee on the street alongside that makes it possible to enjoy the ocean while in safe, full sight of passing cars and neighborhood residents.)

I passed a young man who did not look remarkable in any way, neither scruffy or dangerous—he might well have been another SFSU student from the way he dressed and walked.

About ten minutes later, "something" made me turn around abruptly despite the lack of any unusual sound or other stimulus. There he was, pants open, with a vivid verbal description of what he would like to do with me.

I instinctively yelled, "If you come near me, I'll kill you." He stayed put. After this appropriate beginning, however, I seemed to freeze, my eyes locked on him. I became aware of a voice whispering clearly and distinctly in my ear, "Get out of here. Go, go, just turn and start walking up to the street. Go, just get out." The voice went on persistently, like a litany.

I definitely heard a whisper and clearly formed words. Finally, I was able to come to my senses enough to turn and go away. As soon as I was out of his sight, my paralysis disappeared. I turned and ran across the street to a lighted house. The family let me in and I called the police.

Out of Harm's Way

Angels sometimes behave like a protective mother—human or otherwise—looking after her young.

American G.I. Mike Frederickson was literally grabbed by the ears and whisked out of harm's way by his guardian angel while on overseas assignment with his army unit.

Michael, of Culver City, California, recollects the day his angel saved his life:

I thought it would be nice to say thanks to the angel who saved my life back in 1970 when I was in the Army stationed in Germany, in a small town just outside Stuttgart.

I was assigned to an ammo dump and was part of a sentry group that stood watch over ammo and I had a call from one of the towers that he heard shots being fired.

A staff sergeant and myself heard the whiz of the bullets coming from outside the compound. We went to the top of a hill to see what was going on, and we could hear the bullets going past us.

We went up the hill a little further for a better look when—all of a sudden—I felt a pair of hands grab me by my ears and forcibly pull my head back just as a bullet passed in front of my face.

I could almost feel and smell the heat and speed of that bullet. I just knew it had missed me by inches. I also knew that there were only two people on that hill—the staff sergeant and myself.

Later we found out the bullets were very real. For some reason or another, some old Germans had been sitting in a backyard nearby taking potshots at our compound.

Afterward I had a very eerie feeling knowing that someone had reached out to touch me and save me.

That incident certainly has had a tremendous influence on my life on a very personal level. I had been quite religious as a young boy, but I had drifted. The

incident certainly renewed my faith in God and reinforced the belief that God is indeed for us and not
against us.

It also convinced me of the existence of guardian
angels. Since the army incident I have always been
aware of my angel, whom I know is always close at
hand.

My angel was at my side again just a few years ago,
when I was out walking and was attacked by a fero-
cious stray dog.

I came across the dog when I just rounded a corner.
The animal seemed harmless at first. It ran up to me
and I stopped; then the dog sat down beside me. What
happened next took only a split second.

The dog suddenly made a lunge for my throat. I
recoiled and out of the corner of my eye, I saw the
dog being pushed away by the arm of someone standing right behind me. I actually saw the arm—it was an
arm in a white robe like you see in pictures of Christ.

The dog scurried off. And when I looked around there
was no one there. I only caught a glimpse of the arm,
but I know what I saw. I will leave my story at that.

I am sure there are those who will laugh at my
stories.

Because of that incident in the army and the dog attack incident, I live with a strong, comforting feeling
that I'm not alone.

From time to time, I sense a powerful presence and
know my angel is constantly trying to get in touch with
me. It's a wonderful feeling.

A Canine Angel

Margaret Knodell, a nurse from San Antonio, Texas,
is convinced that her life and the life of her baby were
saved by her guardian angel—who appeared to her in the
form of a dog!

She was walking her baby in a stroller in Dodge City,
Kansas, when a huge dog appeared in front of her at a
crosswalk, blocking her path.

Margaret, now fifty-seven, recalls trying to edge round the dog. But it would not let her proceed.

It wasn't growling or anything. It was just determined not to let me pass. Finally, the dog reared up on his hind legs, pawing the air with his front legs. He towered over me.

That did it! I grabbed my son and ran back the way I came. Looking over my shoulder, I saw the dog had vanished.

Suddenly, a speeding car ran a light at the crosswalk and smashed into another car. The cars careened on to the sidewalk—right where I'd have been if the dog hadn't turned me back.

To this day I'm convinced that dog was an angel guarding over me and my baby.

A Booming Voice

Angels were also guarding over Mary Ellen Brown and her six-month-old son, John, in the summer of 1973, when they were walking in their Concord, New Hampshire neighborhood.

"On this particular day, after a trip to the bank, we were ready to go home," said Mary Ellen, a forty-two-year-old accountant who now lives in Pittsfield, New Hampshire.

Their walk home that day involved crossing a side street that normally wasn't very busy with traffic.

"I had just edged the carriage over the curb when I heard this voice," she recalls. "It was a very authoritarian voice that boomed, 'Put the carriage back on the sidewalk.' It was so emphatic that I just did it."

No sooner had she returned to the sidewalk with her stroller than a tractor-trailer rig sped around the corner onto the street the Browns were about to cross.

"He was going too fast and as he rounded the corner his wheel came up over the sidewalk and just missed the carriage and myself. We both would have been killed if we had been in the spot we were just seconds earlier," Mary Ellen remembers.

Once she realized they were both safe, the shaken mother looked around to thank the person who had saved her and her infant son's lives.

There was no one to be found.

"I didn't think at that moment a guardian angel had done it," says Mary Ellen, who still looks on the incident as a "miraculous" intervention.

Twenty-three years later, Mary Ellen insists, "The idea that it was our guardian angel is as good an explanation as any."

An Answered Prayer

Sandra (Sam) Humphreys of Storrs, Connecticut still gets teary-eyed when she recalls the day a guardian angel answered her prayer to pluck her three-year-old son from certain death out of the path of a galloping horse.

Here is Sam's story:

At the time, we lived on a small farm in rural Connecticut. I was walking with my three preschool-age sons through the many paths that weave through the woods and fields surrounding our farm, where our neighbors have horses. We had all been enjoying a wonderful afternoon, and I think we were all a little giddy with the sense of "rightness" in our world.

My second son, who was about three years old at the time, was running a little ahead of me, dashing a few feet up and running back like a puppy when I called.

As we came around a large pond, I was holding tightly to their little hands, knowing that a disaster takes only a second. I now think it was those few moments of physical restraint that caused my son to break away from me once we were safely past the water.

At any rate, he scampered off, giggling. I could hear him, and through the bends in the path and the breaks in the trees, I could see occasional flashes of bright red and yellow stripes on his shirt.

When he did not return at my call, I was only mildly concerned, for we knew these paths well and since I could still hear him, I knew he was not too far ahead. Nevertheless, I wanted to catch up to him quickly.

Tucking the baby under one arm, and taking a firmer grip on my oldest son, I walked with a firmer, faster stride.

Abruptly the sound of him veered off in a direction I did not anticipate. I paused just long enough to be certain of what I was hearing, then scooped my four-year-old up as well and began to run in earnest.

My middle boy was undoubtedly taking a less frequently taken trail that eventually would make its way up a very steep hill into a pasture of horses. I felt the panic rising in me.

In seconds I reached the foot of the hill and, scanning quickly, felt my heart crash down to my toes, for there was my boy scrambling like a baby goat about halfway up. I placed the baby's hand in my older son's hand and admonished them both to stay put and not to let go, before racing up after the middle boy.

I could not believe that such a little guy could move so fast. Urging him to stop the whole time, I slipped, slid, and clambered up all at the same time.

Without warning, I could faintly hear the unmistakable sound of hoofbeats. Someone was riding very near us. I knew that it was not unusual for the riders to bring their horses running and sliding down this incline, for it was a shortcut to the pond.

I also knew that because they were certainly not expecting my son to come popping up over the edge, they would never be able to stop the horses in time.

Heart pounding, I renewed my efforts, praying all the while that I would reach him. I even remember that it was no specific prayer, just "Please God, please God" over and over.

Everything happened at once, of course. I lunged

up and forward in one last desperate attempt to grab the back of his overalls just as he crested the hill.

To my absolute horror and disbelief, I fell with a crash inches from my child. Helplessly I watched, anticipating disaster, as my son flew backward away from me and landed with a dusty thump on his bottom.

The rider tried frantically to stop her horse, which was now pawing and rearing exactly where my son had been split seconds before.

Unaware of what had nearly happened, my beloved son turned to me accusingly and scolded, "Mama, you didn't have to pull so hard. That hurt."

I scooped my boy into a teary embrace and held him until my heart stopped pounding, despite his struggles to get loose.

The rider, horse now under control, and I gazed at each other in amazement. What exactly *had* happened?

There was only one possible answer—the guardian angels I had heard tales of as a child were looking out for this generation of my family as well.

In the years since, I have rerun this incident over in my mind countless times and I always come to the same conclusion. I look at my son today, now almost a grown man, preparing for college, and still get teary-eyed with a lump in my throat thinking how grateful I am for that moment of divine intervention.

I have also given the whole subject of guardian angels long and careful thought. I figure that I was not overly shocked at their intervention because my family background had long prepared me that they exist.

In my own family, these experiences have been fairly commonplace over the years. My mother's family were all seafarers of one sort or another, and these rugged men and women spoke openly of their angelic meetings.

In addition, I work in a hospice and it is not unusual to hear patients and families tell of seeing and/or speaking with angels.

I think the common denominators for having an angel encounter are, first, a deeply personal spirituality (which is not necessarily the same thing as belonging to a particular religion); and secondly, experiencing the emotion of the near-death situation. In some of the near-death situations, obviously, the individual needs physical rescuing; in another situation, emotional or spiritual rescuing.

How might an individual call up his or her personal guardian angel? I'm certain that we can. Maybe we are not supposed to be able to. Perhaps divine intervention is only at the behest of the divine.

Speaking only for myself, I know that I am profoundly lazy, and that if I had an angel at my beck and call like a fairy-tale genie, I would be far less likely to solve my own dilemmas.

I would not want to abuse the privilege exactly, but most definitely to depend upon it. I am grateful that I do not have that option, for I feel that I am a better person for it.

Angel with a Badge

There are angels in the ranks of New York's finest. One black family from Washington Heights certainly believes there are.

A young friend from New York is not sure whether he believes in angels or not. But he loves to tell this story:

When I was two years old my parents lived in a apartment in the Washington Heights neighborhood of New York City. There were many drug dealers who lived in that building on the third floor. One day, some drug dealers approached my mother because someone spread a rumor that some tenants, including my mother and father, were trying to get rid of all the drug dealers (the rumor was probably true). So the drug dealers started to hassle my mother.

My mother then called for my father, who came to her protection and confronted the drug dealers. The drug dealers were standing in front of the building, all crowded round my father, who admits he was scared to death.

One of the drug dealers was known to be a murderer with a short fuse. He and my father began arguing and, just when it looked as if a fight was going to develop, a white police officer came around the corner.

Quickly, my mother called the police officer over. The cop walked up to the drug dealers and told them to stop harassing my folks.

He warned them that if anything happened to my family he would know who to come looking for and arrest. The dealers left my mother and father alone and walked away.

My mother noticed that the cop had a beautiful face, so she looked at his badge and remembered his name and number. The next day she wanted to thank the officer, so she called the precinct and asked for the cop—only to be told there is no one by that name or number in the precinct. Or on the force, for that matter.

After that, my mother was convinced their savior was an angel. My family never saw or heard from that officer again.

In the Eye of a Storm

Glynn and Lynne Coates of Louisville, Kentucky, are convinced a guardian angel sheltered and protected their six-year-old son when a violent and devastating tornado bore down on their community in April of 1974.

It was during the spring peak of the Midwest tornado season that a series of treacherous storms buffeted the Coates's family home.

Glynn and Lynne were frantic with worry. Their two older children had arrived home from school safely before the storm struck, but six-year-old Collyn was still at kindergarten at the nearby Southern Baptist Theological Seminary.

As tornado warning sirens whined noisily, the Coateses were forced to take refuge in their basement. The storm passed them by, but their anxieties worsened when local radio reports said that a funnel was sighted directly over little Collyn's school.

Desperate by this time, Lynne tried to telephone the school, but got no answer. Glynn raced to the family car in an effort to drive to the school. But he didn't get far. The tornado had caused awesome devastation in the neighborhood and there was no way he could get through.

His distracted wife repeatedly kept trying to reach the school by phone, growing more distraught each time the phone failed to ring. Please, she prayed desperately, please watch over Collyn and the other children and keep them safe.

As she prayed, she began to feel calmer, less worried. Encouraged, she decided to try the telephone one more time. This time a woman's relaxed, pleasant-sounding voice answered.

"Don't worry," soothed the woman. "The children are fine. They were all taken to another building before the storm. Their teachers are staying with them."

Tears of joy streaming down her cheeks, Lynne hung up and waited patiently while her husband drove to the other building to pick up their son, who was returned to her safe and sound.

A few days later, after the area was cleaned up and classes were able to resume, Lynne decided to visit Collyn's school to personally thank the woman who had given her the good news during the worrying crisis.

At the kindergarten, Collyn's teacher expressed surprise as Lynne related the story of the reassuring telephone call. "But you couldn't have spoken with anyone," the teacher insisted to Lynne. "We put a sign on the door, locked the building, and moved the children before the tornado struck. There was no one here—and in any case our phone lines were destroyed by the storm!"

Angel in the Blizzard

As a young lad and an Eagle Scout, William N. Lindemann often roamed alone through the woods around his Great Lakes home, learning survival techniques in the wilderness.

But he never felt threatened or alone on his treks because he always felt a presence with him that he called his "General Direction."

That presence came to his rescue one bitterly cold February day when he found himself stranded in the middle of a vast frozen lake after an intense, blinding blizzard blew up from nowhere.

Blinded by the stinging snow, he stumbled through the roaring blizzard, becoming weaker with each step. "Please, dear God," he cried out. "Help me find my way!"

Suddenly, a loud foghorn blasted through the storm from a rescue station in the general direction of his home. He still couldn't see anything, but he heard a voice call out: "Be careful! The breakwater is open and deep."

As he inched on his hands and knees toward the sound of the foghorn and the calm, firm voice—which, curiously, was quite audible above the howling wind—the voice repeated, "Be careful. Stay to the right, and climb the concrete wall when you reach it."

Lindemann finally reached the shoreline and the safety of the rescue station. "The next thing I felt was being half pulled and half carried inside. A man with dark hair and a beard was there with hot coffee brewing. When I asked him why he was there in the middle of winter, he said he was finishing some research."

Returning to the rescue station the next day to further thank his savior, Lindemann had to dig through a snowdrift to reach the door. There, he found a battered sign that said: CLOSED FOR WINTER.

Only then did he realize it was his guardian angel who had appeared on the banks of the frozen lake to guide him through the blinding storm!

Safe, Strong Arms

Pregnant with her fifth child, Jean Blitz was sure she would lose her unborn baby when her feet went out from under her as she stepped on to the icy porch of her home one winter morning.

She reached out desperately, but there was nothing to grab hold of to prevent from falling. As Jean fell, the terrible thought that she might lose her unborn baby flashed through her mind.

Her protective angel saved the day. Just before she hit the ground, two strong arms caught her and stood her up straight.

"My husband!" she thought—but only for a second. But when she turned around, she was by herself.

Angels on the Beach

Your guardian angel sometimes wears a uniform, as Jennifer Munro found out when she and her baby son were stalked by two drunken thugs on a lonely Florida beach.

Jennifer, originally from Miami, now runs her own successful consulting company headquartered in North Carolina. She tells her story:

In 1975, my son was eighteen months old. He and I waited at the beach early in the morning while my husband went exploring on the other side of the inlet.

Suddenly, I realized we were no longer alone on this very desolate beach—at Sebastian Inlet in Florida. I looked around and there were two very mean and awful-looking men approaching. They began to threaten and try to scare me—which they really succeeded in doing.

They were drinking out of liquor bottles in paper bags, and they looked like they had been drinking for some time. They had long, dirty hair and were missing some teeth and were generally like what you see in scary movies.

I pretended I had to change my son's diaper and stood up from our blanket to go toward a bathhouse, which was nearer the main road. At that time we were still hidden from any passersby by huge sand dunes.

As I started to go toward the bathhouse, one of the men stopped me, but the other told him to let me go. They followed. When I got to the top of the dune, I began to run with my son locked in my arms.

They were closing in on me when a Florida state park truck pulled into a parking area beside the beach. I started to scream for help and ran to them.

The guys who were chasing me jumped into their car and sped off. I was very upset and the two park rangers kept talking to me, trying to calm me down.

They took me to my husband. I was so grateful and so relieved, I wrote down their names so I could write them a note later.

When I was writing to thank them, I called to get the address of their commanding officer. I sent the letter to him. After several weeks I hadn't heard from him, so I wrote again, just to make sure he told them how much I appreciated the help. No response.

Eventually I called on the phone. To my surprise, he told me he had never had anyone with those two names working anywhere in Florida. He said the truck, uniforms, name tags, seals, everything was as I described it, but that no one with those names or even close, were ever there, nor with the national park service either.

I didn't know what to think. Neither did my husband—who also met the officers—or the commander.

A month later, someone who knew nothing about my story gave me Billy Graham's book called *Angels.* In that book, I saw many examples that made me realize that the men who saved me that day had to have been angels.

It has meant so much to me all of these years, although I have only shared this story with a few people.

I guess I was worried that my business clients would doubt my mental state.

Looking back, there have been many other times when I thought I must have been specially protected, including once when my car became airborne during an accident and rolled five times (according to the witnesses and police report), ending up upside down. I walked away from it unhurt.

I feel peaceful about the idea of them being there all of the time. Angels bring a lot of peace.

Shortly before Jennifer shared her story with me, I heard a remarkably similar one from a close friend, Michael G. He had never told this story before, but when he heard I was researching angel encounters he couldn't wait to share it with me.

It bears incredible similarities to Jennifer Munro's encounter—right down to a savior in uniform appearing on a lonely Florida beach. Here is Mike's story:

> In the early seventies, I was just married and loved the Florida Keys. I took my wife there on a camping trip.
>
> We were disturbed in our tent in the early hours by a group of noisy drunks. They were outside our tent, making obscene and violent threats. We felt so vulnerable and terrified. Through the canvas we saw the flashing blue lights of a police car. The hooligans ran off.
>
> I went out and spoke to a young officer. He apologized for the harassment and said the patrol car would stay by the roadside and make sure we wouldn't be troubled.
>
> He was true to his word. In the early-morning light, we both looked out and saw the marked police car still sitting there, about fifty yards from our campsite. "Let's invite the young cop for coffee," I suggested to my wife.
>
> As I walked toward the parked police car, my attention was diverted for a couple of seconds. When I looked toward the car it was gone! I could see clearly

north and south and there was no traffic on the road, not even the sound of a car engine.

Later we went to a police station near the town of Marathon. I was unable to supply our guardian's name, but we were both chilled to learn there had been *no* patrol car in our camp area that night.

Who was the man in the phantom police car? He just had to be our guardian angel.

CHAPTER FOUR

Angels: The Great Comforters

When you are at your lowest ebb in life, you can always call on your angel for comfort. In times of family crisis or bereavement, your guardian angel is only a whispered prayer away, as if he or she senses your anguish and distress, feels your pain, and has flown to your side to be your inspiration in your darkest moment.

Stories about angels in their role as comforters may not be as dramatic as stories told elsewhere in this book, but they are equally moving.

Angels _Are_ Watching You

After the untimely death of her younger sister, forty-four-year-old Peggy O'Connor was racked with guilt and grief—feelings that were only assuaged when she was comforted by compassionate angels.

Peggy, from Buffalo, New York, is a mother of two children aged nine and ten, and has always had both feet firmly on the ground. She is a former flight attendant for American Airlines with a college background, and today she runs her own business. In 1993, she was given an award as one of the top forty "Under 40" businesspeople in Western New York.

She came to believe in the existence of angels in a very powerful and comforting way. Here's Peggy's story, in her own words:

My sister Patty died July 10, 1993, in an automobile accident in which she was thrown from the car. Tragically, she was not wearing a seatbelt.

As she was my only sister and we were only twenty months apart in age, we were naturally very close.

The week prior to her death, we had gone to a movie together. While viewing the movie, I felt a horrible feeling come over me. I turned my head to look at my sister, who was staring at the movie screen, and saw her image appear translucent and surrounded by light.

At the same time, in my own head, all I could think of was that she is going to die very soon (although she was only thirty-eight and healthy). It was a truly horrible feeling and I had to shake it off. I was very upset, although I didn't tell her. I couldn't.

Later, I felt compelled to call my father and told him that I was very concerned about Patty and thought maybe she might have an illness, as she had been doing a lot of coughing. He shrugged it off, but he did suggest to my sister that she go to the doctor to have her cough checked. One week later she died in an auto accident.

The guilt I felt after that accident was very strong. Somehow I felt I had not warned her properly. It was probably for that reason that, immediately after her death, I started having vivid dreams about her. In one, she told me the location of something she had hidden. I told my mother, who went to my sister's house and, sure enough, it was hidden right where she said it was in my dream.

In another dream, she told me she was an angel now and would make herself known to me. How is that possible, I wondered?

I would add here that, in my life, my sister was a devotee of everything about angels. She was a collector of angel artifacts and memorabilia long before this current angel phenomena. She even had a small tattoo of the angel Raphael.

About a month after her death, I was still grieving, still hurting emotionally. One day I was reading an angel book before I left for work. I became upset that a angel had not saved my sister from her death. I slammed the book down and began crying. I said aloud that I just don't believe angels watch over us! How could they let these things happen?

Distraught, I left for work and while driving on the thruway, a car started to pass me on the left. When I looked over, it was a vehicle exactly like my sister's car, the one she was killed in. I mean identical.

I started crying again at the mere sight of the familiar car. But as the vehicle sped up to pass me, it suddenly moved into my lane just ten feet in front of my car. On the bumper was a sticker that said, in bold letters, "Angels ARE watching you!"

The car then sped off onto a ramp. When I looked down the ramp, there wasn't any car to be seen. An angel encounter?

After my sister died, several people gave me books on angels. I read a lot about the angel Raphael, her particular favorite. It was interesting to read that Raphael is often seen with a boy and his dog. My sister raised dogs, and was never without her dog, Arri.

I also understand Raphael's domain is the western sky. Shortly after Patty's death, I was outside at midnight. For some reason, I just needed to be outside. It was a warm Buffalo night and I was really missing my sister. I looked up into the sky and asked her if she was okay. I was crying again, of course.

I immediately witnessed the most beautiful shooting star streak across the sky. What was odd about it was that I was facing the opposite direction when I heard this voice in my head say "Turn around."

It was when I turned to face the opposite direction that I saw the star. It filled me with a really warm and peaceful feeling.

We don't see many shooting stars in our area because of the cloud cover and location. This was the first one I had ever seen!

A short time later, I realized the shooting star was in the western sky—the domain of Raphael!

Yes, although she only appears to me in dreams, I believe my sister is still with me, sends me messages, and that she now enjoys the life of an angel.

Out of the Darkness

Michael Bryant's encounter with an angel—a small, gentle Hispanic lady with a soft voice and comforting hands—was truly a life-altering experience when he was at his lowest ebb one lonely Christmas just a few years ago.

He describes his amazing encounter in a moving letter to the *Miami Herald:*

For almost four years now, I can't think of my accident without thinking of her.

She came out of the darkness to help me out of a car wreck that should have killed me, and comforted me until the ambulance came.

She stayed with me until the police handcuffed me and took me away. I would later be charged with DUI, my life was about to change, and I was forced to take a deeper look inward.

I had woken up one Christmas morning and realized I was truly alone. It was then that I started going to bars to be around others, and then that I started to drink heavily.

I was driving down one of those infamous San Francisco hills when I slid through a traffic light, hit the back of a taxi, and crashed into a street lamp. If I had gone through the intersection one second sooner, I not only would have killed myself but the passengers in the taxi.

Before I could regain my senses, she was there—pulling me out of the car, whispering to me that everything would be OK, that the ambulance was on its way. She was small, Latin, with short black hair. She had a soft voice and comforting hands. She sat with me in the ambulance as they cleaned the blood from my face and hands. And then she was gone.

I wondered who she was, and why she chose to help me. I went back to the scene days later and wandered around for hours. I described her and asked people in the streets if they knew her. Nothing. She came from nowhere, she helped me, and she disappeared.

Years later, I still can't think about the accident without thinking of her. An Angel? She was to me.

An Assurance of Peace

A few days short of her eighteenth birthday, Charmaine Donnelly entered a religious order because she felt her life was out of control.

"It was an attempt to awaken the small, still voice inside me," she says. "I thought the convent would offer me physical comfort and spiritual discovery. Through no fault of the convent, I found neither. I was still in the desert."

Six years later, she left the convent, still emotionally despondent. Her life went into a tailspin—marriages, divorces, failures, dabbling in cults, drug and alcohol use, depression.

Then an angel intervened. Charmaine, now forty-nine, recalled in a *Buffalo News* interview how an angelic presence turned her life around:

"At one low point in my life I happened to be driving in the country by myself. I had this sense that this being was with me. It was the most absolutely exquisite assurance of peace I had ever had in my life up to that moment.

"This peaceful presence stayed with me for quite a while. It looked angelic to me. I could see a light—like when you read near-death experience books and people say there is no description on earth for the light they see."

Sadly, that exquisite feeling of peace passed for Charmaine. And for several long, desolate years, she continued to feel constant despair.

Again she cried out for help—and it came again in the form of a support group of caring individuals who understood her despair because they had travelled the same, painful route.

Up to that point, Charmaine had seen God "as a sort of judge, a quite harsh judge. An Old Testament kind of person," she recalls.

Now she rejoiced, "Suddenly, it was as if someone had turned up the flame under my spiritual hunger. I was learning to live according to a set of principles; to function in the world in a responsible, responsive way.

"I began to feel safe, protected," she says. "Life at last had meaning. Being connected to a spiritual being had a lot of sweetness for me, like a deep love affair."

And one of the most important side effects of her life-changing experience was the return of that angelic light, the comforting presence she had felt on that lonely country highway.

"I was in Hawaii on a retreat and a woman asked me if I knew that there are angels all around me, that we are protected by angels," remembers Charmaine. "This reawakened my conscious connection with angels."

That comforting connection stayed with Charmaine throughout a period when tragedy and despair again threatened her well-being.

"I was diagnosed with a potentially fatal, progressive disease," Charmaine explains. "But I didn't give up."

> I now knew that the discipline of gratitude can transform every hurtful, troublesome, painful, dark situation—so I used my will to be grateful even when I didn't feel grateful.
>
> Now I don't know words strong enough to express what I have—but simply to say it is a new appreciation for the wisdom of God's will and the enormous beauty that the love and support of others offers us. I am glad I have lived long enough to be experiencing the kind of life I have now.

Timely Advice

Angels have always been a comfort to seventy-nine-year-old Regina Ash, who says she has always had the company of a guardian angel since she was a girl growing up in Baltimore.

She's been able to call upon her angel for all kinds of problems in her life—from something as simple as helping her prepare a shopping list to giving advice on how she could help keep her soldier son close to home.

"I always make sure the angel gets the credit," Mrs. Ash said. "I tell people about it."

When she was worrying about her son's imminent deployment to Vietnam from a West Coast army base, a substitute French teacher in the parochial school where Mrs. Ash taught told her how he could avoid overseas duty.

The substitute said that before being shipped overseas, army units would be asked for volunteers to stand guard at the Tomb of the Unknown Soldier in Arlington Cemetery. Mrs. Ash advised her son of this, and when his unit was asked, he volunteered for the job and was accepted.

Mrs. Ash never saw the substitute again. Just a coincidence, perhaps? "But if it happens to you, you know it," she said. "I know it was an angel. What else?"

Troubled Teen's Comfort

Long Island, New York, high-schooler John T. believes that an angel was sent to bring him back to the land of the living after he took an accidental overdose of medication.

Since then, he has been revisited several times by his guardian angel, whom the shy sixteen-year-old now recognizes as an always-present source of comfort and encouragement.

As a result, John plans to become a minister when he graduates.

John says of his first encounter: "I was taking Ritalin for a medical ailment for some time. One day when I was alone, I accidentally took an overdose. It made me feel horrible. Then, all at once, I felt an incredible peace come over me. I heard a voice telling me not to worry, to just relax and I would be all right. When I closed my eyes, I could see myself lying on my bed with someone standing over me. I knew then that I was being looked after and that I would survive." Not long after, John was revisited by his angel.

I had just returned home from high school and was feeling pretty miserable. A school bully had been threatening me, and I was beginning to worry irrationally about the threats. Continually looking over my shoulder—that kind of thing.

This day, being a religious kind of person, I decided to kneel down and pray. A candle was near me, and I heard someone telling me to light it. I did, and the instant I did so I felt as if a weight had been lifted from my shoulders.

I just knelt there for a while. When I finished praying I rose and extinguished the candle. As I did so, I swear the smoke made a hazy outline of a human form for several seconds. I felt a great peace.

John also believes his guardian angel is also helping him overcome his rather quiet, shy, and introverted personality.

Just the other day, some school friends were talking and joking around with each other. Normally I don't join in any of this kind of fun. In fact, most of the time I basically try not to be noticed. But this time I felt someone nudge me, and guide me over to them. The next thing I know, I'm joking with them. I know it was my angel trying to tell me something."

A Match Made in Heaven

Dr. Harry MacDonald and his wife Hope have been married for almost half a century. And if you don't think this is a match made in heaven, then just ask their guardian angel.

Dr. MacDonald, senior pastor at Seattle's John Knox Presbyterian Church in Seattle, and his wife were childhood sweethearts. But as college students together, they were on the verge of breaking off their engagement. As both youngsters had doubts, Harry suggested they pray for guidance.

"In the middle of the prayer," Mrs. MacDonald recalls, "the room was suddenly filled with an overwhelming presence."

A beautiful, glowing white figure filled the doorway and advanced toward them, laying an outstretched hand on each head. "The room was filled with such a sense of peace," recalls Mrs. MacDonald, who later wrote her own collection of angel encounters, *When Angels Appear.* "The message was that God wanted us together. It was so beautiful."

Bearing Up with Cancer

Baltimore author Jane B. Wilson's fascination with angels came about in a most unusual way: She became intrigued initially with angel statues in cemeteries while researching a book about interesting graveyards in and around where she lived.

Gathering information for her graveyard tome, *The Very Quiet Baltimoreans*, Mrs. Wilson was impressed at how graves with angel statues or angel motifs around them seemed more meaningful. "There's a difference if you put an angel on a grave—somehow it's an overpowering symbol of life after death," she says.

For a period of years now, Mrs. Wilson has had cancer, and her disease has been in and out of remission. But she is convinced it is her comforting angels who allow her to bear up when her cancer is at its worst. Her neat Baltimore home is filled with angels in porcelain, cloth, paper, and pictures, mostly gifts from friends.

"Sometimes I think I hear the swooshing of a gown, or feathers of wings. Now I know that sounds like nonsense. But there's so much in this world that can't be explained," says the middle-aged retired librarian.

"I'm going through a bad patch right now, so it's more likely that I'll hear these sounds again in the next few days."

Mrs. Wilson has survived long past the projections of her doctors, but recognizes that her time may be short. And when it comes, she wishes for an angel, sculpted in bronze like the one on her favorite monument—a winged and gowned angel of death in the Baltimore Hebrew Congregation Cemetery on Belair Road.

"If I'm able to afford one after my death, I would love to have one on my grave," she says. "Just to go up and touch one is an enchantment."

Angel at the Airport

Seventy-three-year-old retired science teacher Mary Jane Albrecht of New Lebanon, Ohio doesn't consider herself to be a terribly religious person, but she definitely believes in angels.

An angel came to Mary Jane's rescue ten years ago when she found herself lost, overwhelmed, and distressed in a busy air terminal.

Mary Jane, exhausted after a long school year, was on her way to visit her daughter in Florida. When she got off the plane in Atlanta, she was overwhelmed by the size of the busy terminal and unsure of where to go for her connecting flight.

Out of nowhere appeared this "great big man" dressed in a business suit and carrying a briefcase, who said to her, "You're going to Orlando, aren't you?"

He told her to follow him and he would take her to her gate. The two didn't speak as the man guided her a long distance to the gate and told her exactly what time to expect her plane.

"I turned around for a second and when I turned back, he was gone," says Mary Jane. She didn't think right away that her Good Samaritan was an angel. But, on reflection, it was the only explanation.

"After all, how did he know I was going to Orlando?" asks Mary Jane. "Having an angel watching over you is comforting. And I don't think it's uncommon—I think it happens more often than people realize."

A Child's Comforter

From the tender age of three, Jean Hill Monroe of Houston has been vividly aware of the reassuring presence of her guardian angel, who first appeared to her during a particularly traumatic childhood experience that still scars her memory.

Here is Jean's moving story:

Our guardian angels are always with us. They can tune you in or tune you out. They are here for each of us to help and guide us in fulfilling our obligations and promises here on earth and help prepare us for the after-life with our families, including our brother Jesus.

We all have an angel assigned to us. They have chosen us individually. So it is not a matter of how to get in touch with your guardian angel; it is a matter of keeping in touch with him or her.

This is not just a wishful thing on my part. It is very real. And when we all realize this and work with our angels, we can make this a better world.

I have had many experiences with my own guardian

angel and have always felt his presence. He has been by my side ever since I can remember—even before I was taught that they exist.

When I was three years old, living with my family in Waterloo, Iowa, my mother was in labor with our younger sister and our father found this woman, through a newspaper advertisement, as a babysitter. Unfortunately, he did not have sufficient time to check her references, before dropping us children off at her house while he took mamma to the hospital.

I'll never forget that experience. I had ventured into her kitchen, and saw this crystal bowl full of candy-colored mints on top of her refrigerator. I reached for it and it came crashing down, glass and candy all over the kitchen floor.

She ran into the kitchen in a rage, grabbed me by my arm, telling me that I was a terrible ugly person for breaking her favorite crystal bowl.

She proceeded to drag me to the cellar. I remember her telling me there were all these evil creatures down there just waiting to tear me up and eat me alive. With that, she shut the cellar door and locked it, leaving me terrified in that dark, damp basement.

I do not remember her opening the door to let me out. But I do remember being taken upstairs to a huge bedroom where I was placed in a baby crib bed.

I remember looking about the room from the crib. It was lit up with moonlight coming through the long window to the floor. I saw shadows from the trees outside the window, fluttering like wings on the walls of the room.

But I managed to fall asleep. For some inexplicable reason, I just knew my angel was there to protect and comfort me. I could feel his presence.

I grew up being afraid of my own shadow. But I do believe my angel has helped me overcome some of my insecurities I have had throughout my growing years, and that he is still with me today.

That was my first remembrance of encountering my guardian angel, but it was not the last. There have been other instances I have felt his presence and warmth, and have witnessed the results of his help.

He has always been by my side, to guide me and protect me and others dear to me. He is with me now.

In an Angel's Arms

When Donald E. Styck, of Leesburg, Georgia was just three years old, he had an angel encounter that has been etched indelibly in his consciousness all his life.

Donald writes:

I was a little boy, only three and a half years old, when the angel Gabriel came down and picked me up and took me up in the sky and showed me the pretty trees, the fields and flowers.

It's all so vivid in my memory. I remember the angel saying, "Isn't this pretty." Then he said: "I had better put you down now or your mother will be worried about you." I have a clear recollection of being dropped two to three feet to the earth.

Years later, I had other angel experiences. One I'll never forget is when one of God's angels helped drive my car for me in a blinding snowstorm. That storm caused great damage in our neighborhood. Roads were impassable, trees were blown down, and it was chaos all over. But the little house trailer where we lived was untouched.

An Angel Nanny

No job is too big or too menial for a true angel. Protector or guardian, counselor or spiritual adviser, bodyguard or comforter—or even just a helping hand around the house.

An angel-turned-nanny came to the aid of Jennifer Ailstock, thirty-seven, a school secretary from Arlington, Virginia.

Her angel experience is an "awkward" one, she says.

After all, how can you convince your husband and friends that someone—an angel, she believes—changed the wet bed of her four-year-old daughter in the middle of the night?

Although Jennifer never saw anyone, she swears that she felt a presence as she was preparing to change her daughter's bed. As she approached the bed, she was amazed to see that the sheets were being tucked in with little effort from her. "It was an instantaneous thing—just a small help, but one that made me feel that my drudgery was more than worthwhile," laughs Jennifer.

The Comfort of Celeste

Cynthia M. Cornish-Band was a worrier and took everything to heart until the crystal-clear voice of her guardian angel made itself known to her as she slept.

Since then, she has grown to cherish the warmth and comforting presence of her angel, whom she calls Celeste. Celeste has even introduced Cynthia to other angels, including the guardian angels of her children and husband—although the latter is not a believer in angels.

Cynthia writes:

How do I go about talking to my angels? Mostly I hear the voices during sleep—that place where you're not yet asleep, but not awake, either.

At first I would get very upset and scared when I would hear the voice. I went so far as to consider my mental stability. The voice was very plain and clear. I can at this moment hear that voice and know that it is real.

The voice would tell me to get up and write things down so that I would be able to remember later what I was being told. I have gotten up several times in the middle of the night to write down messages.

I always remember getting up and writing, but I am not always conscious of what it is I am writing at the time. Later, when I go back to read the writing, I am always shocked to get such clear and vivid messages relating to problems or concerns I am having.

The first time I ever heard her voice, my angel told me her name was Celeste. I was scared to death when this happened, and remember jumping out of bed and shaking my husband awake. My husband thought I was going nuts!

Since then, Celeste has also told me the name of my husband's and children's angels. I get messages from her often now. Mostly the messages are to do with difficult things going on in my life.

I am a very good worrier and recently I've gotten a lot of messages about not taking everything to heart. "Learn to be patient with yourself" was a message I received recently.

I'm really learning to listen, though, and I think it is making a big difference in my life. I am not really a religious person, though I would say that I am spiritual. I feel really strange, though, in talking to others about my experiences. People just seem to not understand.

I believe there is a reason for being touched by these guardians. I just haven't figured out "why me?" yet. I do, however, find myself relying more and more on my angel to guide me with life.

I received a poem from an angel named Peter—whom I understand to be my husband's guardian angel—that I'd like to share. It was given to me in one of my dream states in June of 1994:

There are two angels in heaven
who are so very dear
we feel their presence daily
and always know they're near.

We hear their voices singing
we see them standing tall

with wispy wings and halos
and harps that play so loud.

They know we miss them dearly
though they remind us every day
that though we cannot see them
they'll never go away.

They made our match in heaven
because they truly knew
the love we give each other
would be forever true

The neat thing about this poem is that it came to me two days before I was to be married. My husband-to-be had just lost his father in an accident and my grandmother had just passed away after suffering from cancer. And we were both really missing them.

I really believe that I was given the gift of the poem to help me to understand that our loved ones were with us in spirit and that they approved of our love and commitment to each other.

Before these experiences, I never really thought one way or another about angels, but now I am a firm believer. I try to always listen to that little voice in my head, because now I know that it is truly for my own good!

So I have found a really special someone who has wrapped her arms around me and cares about me. I firmly believe that that voice comes from my loving guardian, who saw hopelessness and despair in my life and knew that I needed the help.

I think that we are all guided by an angel. I also believe that that angel is with us for eternity. I believe that humans are lacking hope. We see and hear so many sad and terrifying things that we have all become very numb. It is my belief that the angels are out in swarms trying very hard to give us back that hope so that we can once again become close to God.

A Troubled Teen's Guardian

As a troubled, suicidal teen, Mandy, faced death on two dramatic occasions—but in each case she credits her guardian angel with saving her life. Brought up an air force brat, moving frequently to homes in different parts of the country, Mandy first became aware of the presence of angels when, as a schoolgirl, she was living in Montana, where her father was stationed. In a home there, which she also believed was haunted, she had her first angel experience. Here's Mandy's story:

This home in Montana was the place where I first became close with my angels—I believe there were two of them. My brothers and I believed there were ghosts in the house, so I began reading books about the paranormal.

One day I was in my basement bedroom, laying on the floor reading. I had been reading for quite some time, and was totally engrossed in the book, when suddenly, I just rolled over.

I had no thoughts about rolling out of the way—not even an inkling! If my own muscles hadn't rolled me over, I would have said I was pushed. But right after I rolled over, a clock came flying down where my face had been! The clock had been sitting on my vanity, unplugged, more than three feet away from where I was lying. There was no way the clock could have just fallen that far.

It is my belief that the ghost was angry at me, and my guardian angel made my muscles move me out of harm's way. Kind of strange to have two paranormal forces working at once, wouldn't you say?

I know it makes me sound crazy, but two of my brothers can confirm that a ghost existed. The whole time I lived there, I could sense two other "spirits" keeping the ghost at bay whenever he got angry.

The only thing that let me sleep at night was reminding myself that the Bible said God protected children. I had a lot of faith that He did just that.

That incident made me start thinking of the existence of guardian angels. And these two other incidents in my life convinced me 100 percent that we are being looked after.

I was a teenager, living in Anchorage, Alaska, and was deeply troubled. I had begun to run away from home frequently, and had suicidal thoughts. One day I walked into a major and busy street. I walked directly toward a speeding car headed straight toward me. Somehow, it got past me without touching me, and I cannot fathom how it could have! It really didn't have time to veer away, and I was staring right at the bumper, ready to be nailed, when suddenly, it was past me! I wish I could remember more of the details of that day, but I can't.

Another time, when I was about fifteen years old, we kids were basically on our own and this got me very depressed, thinking no one really cared about me.

I grabbed my prescription of pills for my sore throat and started taking them, one at a time, while I cried and prayed to God. I just wanted to die. That one time in my life I think I was the closest I had ever been to my soul.

But I kept hearing a voice telling me that I could *not* do this. God would not allow this. I would face a worse punishment after death if I took my own life. This was not an escape.

At that point, it was like there was a voice in my head warning me not to commit suicide, that God couldn't give me another chance if I took my own life by my own choice. That was the only thing that stopped me.

I have had many other instances where I've heard these "voices" and determined that God was talking to me. Along with these voices comes a strong feeling that pulls you in a certain direction, or path in life.

Many times, I cannot fathom why this is being

done, but I have learned to listen to these "intuitions," if that's what you want to call them. While we have our own wills, it's always best to try and follow His.

CHAPTER FIVE

Angels: When a Life Is at Stake

When it's a matter of life and death, you can count on your angel being there to save your skin, as these following remarkable stories attest.

In a life-threatening situation, you don't even have to holler for angel help; you don't even have to be an angel believer—most of these survivors weren't!

If a life is at stake, your guardian angel can appear, without prayers, without begging. Spontaneously, as it were—to extricate you from the most seemingly-fatal predicaments.

Underwater Angel

An angel appeared to rescue diver Debra Pruett in the murky depths of a river as she was about to slice her trapped finger off to save her life.

With just five minutes of air left in her tank and her finger caught in the door of a submerged car, firefighter Debra Pruett was faced with a life-or-death decision—she had to cut her finger off or drown.

But just as she was about to slice into her skin, Debra says, her hand and her life were saved by an angel!

"I was moments away from death when out of the darkness a strange light appeared," recalled Debra, mother of two. "It was an angel. Nothing will ever convince me otherwise."

Coincidental with the appearance of the comforting light, Debra's trapped finger slipped free and she found herself swimming to the surface and safety.

Ironically, Debra—something of an angel herself—was risking her own life to rescue a baby she believed was still trapped in the car when her guardian angel lent a hand.

The riveting drama took place October 14, 1991, when Pruett and other divers with Nashville, Tennessee's elite fire department rescue squad dove in search of a despondent woman who'd driven her car off a ramp into the Cumberland River. Debra found the woman and dragged her to the surface. Then she went back into the murky depths to search for a baby reported to be in the car.

By the time she found the car again, the brave rescuer had less than six minutes of air time left in her tank. Determinedly, she reached to open the car's door when a sudden shift in water pressure slammed it on her middle finger! She frantically tried to open the door, but it wouldn't budge. "I knew I'd drown if I didn't take my knife out and cut off my finger. I decided to do it.

"I prayed: 'Help me, God. Please don't let me die like this.' That's when the angel appeared. I turned and over my shoulder I saw this bright light. The light came within arm's length, and then it was gone. Suddenly my finger was free."

Debra scrambled to the surface and was pulled into a boat by two other rescuers. Fortunately, there was no baby in the car, she was told.

She was curious about the light she had seen, thinking perhaps it was one of her colleagues who had come after her. She asked her supervisor which diver had gone down and tried to rescue her.

"Nobody," responded her puzzled chief.

"That's when I knew it had to have been an angel," says Debra.

Saved from Killer Sniper

Olivia Sue Lambert was a student at West Virginia University when a protective angel in a long luminous robe appeared to her and a friend in broad daylight with a warning that saved them from dying at the hands of a psycho killer.

Olivia, of Phillipi, West Virginia was out for a walk on the university campus one clear summer's day in the early 1960s with Alun, a fellow graduate student, when the angel appeared.

The young couple were nearing the Monongahela River when the angel suddenly confronted them and said, "Go no farther. You are in grave danger. Turn around and go back the way you came. Go slowly. Now."

For years the incident was lodged firmly in Olivia's mind. "Then one day, several years later, a headline in the local paper caught my eye. 'Morgantown Sniper Strikes Again'.

"I read with horror about a person who had randomly killed over a period of years, always striking in broad daylight, using a high-powered rifle atop a ridge overlooking the Monongahela River.

"Realizing Alun and I had been saved that day by one of God's angels, I whispered, 'Thank you, Lord.' "

Angels on the Cliff

Probably the most dramatic intervention of guardian angels ever reported is the story of Chantal Lakey, which has been documented in *Time* magazine and in a dramatic network television reenactment.

A band of protective guardian angels led Chantal to safety as she clung desperately to the face of a four-hundred-foot sheer cliff, her hands and feet unable to find a firm grip on wet rock as slippery as ice.

Seconds before, Chantal watched in horror as her beloved fiancé, Dale, toppled to his death on the rocks
below. She was certain she would follow him.

"Oh, God! Oh, God!" she screamed at the top of her
voice. "Please help me!"

Chantal and Dale, driving from a visit to Eugene, Ore-
gon to their home in San Diego, had stopped to enjoy
the rugged scenery atop the coastal cliff on California's
scenic Highway 101.

They hiked a winding trail to a spot called Lookout
Point, where they could see the Pacific Ocean. En-
tranced by the scenery, they decided to continue down
the trail to the ocean's edge.

"Very soon we realized what a foolish thing we had
done," remembers Chantal. "The path was fast becoming a sheer cliff. But it was too late to turn back—the
climb up was too steep. There was nowhere to go but
down. To make matters worse, it began to rain—a soft,
light drizzle that turned the loose rock as slippery as
soap."

As Dale inched his way down, he paused on a tiny ledge,
reaching his hand behind him to help Chantal find her
footing. Then, as he was looking upward at Chantal, he
simply fell off the ledge to his death on the rocks below.

Chantal went completely numb, trapped in a real-life
nightmare unfolding in front of her eyes. She had no
idea how to descend the cliff and she prayed and
screamed, convinced she was doomed to share Dale's
fate.

Then came the miracle: "I suddenly felt as though the
gateway between heaven and earth had opened up. And
I saw angels all around me like a wall of protection,
holding me up, closing in around me to keep me from
falling off the cliff.

"The next thing I remember is looking up and seeing
the cliff high above. Somehow I had managed to descend
more than three-hundred feet of slippery wet shale
safely, and I was about seventy-five feet above the
beach. I have no idea how I did it, but I am convinced
that the heavenly beings who had surrounded me high

on the cliff supported me in some way as I came down. I felt their presence all around me."

On the beach safely, she made her way to the main highway, where she flagged down a passing motorist. A rescue team later recovered Dale's lifeless body. They marveled how she had been able to descend that sheer four-hundred-foot cliff.

"How you got down that rock face safely is beyond me," one rescue team member later told her. "Chantal, you're a living, breathing miracle!"

A Businesslike Savior

A soft-spoken businessman type in a dark blue suit with a white shirt—who looked remarkably like the late actor James Mason—appeared out of nowhere to come to the aid of two Chicago teenagers involved in a life-or-death situation.

More than thirty years later, one of those boys, Lawrence Gray, now a forty-seven-year-old computer software salesman is convinced that the quiet stranger who came to their rescue and averted a tragic drowning that fateful day was a guardian angel.

Lawrence Gray, a Vietnam veteran and father of two, with degrees I accounting and business administration, recalls vividly the experience that happened when he was just sixteen:

A friend and I went swimming in deep water off a seawall in Lake Michigan, off Foster Park on the north side of Chicago. It was April of 1964 and we were on spring vacation. The day was extremely warm (83 degrees) for April—hence there were not many people around and the water was still cold (probably 50 degrees).

I was going to sun myself while my friend swam. He dove in, then swam back to the wall, but could not get up because the handhold was too high to reach. We had been in the same location many times the year before but the lake level had dropped and made it impossible to get up the wall.

The waves were also high that day and that caused my friend to get smashed into the wall each time a wave broke. He was being beaten into the wall constantly. Along with the cold water, it was quite an ordeal. Trying to scale the wall he cut his foot, and that was also a problem.

I tied two towels together and was able to hold him up but couldn't pull him out of the water. This holding on went on for at least thirty minutes, but the moss-covered seawall was too slippery and made it impossible for either of us to get a foothold.

I weighed about 140 pounds and my friend about 180 pounds, so it would have been difficult for me to haul him up. And after those painful thirty minutes, I was exhausted from trying.

All of a sudden a man in a blue suit appeared and asked if he could help. With one hand he pulled my friend out of the water, which was a significant feat of strength since my friend weighed 180 pounds.

After my friend was safe the stranger just disappeared! I could see for a mile and there wasn't anyone around and I did want to thank the man. My friend didn't believe me but that guy in the suit simply vanished!

The rescuer was a white businessman-type with a blue suit and blue-gray hair. He reminded me of the movie actor James Mason. The only words he spoke were, "Do you boys need help?"

I don't have any other explanation for this incident, other than that he must have been an angel. As I am convinced this incident happened to me for a reason, I think it important to share it with anyone who wants to listen.

Costa Rican Angels

During the harrowing sixty-six days they drifted aimlessly in the giant Pacific Ocean, Miami couple William and Simone Butler, both in their fifties, prayed fervently for angel intervention.

Their prayers were answered. As sharks were closing in on their tiny liferaft, the starving couple were rescued by a Costa Rican coastguard patrol. Incredibly, the patron saint of Costa Rica is the Virgin of the Angels!

That's why, just a few days after their miraculous rescue in August, 1989, the Butlers made a pilgrimage to the small cathedral town of Cartago on the Pacific coast to pay homage to the tiny country's Virgin of the Angels.

Hundreds of townspeople who had heard about the amazing rescue gathered outside the cathedral as the Butlers went inside to offer up their silent prayers.

"Long before our adventure on the high seas, we had heard of the great devotion the Costa Rican people have for the Virgin of the Angels. And while we drifted on the high seas we prayed constantly that she would help us," said Bill Butler.

The couple's adventure-turned-ordeal began on May 24, 1989, when they began their voyage from Panama to Hawaii in a forty-foot sailboat. Whales attacked and sank their boat June 15, and they escaped onto a liferaft with only a fishing line and a water filter.

Sharks were their constant companions as they drifted for more than two months. They had to eat raw fish to survive. Bill Butler lost 50 pounds, his wife sixty.

That's the pathetic state they were in when the Costa Rican Coast Guard found the Butlers on August 19, drifting aimlessly about twenty miles off the port town of Golfito.

But doctors at the hospital in Golfito later pronounced the couple in "remarkably good condition" and they were released after just a few days of treatment.

"That's why we felt we had to come to the Virgin of the Angels Cathedral in Cartago," said Simone Butler, "to personally give thanks to the Virgin of the Angels for helping us survive."

The Coffee-Colored Angel

A tiny coffee-colored lady with a sad face and beautiful expressive eyes saved Rita Staropoli from being crushed to death when she fell in front of oncoming traffic in a busy New York street.

Like other classic angel intervention stories, the unlikely hero vanished into the crowds without waiting to be thanked for her heroic act.

About twenty-five years ago, I came out of a department store in Brooklyn, New York, and saw my bus pull up across the wide avenue [Mrs. Staropoli of Plantation, Florida, wrote to the *Miami Herald*].

The cars were stopping at the red traffic lights. Carrying a heavy shopping bag, and burdened down with a heavy, fur-lined coat, I started running across the avenue to get to the bus. Halfway across, my rubber-soled shoes caught on the asphalt, and I fell down face forward.

The traffic lights changed, and I heard the lines of autos start their engines. My mind screamed, "I'll be killed!"

Suddenly, a pair of strong hands pulled me up to my feet, and the person and I rushed to safety. I turned around to see who had dashed out into traffic and rescued me. It was a small coffee-colored lady. I outweighed her by fifty pounds. She had a rather sad little face, and her eyes were remarkably beautiful.

She took a small package with an antiseptic towel out of her purse and handed it to me. In a very sweet voice, she said, "Wash your knee. It's bleeding. I work in a hospital." Then gently, she said to me: "You don't have to run for a bus."

Speechless, I stared wildly into her beautiful eyes, and she lowered them and walked away into the busy crowd.

Faster Than a Speeding Bullet

"I'm alive because angels are faster than bullets!" says fourteen-year-old Jan Zonyk, who credits his guardian angel with saving his life after a bullet was fired straight at his heart.

Jan's brush with death came as he was showing off his father's .32 caliber pistol to some young friends. One of his young companions started playing a kind of Russian roulette with the deadly weapon.

Believing it unloaded, he started pointing it at his pals. "Do you trust me?" he asked each in turn, before pulling the trigger as the hammer clicked on to empty chambers.

It was Jan's turn. This time the gun fired for real.

"There was an explosion. I looked down and saw blood oozing from the front of my shirt," remembers the Michigan City, Indiana, boy.

Incredibly, the speeding bullet had been deflected by his St. Christopher's medal, which his father had given him only two days before.

The deflected bullet lodged in Jan's lower abdomen and he had to undergo emergency surgery. Luckily, he survived without permanent injury. But doctors told him he would have died if the medal had not diverted the bullet's deadly path.

"I'm just thankful my angel was with me to give me a second chance at life," says the lucky boy.

Two Angels in Brooklyn

If it weren't for the intervention of a couple of angels, two of New York's finest might have been blown to heaven.

Officers Vincent DeSantis and Anthony Agugliaro were pulled to safety on November 13, 1994, from a wrecked truck that was carrying highly flammable oxygen tanks and leaking gas.

"It was clearly a case of role reversal and I'm attempting to locate them so we can give them a commendation," said Sergeant Jack Cambria after the incident as he pored over police reports trying to find out the identities of the two mysterious heroes. "What they did was very heroic. They're lifesavers."

"The truck could have rolled over or caught fire," said Sergeant Arthur Mattor, who arrived on the scene after the rescuers disappeared. "They definitely put their lives on the line. I've been on the job for thirteen years and I was overwhelmed by the sight of the truck," he said.

As members of the elite Emergency Service Unit, Officers DeSantis, thirty, and Agugliaro, twenty-five, usually do the rescuing. But early this Saturday morning, as they raced to a wreck, their truck was struck by a car that ran a red light at Sixty-third Street and Bay Parkway in Bensonhurst, Brooklyn.

The police truck flipped upside down and its rear compartment was torn from the cab. Gasoline stored in the rear compartment spilled into the street. One spark could have set off the oxygen tanks.

Then, out of the blue, the angels appeared.

Sergeant Mattor feared the worst when he arrived on the scene. "I didn't think they could have survived," Mattor said. "I looked in the cab and nobody was inside, so I thought they had been ejected. Then people on the street told us the cops had been dragged a half block away."

The two rescuers left the scene without giving their names.

On Land and Sea

As a U.S. Navy diver and bomb disposal expert, Rudy Smith has been in a few tight scrapes in his time.

But on at least two occasions, this macho twenty-year-old man has given thanks to his guardian angel—or angels—whom he credits with extricating him and his buddies from alarming predicaments.

A father of two from Michigan, where he grew up the second-oldest of six sons, Rudy currently lives with his family in Kaneohe, Hawaii. As he nears completion of his military service, which has involved him in such activities as bomb disposal work, deep-sea diving, demolition, parachuting, and training sea lions and dolphins, Rudy is looking toward writing for a living. That's why he is able to articulate his own angel encounters in such dramatic fashion. In his own words:

Location: Yorktown, Virginia. No previous contact of the mystical nature. Not, repeat *not*, biblically oriented or religiously indoctrinated. Agnostic maybe, atheist maybe.

Job description: Loading wooden boxes (by hand) and one piece at a time with extremely sensitive explosives—live fuses, civilian fireworks, raw high explosives.

When one box was full, about 150 pounds, we used a forklift to carefully place it on a flatbed truck, which would then inch, emphasis on inch, down to the place where a crane would slowly lift box off truck and place in large hole to minimize kick-outs.

There was I on forklift with six people on my left just watching—no time for a bump, thump, jostle or oops. Intense concentration.

Box makes it to flatbed, and, as I slowly back off, a voice behind me distracts my concentration with a soft "Rudy."

I turn, for a split second, to see who's there. It's not good to run over a soft-spoken comrade's foot. But there's no one there?

I look back and witness the box begin its slow-mo descent to the ground. Inches from its destination, the corner of box tilts. I jam on my brakes. I inhale and scream at the same time.

I'm sure it's all over, for all seven of us. Before box hits ground, the voice distracts me again, with an ominous message, "As you forgave, so shall you be forgiven."

The box of explosives hits the ground and begins to disintegrate. Everyone is frozen, in shock. Its volatile contents begin to fly in all directions. A detonation begins and the fireball engulfs us, taking the oxygen away from our lungs and blinding us.

Suddenly everything goes quiet. Everyone is still standing. Unhurt. Unscathed. Like it didn't happen. Frozen in another time and place? Yet, undeniably, the ground is covered with explosives and ordnance.

My first thought is to make sure everyone is okay. They are still frozen. I shut off the forklift. Adrenaline begins to flood my body and my heart begins to pound wildly. "My God," I say to myself, "I almost killed them."

I am numb, no longer a body, I am awareness, I am thought without a body. For the first time in my life I am aware that I *am.*

Suddenly, yet cautiously, my six companions begin to move. They kneel down and silently begin to clear away the still-dangerous, deadly debris surrounding their feet. They cannot make a false step. It's still too dangerous.

I stoop down to help. Silent seconds, then minutes pass. Everyone has worked themselves into a circle, cautiously clearing the debris.

The shared adrenaline begins to subside, and I see myself at a court martial. I see myself being discharged dishonorably. I see myself being kicked out of the organization I've become so much a part of.

Then one of my companions speaks. "Don't worry about it, Rudy. It was an accident."

Later that evening we are drinking beer at a local pub. It's not a cheerful event, the post-traumatic blues have taken the last of our oxygen away.

Until ... until a brave soul, not myself, says, "I know this might sound crazy, but I could swear when that box was falling I heard a voice."

I laughed. Ha. "No really, laugh if you want but it said something about being forgiven." I had heard the same message. Someone else jumps in, "I heard it too, it said something about being forgiven because I forgave."

"Before long all seven of us confirmed we heard the same (in our head) voice.

Years go by. There are major life changes for all seven guys. Mystical things, coincidental things, begin to happen more and more. Too many to be coincidence.

Now I understand everything in life is on purpose.

Fast forward a few years for Rudy's other angelic encounter:

The date: November something, 1992.

Location: Kanehoe Bay, Hawaii, ninety feet below the surface of a very big ocean.

Job description: A pleasure trip, gathering lobster on what should have been an uneventful scuba dive. I had made two dives earlier in the day in connection with my work—training sea lions.

My dive partner and myself had anchored our Zodiac boat and quickly descended to a ninety-foot ledge. Our goal was to get in, grab some groceries, and get out.

Previous dives had left too much residual nitrogen in our blood to waste any time. I had no desire to get decompression sickness. I am allergic to pain.

Our destination was a cave which we knew held an abundant supply of spiny lobster. To enter this cave one must take off one's dive tank completely and slide it into the tunnel first.

The two of us entered the cave slowly. We each slipped our tanks back on and began to pick and choose our menu. According to plan, I moved clockwise and my partner moved counter-clockwise. Everything was going perfectly.

Then I heard the voice: *"Get out."*

I was startled, I knew the voice wasn't that of my dive partner, but I didn't panic. There was nothing to panic over. At least not yet.

Suddenly, out of the murky depths, appeared a huge moray eel, eight or nine feet in length. To put it mildly, it was somewhat upset at finding us in its lair.

This normally docile creature began snapping at our bags and rolling across the bottom of the cave with writhing and twisting motions.

In a matter of seconds everything went dark. The turbidity was so severe the only thing I could see with my light was the fine particles of sediment suspended directly in front of my mask. Not good. Not good at all.

It's at this point where a diver, even a veteran diver, loses all sense of direction. And panic means death. My partner began to panic and ricocheted off the walls, desperately trying to escape. This panic began to take over me, as I too worked the walls looking for the narrow way out.

Seconds soon turned into minutes, and soon we had exceeded our bottom time and were almost out of air.

It was at that point . . . the final point . . . the point of no return . . . that I felt something grab me and start to forcefully guide me. I assumed it was my buddy.

In an instant I was surrounded by blueness and light. I was free. I was out.

I looked for my buddy, but he was nowhere to be seen. Checking my air supply, I knew I only had two minutes left. If I surfaced now I would probably be bent. I turned and tried to go back into the cave entrance, but my tank clanked against the narrow opening of the tunnel.

How, I wondered, had I managed to get out of the cave with my tank on? I started to pull off my tank, thinking maybe I can go into the tunnel just far enough to grab part of my buddy if he swam by.

But I wasn't thinking clearly, and whatever air I had disappeared. I was forced to start my ascent.

Fear gripped me, and an overwhelming feeling of desperation tried to hold me on the bottom. I had left my buddy, my dive buddy, in a cave to drown. You never, ever leave your buddy.

When I hit the surface, I grabbed a spare tank from the boat. But just as I was about to go down, my buddy's head popped to the surface. He was gray, ashen, marbled. He was scared to death.

I pulled him in the boat and asked him if he was okay. He nodded a silent and terrified "yes." I started up the boat and headed back for shore. I knew we would be feeling the pain in our joints quickly. Hopefully the nitrogen bubbles wouldn't hit a main artery or a nerve center and paralyze us or cause us to black out.

Strangely that pain never came. The color in my buddy's face returned slowly, but he couldn't talk for several hours.

Later, a few beers later, I asked him how on earth he managed to get out of that cave. He responded, "I thought you pulled me out!"

So there you have it. This is the first time I've ever talked about that experience. It gives me chill bumps just remembering it.

So, are there guardian angels at work? Since these experiences I have given them a lot of thought. Why were we saved when so many people don't make it? Can our subconscious shut off our conscious mind, so the super-conscious can take over and save our silly adrenaline-addicted behinds?

After these angelic interventions, I have tried to make unsolicited contact through traditional meditation. Unsuccessfully.

But I still routinely experience profound bliss, peace, and clarity through mystical revelation and awareness—although I have not yet found a *way* to contact the *voice* that was my savior.

It seems it only shows up and does its thing when it absolutely feels it *has* to.

As a mucho macho skeptic—a military man—I am not into hocus-pocus stuff. And, had I not experienced these things firsthand, and had I not been firmly grounded (sane), I would never have believed what happened to me.

The Young Man from Angell Street

It's probably no accident that twenty-eight-year-old advertising executive Will Burns lives in—get this—Providence, Rhode Island, on Angell Street.

Will is not formally religious in any way, but he believes it was a combination of providence and angels that saved his life on two separate occasions. Here are Will's stories:

Once, on the evening of my cousin's funeral—he died of cancer at age twenty-four—my family was sitting by the fire in our living room when we heard a huge crash outside. We all knew it was ice sliding off the roof, but my father asked me to go check it out anyway.

I walked outside and along the side of the house where the sound came from. Once my eyes adjusted, I saw there was a fresh pile of ice that surely was what made the sound. It was absolutely silent at this particular moment and I was in a peaceful mood.

As I stood there looking at the ice fall, a feeling came over me of intense, electrifying fear. Almost as if the bark of an attack dog broke the silence (it didn't, but I felt like that), I instantly turned and ran—even though there was not the slightest indication of anything threatening.

At that moment, another huge five-hundred-pound sheet of ice fell exactly where I was standing seconds before. Whew! Was it a premonition? An angel, perhaps?

Another time I was swimming at a friend's camp beside a lake. I grew up around a nice clean pool and don't love swimming in the lake, but it's not bad if you stay near the surface.

On this day, I was about thirty yards out just swimming around pointlessly, barely underwater, when an intense feeling of "I'd better dive down deeper" came over me. As I said, I hate the thought of swimming deep in a lake, but at this second I really felt I should. So I did.

That second, the rudder of an out-of-control sailboat whizzed inches above my head and proceeded to crash into the dock. If I hadn't listened to that warning voice and swam deeper, you would not be reading this.

Another of my stories isn't so much an angel encounter experience as it is an "awareness" session. My sister lives in Bellingham, Washington, and is very much into psychic healing, as well as angel experiences.

I guess I am too, but she takes the cake. Anyway, I went to visit her and she took me to a psychic for a reading. I had one question I planned to ask: "What is this presence I always seem to feel around me?"

After about ten minutes of meditation and looking at me—and even before I asked any questions—the psychic began to cry. She said she had never seen such protection. She saw five angels above me in a circle, and a spirit guide in my aura.

This floored me, not only because of the angels, but because that was the answer to my unasked question! Apparently, the spirit guide is named 'Bashar' and he has traveled with me through many of my lives and is a "high-ranking spirit guide."

I often wonder why I am so protected in life. I appreciate it, mind you—but I still wonder why.

CHAPTER SIX

Flesh-and-Blood Angels?

Yes, there are indeed flesh-and-blood angels!

Time and again during my research for this book, I've spoken to persons who are convinced that their guardian angels exist in the form of a living, breathing, eating, sleeping human being, be they spouses, children, relatives or just special friends.

But how can this be? Aren't angels supposed to be spiritual entities, heavenly messengers, protective guardians with miraculous powers? The answer is: Yes, they can be all that—and more.

A dear friend and lay pastor, John McKenna of West Palm Beach, Florida, makes a strong argument for earthbound angels we might know as merely relatives or friends.

"We are told that angels can appear to us in any form they want—so why can't they be everyday dear friends or beloved relatives?" reasons Pastor McKenna.

> There are people we know in our everyday lives who are truly angels in thought, word, and deed. They seem to exist just to make our lives brighter, and the world a better place to live in.
>
> Is it not possible that these special earthbound people are here for a higher purpose? Could they not be imbued with an angelic spirit?
>
> I'm sure we all have special friends who deserve to be dubbed "angels."

I was thinking of these words when I received this letter from Clifton Keene of San Antonio, Texas, who presents this heartfelt argument for the recognition of human angels.

Although he hasn't had any dramatic heavenly angel interventions to report, Mr. Keene would like to publicly acknowledge his own special angels, Kelli and Samantha. He writes:

> I have some long-held ideas and beliefs about angels. I am positive that angels are around us at all times—in the form of our closest friends.
>
> And why not? How else do we stop ourselves from things that may hurt or be harmful? It's because of those special, kind, caring, and compassionate souls who are our friends—the true angels of the world.
>
> I have been blessed with friends I feel very close to, and I believe with all my heart that they are angels assigned to watch over me. I'd like others to realize that they too could be similarly blessed.
>
> I've almost lost track of all the times these thoughtful beings, my closest friends, have been my guiding light in times of darkness and sorrow. That's why I want to honor them publicly.
>
> I'm very proud of these angels, and I want this letter to be my way of thanking them in a very special way . . . to show them how much I really love, respect, and care about them for all they have done.
>
> These angels' names are Kelli and Samantha. And they're two of the nicest "people" I or anyone else could ever possibly meet. I want this letter to be testimony of how grateful I am for their presence and influence in my life.

A dear colleague, Catharine Rambeau, a journalist from Lake Worth, Florida, also added her thoughts on the comforting spirit of human angels. She told me:

> About ten years ago, a dear friend of mine died of cancer after a long and noble fight. A memorial service was held for her in Detroit at Wayne State University's theater.
>
> Lucy was a true Southern belle, as well as one of

the strongest, funniest, most loving people any of us knew. At the service, her husband and friends and coworkers spoke about her, telling tales of her life and her endlessly endearing ways.

Sitting in the third row of the theater with no one in front of or behind me and no one on either side, I thought of Lucy and how much she had inspired everyone who ever knew her well.

Suddenly I felt someone gently grasp my ankle; I could feel a warm hand holding it affectionately. And I started to smile.

Then I said, very, very quietly, "Now Lucy, you stop that right now!" And it disappeared. I thought then, and I still think, that it was Lucy's way of saying goodbye. She knew how much we would miss her, and I still do.

A Very Special Angel Gift

If you're skeptical that flesh-and-blood angels can live among us and work miracles, this touching letter by Brenda J. Kirkman, of North Dade, Florida, which appeared in the *Miami Herald* on Christmas Day 1994, should remove all doubts:

This is our angel's second Christmas.

This one is special. It is a precious time in all three of our lives. There may not be a whole lot of it left. We don't know.

When I married my husband Chuck less than two years ago, I thought all my dreams had come true. Our wedding was at sunset, by a lake. The sky was a brilliant red. Chuck said I glowed like a neon light. We both had good jobs, a car, and were starting our home. Everything was coming together just right.

A few months later, our daughter Lauren was born. I felt from the start that she was very special.

I didn't know how special at the time.

When she was ten months old, Chuck was hospitalized with acute anemia. After a week of more tests, he was diagnosed with HIV. One week later, they told me I was HIV-positive, too. We were scared for our little girl. Her tests came back indeterminate.

Chuck had to quit his job. I gave mine up when he was in the hospital. The car died. We had to move in with my mother. Our whole world changed. We hit rock bottom.

Yet all through the ups and downs, the fears, the tears, the denial, the anger, our angel was with us. The littlest things make her so happy. She brightens our lives.

I began to see that God gave her to us to better understand and know that our lives are not that bad.

She has made our acceptance of HIV/AIDS much easier than anyone could imagine. Just when I feel that my world will fall apart, my angel suddenly comes up and gives me a hug, as if she understands my anguish.

Looking back, I know that we needed her more than she needed us.

Just recently, Lauren's blood tests came back negative. No HIV. We learned there is about a 75 percent chance that a baby born to an HIV-positive mother will be negative. Nobody understands how it happens—but it takes about sixteen to eighteen months to be certain.

Knowing this, I can rest easier. I know that our Lord sent us our guardian angel to help us understand the true meaning of love and of life. No words can ever express my love for this angel from heaven. We are blessed. She holds us both together.

I have been writing a diary on a computer disk every night after she goes to sleep. Chuck is making videos. These are for her, so she will one day know how much her mother and father loved her.

Chuck's family members say they have never seen him happier. We are going to have a wonderful life— no matter how long it is.

That's what makes this Christmas so special. If we had known about being HIV-positive a few months sooner, we would never have gone through with the pregnancy. And she wouldn't be here.

We are truly blessed by our angel.

Parking Lot Angels

Angels pop up in the most unexpected places. For an elderly couple, Josefina and Dominick Di Martino of Miami Beach, it was a family of angels who came to their aid—in a parking lot.

The Di Martinos had been shopping at a local market and had just left the store with a number of heavy packages when a violent storm struck. The overburdened senior citizens felt helpless until their angels showed up.

From the moment we left the store we had a problem: The rain was falling very hard, and there was so much wind that the umbrella turned inside out.

My husband had a heavy package and a cane. I carried packages, too. We couldn't run, so we stopped, not knowing what to do. A car stopped with a couple and two kids and offered to help. "No thanks," said my husband, but I trusted them and accepted. The wife was so nice—she fixed my husband's umbrella, took his heavy package and helped us into the car.

They took us home safely. We didn't have words to show them our gratitude; maybe this letter will help. They were our angels.

An Angelic Tutor

Angels can be on your shoulder at the most difficult and stressful moments of your life—they can even help you sail through a difficult examination or test with flying colors.

A thirty-three-year-old lawyer, who prefers to remain anonymous, credits her guardian angel with helping her pass the bar exam.

"I'm not religious," she insists. "I'm very logical. But growing up, I had a neighbor who was kind of a second mother to me. When she died, I started talking to her in my mind, and last year when I was studying for the California bar, I had 'conversations' with her every night.

"Tests always make me panicky, and this one is three days long! As I walked into the exam room, I said to her, 'You've got to take over for me. I can't do this myself.' Then I turned to the first case: The litigants had the same name as my neighbor. It was as if a huge weight had been lifted off my shoulders. I breezed through the test—and passed."

To this day, this lawyer refuses to believe that what happened was mere coincidence and continues to "talk" to her guardian angel when she's worried.

A Cabbie's Comfort

Buffalo cab driver Harold Wilcox was sure he was about to be robbed.

"When you drive a cab—you just know. You sense things," says Harold recalling the night three young men slid into the back seat of his cab. "They were ready," he said. "I saw it in their faces."

Then one of them saw the statue—and stopped. He put out his arm. He said, 'No, not this man.' Just like that. And they didn't rob me."

The "statue" is a small Infant of Prague that stands on Wilcox's dashboard—a St. Jude medal and chain draped over it, a tiny globe of St. Christopher behind it.

And sixty-year-old Harold believes his guardian angels protect him as he plies his trade throughout western New York.

"I have had so many things happen in my life—to the point of hearing Him tell me what to do," the devoutly religious cabbie told the *Buffalo News*. "It's kind of scary at times—but it's Him and I hear Him."

Just a Face in the Crowd

Miami resident Joan Lyons was distraught when she discovered that her sister, who had been visiting from Macon, had misplaced her wallet during a visit to Miami's busy passport office.

Upset at the loss of the wallet and without a clue where they might have left it, the sisters stood on the crowded platform of a commuter rail station as they prepared to return home, wondering what to do next.

That's when a Spanish-speaking stranger appeared out of the crowds on the busy platform to tell them where the missing wallet could be found. Ms. Lyons tells her unusual angel story in a letter to the local newspaper:

While on the crowded platform, we lamented the consequences of the lost wallet. Then a southbound train stopped where we were standing.

As commuters poured out of the open train door, a man speaking Spanish approached us and said "Purse. Passport." Puzzled, we answered "What?"

He repeated, "Purse. Passport office." My sister and I looked at each other and nodded in agreement. When he was sure we got the message, he turned and disappeared into the crowd. We shouted "Thank you, sir!" and raced down the stairs and through the terminal. On our way back to the passport office, we marveled at the timing of the man's appearance.

Breathless, we approached the security guard at the passport office. He recognized us and gave my sister her wallet. It had fallen out of her purse when she loaned a pencil to a man applying for his passport.

To this day, we still speak of the Spanish-speaking angel who appeared in a crowd of Metro commuters and directed us to the lost wallet in massive downtown Miami.

On Their Shoulder

Just as it's comforting to feel that earthbound angels are all around us at all times, as family members or as compassionate strangers blessed with the angelic spirit, most angel witnesses I interviewed are confident and comfortable in the belief they are looked after twenty-four hours a day by more ethereal presences.

The Twelve-Foot-Tall Guardian

A twelve-foot guardian angel appeared to Caroline Sutherland in a thirty-second burst of heat and light and totally changed her life.

Caroline was a counselor at a holistic medicine clinic in Seattle where she arrived at seven-thirty one morning, fresh from several days of intense meditation and glowing with a sense of peace and inner warmth.

She suddenly realized she was not alone in the clinic.

> I felt there was a heat and a light in the room. I looked up, and the whole back wall of this small room fell away.
>
> Standing there was a twelve-foot-plus guardian-angel being. The figure had wings and a head and a flowing effervescence aswirl in beautiful colors, like the aurora borealis.
>
> Everything was telepathic. The words I heard in my mind were, "Behold the angel. Will you do my work?"
>
> The presence was so strong and so vibrant, and the room was filled with light and love. My heart was tin-

gling. There was no mistake in my mind it was a guardian angel, no doubt at all.

I felt a great sense of peace and love. The whole experience lasted thirty seconds, but it felt like a lifetime.

As a direct result of that angelic encounter in the mid-1980s, eight years ago, Caroline launched a new career—running a business she calls My Little Angel, selling stuffed dolls and self-help audiotapes, aimed at reducing stress and enhancing children's self-esteem.

"I believe the angels were behind me all the way in this new project," says Caroline.

Angels in the Cockpit

Angels can be beside you—on your shoulder, as it were—even when you can't see them.

Janice Gravely can attest to this. Her husband died suddenly at the controls of their new plane. Passenger Janice panicked, then prayed.

She felt an overwhelming peace despite the terrible peril she faced. She was able to control the plane and two hours later, after running out of gas, she crash-landed—and miraculously survived.

Pastor Thomas Moore is also convinced that an angel's intervention saved his life while he too was behind the controls of a small plane lost in fog and about to crash.

Pastor Moore had given up all hope of surviving when a calm, soothing voice began giving reassuring instructions, the voice echoing confidently in the cockpit of the lost plane.

"He was talking like anyone else. We thought it was a controller from an air tower on the ground," he remembers.

"In this case, the ground was completely covered with fog, and the controller had lost all contact with us. No one could see us. We did not know where we were and about to land on an interstate just a few feet from a bridge.

"That's when the voice came on loud and clear and said, 'Pull it up. Pull it up'."

The pilot obeyed the voice, pulled up, and narrowly missed hitting the bridge. Moments later, he was able to land the plane safely.

Could it have been a helpful radio ham on the ground giving instructions? Says Moore: "If you take any miracle, you can always figure out some sort of explanation. But I believe it was an angel!"

Many other pilots are convinced that there are angels flying with them in the cockpit of their planes—copilots who even take corrective action at the controls if they sense danger.

"I think my guardian angel was or is a pilot sympathizer," one pilot, Steven F., told me, reporting that on several occasions while flying he has had an awareness of something important beside him, a presence that seems to make itself known by "a feeling of a cool chill."

Steven told me: "It just seems that whenever I am in need of intervention, it is there. One time, when my autopilot failed at night and turned me toward the mountains, I noticed it within a few seconds even though I was busy reading maps.

"Also, on two take-offs where I have been in danger, I had a very noticeable uneasiness in my stomach beforehand for no apparent reason. Now I listen to that feeling."

Enormous—But Beautiful

Jeanetta Tillman, of Fort Myers, Florida, was only six when she had a vivid and miraculous vision of her guardian angel—a tall, serene being in white and gold with fluffy wings! This is, incidentally, one of the only accounts I came across where angel wings were described.

Writes Jeanetta:

Angels to me are very real indeed. They are serene beings, enormous in size, and very beautiful.

When I was about six years old, my cousin and I were playing around at home, wrestling with each other, when a great big picture hanging on the wall by just a nail, crashed down on me, hitting me right in the face.

"My whole face blew up like a balloon. One of my eyes was really hurt, and I had difficulty seeing out of it. My other eye was just slightly bruised. I remember my mother screaming when she saw my face.

She took me in her arms, put ice on my bruises, then took me upstairs to lie down. Shocked and hurting, I was lying in my bed, looking out of the window toward the sky.

I was conscious of a bright light in the sky. Suddenly, as if out of nowhere, my angel appeared to me. He looked at me and smiled.

I'll never forget that encounter. He was so enormous, with big fluffy white wings and the most beautiful flowing blond hair imaginable. He was wearing a white robe and he had a golden girdle around his waist. The sandals he was wearing were also gold.

I consider myself a firsthand witness that angels do exist . . . and they are just as many of us imagine them to be. On this occasion, my angel simply smiled, waved at me, then disappeared. I know he came to look in on me to make sure I was okay.

I knew them angels were very real and walk among us. I feel my angel around me now every day of my life. I am twenty-three years old now, but that encounter is something I will never forget as long as I live. That memory is very special to me, my most cherished of all my memories.

So to people that do not believe, I can only say: Yes, they are very real, and we all have one from birth. I can't speak for others, but I know my angel is with me every minute, twenty-four hours a day.

Visions and Dreams

A devoutly religious man, Marvin Wingo's protecting angels appear to him only as visions and in dreams—but he is as convinced of their power and actual presence as if they were flesh and blood.

Reports Marvin, of Abilene, Texas:

I've spoken to angels many times, beginning in 1981, but it has always been in visions and dreams—see Numbers 12–6; Job 33:14–16.

My first encounter, in 1981, happened in a dream vision after I had been praying. I felt an invisible vacuumlike force sweeping me up and away at an incredible speed. Then I felt myself being set down in a lush green meadow. Nearby, I could see a river banked by tall green trees and other lush greenery.

As I looked around wondering, "Where am I? How did I get here? Which direction should I go to get back to where I came from—if I *can* get back?" I felt a great peace within myself. Everything was so quiet and still.

Suddenly, from across the river came the sound of human voices. They were praying loudly, giving thanks to the Almighty. Since I couldn't see anyone, I decided to move closer to the river.

But before I could take my first step toward the water, I was confronted by this awe-inspiring figure. He was standing only twenty feet away from me. He was tall and humanlike encased in a bright light. Looking at him was like staring through the brightness of the sun's reflection off a mirror, but my eyes did not seem to hurt.

In normal tones, he spoke my name, "Marvin." I asked, "Are you my guardian angel?" For almost a full minute, he stood looking at me as if carefully considering my question. Then he replied, "Well Marvin, you could say that ... for I am your defender, and certainly won't let anyone harm you."

Marvin has seen and spoken with his protector and other angelic figures several times in dreams and visions over the years and has received comfort and guidance.

"My angels have always been very kind and polite—and several times I've seen and talked to the same tall angel I first met in 1981."

It was also through a vivid and very realistic dream that Roger DiPaolo first met his angel when he was only three or four years old. The encounter was very real to him and has remained imbedded in his memory all his life.

Says Roger:

I don't claim my "encounter" to be a particularly exciting one, nor can I ever verify that it actually happened. It did (and still does) seem very real to me.

I have always remembered this as a dream, although I've always had the feeling that it really did happen and it was intentional that I remember it merely as a "dream."

I was living with my mother and grandparents at my grandparents' home while my father was overseas in the military in the early 1960s.

In the dream I am standing in the end of the driveway behind my grandparents' house looking towards a low rock wall that separated the driveway from the patio directly behind the house.

Facing me, I see this "being"—or is it an angel? I am aware that this angel has brought me outside from my bed to talk to me here. I'm not quite sure how I got outside, but a brief image of floating above the area behind the house seems to flash into my mind.

As we're standing there facing each other, the angel begins to "talk" to me, but without actually speaking. I am not afraid. As a matter of fact, I feel a strong sense of security, along with a sense of love, caring, and concern emanating from the angel.

I feel as comfortable with the angel as I would feel in the presence of my parents—maybe even more so.

The angel does not have wings like any of the religious stereotypes that I may have been exposed to.

The angel was a slender being, dressed in white clothing. The clothing was unfamiliar to me, and not distinctive in any way, except that it almost seemed to glow with its own light.

I cannot picture a face, even though other details are clear. If there was any kind of clear face, I certainly could not see any mouth moving as I was being "spoken" to.

The angel seemed tall to me. But, remember, I was a young child and it is possible that the angel was no taller than an adult human, possibly even shorter.

I cannot remember the angel's exact words. I don't even know if the communication between us was in words or in the form of mental concepts. But the basic message relayed to me was, "You never need to worry or be afraid. We will always be with you and watching over you throughout your life."

A Broad, Friendly Smile

Although a guardian angel saved her life when she was fourteen years old, it was several years before Sandy Lawson, now a grown woman, was actually able to see and talk to her protector.

Initially, Sandy was only able to hear the voice of her angel. But to her delight, she was recently given a clear mental picture of her savior—a blonde-haired, slender woman with the world's friendliest smile. Here's Sandy's story:

In the summer of 1981, when I was fourteen, my friend Cheryl and I were walking back in the cranberry bogs of New Jersey, headed for the swing—a rope hanging from a tree that teetered on the edge of a small dug-out canyon.

It was a hangout for all the local kids, the equivalent of the corner store to town kids. Anyway, there were dams, also known as sluice gates, all over the bogs. These control the level of the water on either side of that particular section of bog.

The dams were constructed from wooden boards, and they operated by simply removing or adding a board or two, thereby slowing down or stopping the flow of water.

On this day, we were dawdling at a large double dam, which we called "the bench." It was draining at the time, quite a strong flow too. I decided to stand on the outer edge of the board that the water was flowing over to get a closer look.

When I satisfied my curiosity, I looked up and realized I would have to make a real strong jump, at an angle, to get back up to firm ground.

I'm quite small, and was even smaller then! I was really nervous. I really wasn't sure I could make the jump. And if I missed, I would go straight down into the dam, where I would surely drown from the water pressure holding me down.

I really began to doubt myself at that anxious moment. But I couldn't stay there all day. My friend had run off to look at something else, so I forced myself to jump.

It was a puny, scared little jump—and the farthest I got was about halfway. I could feel my body swinging in an arc down into the fast-flowing waters of the dam.

I remember thinking, "Oh, my God, I'm really going to die now!" I couldn't grab so much as a fingerhold with my hands. In less than a moment, my body's weight would yank me off the board and down into the dam.

But just before I got to that point—and I mean *just* before—my legs suddenly swung back forcefully, as though something shoved me hard, though I couldn't feel anything touch me.

It shoved me so hard, in fact, that not only did I swing out from the dam, but I actually felt being *pushed* upward. I was propelled upward to a spot where I was able to get my elbows onto the board, grab into the groove between the boards, and haul myself up and outta there *fast!*

Just then, my friend came back and I told her what had happened. I said it must have been my guardian angel, because I couldn't have physically done it myself. What happened to me that day went against the laws of physics. My friend Cheryl agreed with me.

Boy, was I ever relieved! I thanked the angel, and we went on to the swing. Doncha just love a happy ending? I do!

Later in life, Sandy got the chance to thank her angel in a vivid face-to-face encounter.

Not too long ago, I got to thinking about that guardian angel who saved my life when I was fourteen.

For some time I've always paid heed to "voices" that I listen to. I used to attribute these voices to simple intuition. But now I attribute them to angels. And faith. The voice I always heard was female.

A few days ago, I was pondering this, and—for the first time—with the voice came a mental picture. It was of a white woman, thin, maybe around thirty-two years of age, with, a broad, friendly smile. I couldn't see anything else.

Then just last night, I wondered, "What about the rest of the face?" I saw the smile again, then saw the whole face, a little neck. The rest was darkness, although she appeared to be wearing a white draping gown.

It was a pleasant, though not beautiful, face. She was the kind of person who isn't really physically beautiful, but you think they are because of the beauty of their heart. In fact, it was a very heart-shaped face, wide across the cheekbones, with a narrow tapering jaw.

She had golden-blonde hair, shoulder cut. But I remember most of all her broad, friendly smile. That was the thing that stood out most. I didn't notice her eyes much, although they seemed to be smiling too.

Of course, my angel could be some kind of self-fulfilling fantasy, because in some respects she does match the classical renderings of angels: White robes, golden hair—although not the face. And she did look like she could gain about ten pounds. Of course, I didn't see any wings at all!

To me, nevertheless, she seems like a "real" person, as opposed to an idealized version of an angel.

CHAPTER SEVEN

Angels: The Great Healers

A band of merry angels makes a desperately sick child laugh and speeds her on the road to recovery ... a winged cherubim visits an ailing pastor in hospital ... and an angelic vision inspires a paralyzed teenager to walk again.

These are just a few of the uplifting stories about the miraculous healing powers of angels you will find in this chapter.

Inspired to Walk Again

For two weeks after a serious auto accident, high school senior Michele Daly was in a coma. When she woke she was totally paralyzed and told she might never walk again.

In the depths of despair, she was visited one night in her hospital room by an angel and the comforting spirit of her dead grandmother.

These visitations have inspired her to walk again and she is today making a slow but steady recovery. Michele, who attends Rutherford High School in Rutherford, New Jersey, and hopes to attend college soon, is still working hard in therapy.

She reports:

My grandmother, with whom I was extremely close, died suddenly in October of 1992. I was too sick to go to the funeral in Florida, so I never really got to say goodbye to her. But I always believed she was still with me.

On September 3, 1993, I was in a car accident with my friends. I woke up two weeks later completely paralyzed, to find out that I broke my neck. I was only sixteen, and I was scared to death!

Every night I kept praying that I would walk again. I also prayed to stay alive, because my heart stopped twice. I would wake up some nights hysterical after having horrible nightmares.

One night I was lying in ICU and I looked down at the end of my bed. I saw a beautiful glowing light; I remember feeling very warm and safe. Nothing was said but I remember feeling my grandmother's presence. I believe she came to comfort me and to tell me that one day I will walk again.

The Lady in Green

Another equally dramatic account—with an even happier ending—is the 1986 story of twenty-four-year-old Georgia truck driver Joe Tucker.

Joe was dying. Fluid was building in his brain and the pressure was slowly killing him. Doctors didn't give him much hope. The one thing that *might* save him, they said, could also kill him—a difficult operation that involved removing the entire top of his skull and actually removing his brain.

The young trucker had no choice but to agree to the procedure. But knowing the consequences, he insisted on one thing: That he marry his longtime sweetheart, Joyce Womack, first—so they could at least have a few hours together as man and wife.

As orderlies hovered outside, waiting to whisk Joe to the operating room, Joe and Joyce got married in an Albany, Georgia hospital room.

Tears welled in their eyes as they held hands and exchanged vows. They held each other close and talked in hushed tones, and with uncertainty, about their future together.

Joe's new brother-in-law, Mike Womack, joined them in the room to extend his congratulations. As they were talking, the door opened and a beautiful young woman, wearing a striking green dress, quietly walked into the room and joined them.

"She was in her thirties, tall and attractive," remembers Mike. "I'll never forget that green dress." Nor will Joe and Joyce.

The woman walked over to the group and said quietly, "You don't know me, but I know you." Recalls Joyce, "She told us she had been sent by God to pray for us— and we prayed."

After the prayers, she told Joe that it was time for a miracle and that there would be no need for surgery. Then she left the room as quietly as she had entered a few minutes earlier.

Joyce sat stunned for a few seconds, before dashing into the corridor to find the woman in green and to thank her for her concern and kindness. But she was nowhere to be seen. And the nurses and orderlies outside could not remember anything about the visitor in a green dress.

Then the doctors arrived for a pre-op examination. They were speechless as they examined the patient they had pronounced a dying man earlier that day. Joe's critical condition had cleared up completely. There was no need for the life-threatening surgery!

The following day Joe was released from the hospital. His physician, Dr. John Testerman, could only describe the miraculous recovery as "an amazing turn of events."

Today Joe and Joyce Tucker still pray to their personal guardian angel, the mysterious lady in green.

Stranger on the Doorstep

Thomas, a six-foot, six-inch-tall black man with piercing azure-blue eyes, rang the doorbell of cancer victim

Ann Cannady. He raised his right hand, and informed her she was now cured of her ravaging disease.

That was almost twenty years ago. Today Ann Cannady is living proof of the incredible healing powers of angels. And proof that our guardian angels can come in all forms and sizes—at the most unexpected moments.

Here's the moving, dramatic story Ann recently recounted for readers of *Time* magazine:

It was in July 1977 when a third test result confirmed I had advanced uterine cancer—and cancer is a terribly scary word. My husband Gary, a retired Air Force master sergeant, had lost his first wife to the same type of cancer and did not know whether he had the strength to go through it again.

We spent the next eight weeks scared and praying, praying and scared. I kept begging God, saying, "Please, if I'm going to die, let me die quickly. I don't want Gary to have to face this again."

Her prayers were heard—and answered in a most amazing way. Years later, the memory of the following incident remains vivid.

One morning, three days before Ann was to enter the hospital for surgery, Gary answered the doorbell. Standing on the step was a large man, a good inch taller than the six foot, five-inch Gary.

"He was the blackest black I've ever seen," says Ann. "And his eyes were a deep, deep azure blue. The stranger introduced himself simply as Thomas. And then he told me that my cancer was gone!

"How do you know my name? And how did you know I have cancer?" stammered Ann. Dazed and very much confused, the Cannadys invited the mysterious stranger into their home.

"When Thomas came into the house, he told us we could stop worrying. He quoted scripture to us—Isaiah 53:5. 'And with his stripes we are healed.' "

Ann, still confused, looked at the man and demanded, "Who are you?"

"I am Thomas. I am sent by God."
She'll never forget what happened next:

He held up his right hand, palm facing me, and leaned toward me, though he didn't touch me. I'm telling you, the heat coming from that hand was incredible. Suddenly I felt my legs go out from under me, and I fell to the floor.

As I lay there, a strong white light, like one of those searchlights, traveled through my body. It started at my feet and worked its way up. I knew then, with every part of me—my body, my mind, and my heart—that something supernatural had happened.

I passed out. When I awoke, my husband was leaning over me asking, "Ann, are you alive?" and pleading with me to speak to him. Thomas was gone.

Still weak from the encounter, I managed to crawl over to the telephone and called my doctor's office and demanded to speak to him right that minute. I told him something had happened, and I was cured, and I didn't need surgery. He told me stress and fear were causing me to say things I didn't mean.

In the end they reached a compromise. I would show up at the hospital as scheduled, but before the operation the surgeons would do another biopsy. They would keep the operating table at the ready. If the preliminary test came back positive, they would proceed as planned.

When Ann woke up, she was in a regular hospital room, the doctor at her bedside. "I don't understand what's happened," he said, "but your test came back clean. We've sent the sample off to the lab for further testing. For now, though, you appear to be in the clear."

There has been no recurrence of the cancer. At first, Ann was hesitant to talk about it for fear that people, including her children, would think she'd "lost it."

They didn't. Even her doctor, she says, acknowledged at one point that he'd "witnessed a medical miracle."

A Mother's Worst Nightmare

Magazine editor Carole Moore was faced with a mother's worst nightmare when her eighteen-month-old daughter Allison suddenly stopped breathing.

Frantic, she ran into the hallway of her New York apartment building screaming, "Please, somebody help me! My baby's not breathing!" But no one was around.

Carole's nightmare began in the quiet of her living room in New York in the spring of 1990, where she was playing with her daughters, Julie, almost three, and little Allison.

Allison began crying for some unknown reason. As Carole tried to comfort her, the toddler's wails grew louder and louder, then suddenly stopped. The baby slumped over, her lips turning blue from lack of oxygen. She did not respond to initial efforts to revive her.

That's when Carole grabbed the limp child and headed for the hallway. When she could find no one there to help, Carole suddenly felt a deep calm settle over her.

"Relax," she told herself. "You took a class in child safety last year. You know what to do."

With little sister Julie watching wide-eyed, Carole lay Allison on the hall floor and began mouth-to-mouth resuscitation. "My terror just disappeared," Carole says. "Something took over, and it was almost like I had stepped outside myself. I could see myself doing what I had to do." Miraculously, little Allison slowly recovered.

It was later that evening—after the doctor had diagnosed Allison's illness as croup and the baby was sleeping peacefully—that Julie crawled into her mother's lap and asked quietly, "Mommy, who was that man who had his hand on your shoulder?"

"What man, honey?" Carole asked.

"The man, Mommy. The man who had his hand on your shoulder while you were helping Allison breathe."

For weeks after the incident, Julie couldn't forget the

stranger seen only by herself. She cried tears of frustration that her mother hadn't seen the stranger too.

"It gives me goosebumps every time I think about it," says Carole, years after the incident. "I've always felt that spiritual things like this can happen, and it makes me feel good that it has happened to Julie.

"I think a lot of people could have these experiences if they'd just open up a little bit more. It's also made me believe more strongly in the afterlife. I used to be troubled by the thought that I'd die and never see my loved ones again, but now I feel that there is something beyond death."

Angel and the Hairdresser

Customers of former schoolteacher Sharon Courtier, who runs the angel boutique called Angels on Wing in Fort Lauderdale, often share with her their own angel stories.

One recent customer with a remarkable story to tell was a hairdresser who was inspired to change his life by a mysterious woman with light hair and beautiful eyes.

The woman visited his salon to get her hair done at three-thirty every Thursday. After a few weeks of appointments, she got to touch all her hairdresser's problems. And she eventually—where others had failed—convinced him to seek help for his drug habit. He sought help and the professional counseling was working. He couldn't wait to tell his caring customer he was coming clean. But she didn't show up for the next appointment.

"He went to the book to look for the appointment and it wasn't there," says Sharon. "To his surprise, the other hairdressers in the salon said they had never seen this woman before. So he checked the appointment book and found all the spaces blank for three-thirty on Thursdays.

"I get goosebumps just thinking about that story," Sharon admits.

In Moments of Despair

"I know now that I'm not alone," says forty-year-old Deborah Deckelman of Pennsylvania, who is convinced an angel saved her during a dark and depression-filled period in her life.

A bitter divorce and custody battle had left Deborah despondent. Then two close friends were killed in accidents.

"I wanted to die," remembers Deborah, who was so depressed because she felt she was losing everything that she decided to check herself into a hospital.

In the hospital, she was having dark thoughts. One particularly bleak night she was laying awake when a woman, a stranger with silver hair and clear blue eyes, appeared at the foot of her bed.

"Deborah, I know you are thinking about a pit or a grave," said the woman quietly. Deborah was in shock. That's exactly what she had been thinking about.

Gently, the woman placed her hand on Deborah's forehead, then over her heart, and together they recited the Lord's Prayer.

"Scratch away at the darkness a little each day and soon the light will shine through," the silver-haired stranger told her. After promising that she would be with her always, the woman quietly left the hospital room.

A few seconds later, a nurse entered the room and a puzzled Deborah asked who the strange woman was. She was chilled when the nurse replied, "There was no one else here."

The penny dropped. "That's when I understood," said Deborah, for whom the encounter was a major turning point.

"My guardian angel had come to me when I needed her the most."

An Unlikely Angel

Television weathercaster Rob Kress was desperately worried about his baby daughter—until he bumped into an unlikely looking angel in a hospital lobby.

"I hear your daughter is going home tomorrow," said the bearded stranger in dusty work clothes.

Rob, who works in Detroit, looked down for a moment, thinking of six-month-old Katie, who just came out of a delicate operation. If all went well, she could go home in ten more days, the doctors had said.

But when Rob looked up again, the man had disappeared! Amazingly, Katie was completely healed by the next day, so the doctors let her go home.

"I have no doubts that man was an angel," Rob says. And the experience changed Rob's life. He has since joined a Bible group and studied faith healing, and is writing about his remarkable experience.

All-Night Vigil

After Ralph Wilkerson broke his neck in a construction accident, doctors gave little hope for his survival.

He fell into a coma and doctors told his wife that he would die within three days. But that was before his guardian angel came along.

When a nurse entered his room, expecting to find him close to death, she instead found him sitting up, wide awake. He told her, "I saw a brilliant light in this room. An angel stayed with me all night."

Wilkerson was completely healed and from that day on has lived a normal life. Doctors have never been able to explain his recovery.

Angel Road Signs

Although Marlene Wiechman, of West Point, Nebraska, has never seen angels, she believes their intervention saved the life of her six-year-old daughter. She explains:

> Emily had a stroke at seven months, and she's partially handicapped. Last year, we went on vacation with my parents to Yellowstone National Park.
> On the way home, driving through Wyoming, Emily said she didn't feel well. She started vomiting, and her eyes weren't focusing. We needed to get her to a hospital, but the nearest town, Rock Springs, was seventy miles away.
> Emily kept getting worse, and as we approached Rock Springs, I prayed we'd find help quickly. Just then, we saw a blue-and-white hospital sign. There were three or four more signs that led us straight to the emergency room.

At the hospital, a doctor quickly diagnosed Emily as having a seizure and stabilized her with anticonvulsants. After the crisis was over, her mother casually mentioned to the doctors that the eye-catching blue-and-white signs on the highway had been helpful guides. "The doctor looked at me and said, 'What signs?' He said he traveled that road every day, and there were no hospital signs. But all four adults in our van had seen them," says Mrs. Wiechman.

"We went back and looked again. They were gone. I called someone at the local Chamber of Commerce, who said there had never been any hospital signs on that route. I believe they were put there for us by God or his angels."

A Roomful of Angels

Warehouseman Stan Andrews stood by his sick daughter's hospital bed and prayed that she could see angels. Incredibly, the desperately ill toddler began laughing out loud and reported the presence of angels all around her!

Stan, a parts warehouseman for a car manufacturer and a member of Mount Zion Baptist Church in Snellville, near Atlanta, has never forgotten that inspiring, healing moment.

His daughter Tracie was almost three years old when she was admitted to hospital after being diagnosed with leukemia. Her caring father sat at her bedside reading the Bible to his scared little girl.

As she began to cry, Stan reassured her that Jesus and his angels were protecting her. Tracie replied, "No, he isn't." That's when her father prayed, "Lord, let her see your angels."

Suddenly, Tracie started laughing and looking around the room and told her father she saw "Jesuses." She said the room was full of them and they were "big and pretty."

When her father asked where the closest one was, she turned toward the right side of the bed and appeared to be touching something. Then she turned to the left side of the bed.

"In five minutes she was sound asleep," he said. "It was the first time in five nights she didn't wake up in pain."

Stan and his wife, Sheila, were soon able to take little Tracie home with them. He continued to read the Bible to her, praying all the time for the comfort and hope that the child would survive.

After three and a half years of arduous chemotherapy treatments, Tracie went into remission. But Stan was convinced, all through the treatments, that Tracie had taken her first step on the road to recovery after the angels visited.

"Angels are ministering servants of the Lord," he said. "It's all through the Bible. They are sent to send messages or to protect God's children."

Encounter with a Cherubim

Although he had always believed in angels since his religious conversion as a child, the Reverend Carl C. Williams of Bartlesville, Oklahoma, never thought he would encounter an angel face to face.

On October 3, 1994, Pastor Williams, in the hospital in acute pain, was visited by a chubby cherubim who washed his pain away and filled his heart with joy. Here is his moving story:

> Three days after painful surgery in the hospital, I found little rest, day or night, since the pain was quite severe. I tossed upon my bed each night and prayed the Lord would ease the pain and help me through the night.
>
> After the third night, at daybreak, my prayers were answered. And what a surprise it was! I was awakened by an arm brushing against my face.
>
> As I looked up I beheld a chubby child, wearing a pale blue gown, standing beside my bed. At first I thought it was one of my grandchildren, but they are all of a very slim build.
>
> Then, I knew it had to be a celestial being, since my door was shut and none of my grandchildren had entered. He had a golden vessel in one hand and, with the other hand he began dipping into the vessel and began anointing my pillow all around my head. I started to speak but he faded from sight.
>
> That little cherubim, sent from heaven, brought me new hope and healing, filling my heart with great joy. My spirits were lifted and I began to heal. The pain subsided. What transforming power that precious little

cherubim brought to me in those particularly difficult moments!

After the incident, I sought Webster's dictionary
definition of a cherubim. He states that a cherubim,
is "an angel of the second-highest rank; a beautiful,
usually winged child, a chubby and rosy person."

Amazingly, the cherubim returned on November 3,
exactly one month from the first appearance. I was
awake at 2 A.M., when I heard a great rustling noise
in my room, like a large bird flapping its wings.

A dazzling white being appeared over my bed with
large wings. As the angel hovered over me, I lay mo-
tionless, startled and amazed. How exquisitely beautiful were those pure white feathers! Slowly, those large
wings descended and completely surrounded my body.

I felt a very warm, protective spirit over me. I began
to wonder if the angel would carry me away. But
slowly the wings lifted; the angel ascended and disappeared. He left me with a great sense of peace and
security. His message to me was that as long as I
abode under the wings of the Almighty I would be
secure from all fears.

Since then, I have pondered over these two encounters, have studied the Scriptures, and have come to
the following conclusions about God's holy angels
which I'd like to share in this book:

1. *Angels are powerful:* God created them before
the foundations of the earth were laid (Job 38:4–7).
Man was created lower than the angels because he
was made subject to death (Hebrews 2:7,9), and angels
are immortal.

They never die (Luke 20:36). They are greater in
power and might than we are. They excel in strength.
An angel rolled back the heavy stone from the entrance to Jesus' tomb when he rose from the dead.
When Peter was delivered from prison the angel had
superhuman power to cause the chains to fall off him
and to open the iron gate that was securely fastened.

Angels are powerful also in movement. They can
travel rapidly from place to place. They move from
place to place instantaneously. But they have no
power over men, except when God gives them the

power. So they are not to be feared because of any harm they might give us. Nor are they to be worshipped. Holy angels do not accept worship from men, but they exhort us to worship God. Angels are powerful enough to penetrate closed doors and walls. They can materialize at any place God may send them.

Angels also are powerful in number and in organization. In Daniel 7:10, God is ministered to by millions of angels, with hundreds of millions more standing before him. God has his angels organized into ranks and they have certain thrones, dominions, principalities, and powers (Colossians 1:16). Michael in the Scriptures is represented as the archangel, and Gabriel is also mentioned as one of the archangels.

Not only are angels used by God as ambassadors to people on earth, to administer to our needs, but certain angels act as administrators in His Kingdom, recording not only births and deaths but religious conversions—for "the angels in Heaven rejoice over one sinner who repents."

2. *Angels perplex the world:* Angels can appear to humble and reverent people—but those who are arrogant and scorn His name never see angels.

The shepherds on the hillside, tending their flocks, were chosen to hear firsthand from angels that Jesus was born that night in Bethlehem. The shepherds were, at first, filled with fear, then awe and amazement, perplexed by it all. But they obeyed the message and were filled with great joy when they found it was actually true what the angels had said.

God delights to condescend to people unexpectedly. And these unexpected moments can be perplexing at times—but the surprise element intensifies the excitement and joy.

3. *Angels provide for our needs:* When we are low in spirit, dejected, lonely, or in deep pain, angels love to bear us up and put a new song in our hearts. They take a deep interest in humanity. They can provide food and water in a dry and parched land and they can sustain life under life-threatening circumstances. In Bible times and even today, many bear witness to

the fact that angels came to their aid when they were alone.

4. *Angels protect us:* When we are in danger, God sometimes sends angels to warn us and shield us from all harm—as He did for Lot and his family.

He protects His own by using angels to warn of impending doom, and make a way of escape. The songwriter said it right when he said, "Under his wings my soul shall abide, safely abide forever." What a place of refuge under His wings!

5. *Angels proclaim God's message of redemption to mankind:* Holy angels gave God's messages to the prophets of old, predicting the very time and place Christ was to be born (Luke 1:11, 2:9). They still proclaim this wondrous message through his ministers and saints today. They proclaimed the resurrection of Jesus, and they were present with the disciples at the ascension to comfort them.

6. *Angels prepare the souls of the saints:* At the hour of death from this life, they bear the souls of men on their wings, as they fly away to present them before the Lord and usher them into His glorious, eternal kingdom, just as they bore the soul of the beggar Lazarus to paradise.

So have no fear. For if we are sheltered underneath those wings of love, nothing can harm us. Even at the hour of death, we shall be borne up on the wings of a snow-white angel and fly away to be forever with our wonderful Lord and Savior.

CHAPTER EIGHT

Good Samaritans of the Highway

If you're looking for an angel experience, you need go no farther than the nearest highway.

Stories of angel Good Samaritans of the road are legion. Not only will they fix flats, they will act as traffic policemen and prevent accidents.

If you're really in a fix they'll even drive your car for you—and they seldom stick around to be thanked.

Here you will read just a few of the remarkable stories I was told about these gallant angels . . . the black angel in a white Cadillac . . . the angel in white tennis shorts . . . the angel in a flannel shirt and corduroy pants . . . and a host of other highway saints.

The Black Angel in a White Cadillac

A Los Angeles woman named Carmen reported the following intriguing angel encounter to a computer forum on angels in August 1994:

> Since we're talking of angels, I am reminded of an incident in my life almost twenty years ago. Without going into detail, I'll just say that I was driving to a girlfriend's home and found myself in the street around 3 A.M. after my car died on me.
>
> My six-year-old son was with me, so of course I felt

vulnerable and afraid for our safety. We started walking down the street and I saw a big white car pass.

It came round the block again, slowed down, and a man in white rolled down the window and asked if we needed help. I can remember that he appeared nonthreatening.

I found myself accepting his help and we climbed into his big white Cadillac, and we drove in silence across the city directly to my friend's house.

We didn't exchange any information other than my destination. And I never saw him again, didn't find out his name, where he lived or anything. Nor did he make any personal enquiry of me.

It hadn't occurred to me until recently that it's possible that this was an angel.

Carmen's story prompted George C. to tell the forum about a similar and just-as-amazing encounter in 1960 which made him and his wife confirmed angel believers.

He remembers clearly the incident which occurred near Quantico, Virginia:

Driving south on Route 1, we came to a hill. Cresting the hill, we encountered a wind and rain storm which swept up from nowhere.

The force of the wind lifted up the front of my 1955 Mercury, leaving me with absolutely no control. The car went to the other side of the road, spinning three times as it careened downhill, just missing oncoming traffic.

When the car reached the edge of the roadway, it rolled over twice and finally came to a halt against a telephone pole. The car ended upside down in a foot of mud.

The passenger side was crushed flat. But my wife escaped any major injury by being tossed to the rear seat. I remained in the driving position with my hands almost welded to the steering wheel. My side of the roof was flattened to the top of my head.

Dazed and not fully functional, I sat upside down until I heard the door on my side open, and a huge hand reached in, gripping my arm. The powerful hand lifted me out of the vehicle in one action.

I was suddenly upright facing a black man whose size matched the size of his hand. He spoke in a low tone at first, saying, "You must have gone to church today, because somebody's looking over you," and ending in thunderous laughter.

I realized my wife was still in the car and I called to her to come out. She did. "You dropped your wallet," said the black man, in a gentler tone. He picked my wallet up and handed it to me.

My wife and I both observed silently that he wore a white suit and appeared to drive a white Cadillac nearby.

At that moment, a Virginia state trooper pulled off the road and our attention was diverted to the police officer. He asked us to step away from our car, which we did.

I started to explain what had happened, but he interrupted me and said he had observed what had occurred and believed there was no fault by me. When he saw the accident occur, he had proceeded directly to us.

I told him how the black man had opened the door and lifted me out, then returned my money. The trooper stated, "What man? I came here immediately. There was no one else."

He was correct. There was no one else around!

It took five days for all of this to sink in as my wife and I contemplated the events surrounding the accident. What happened that night has remained with us almost thirty-four years later.

May an angel always be a part of your life.

Since George C. filed his report, Carmen has confirmed that her angel in the white Cadillac was also a black man!

A Timely Warning

Suenette Hunsberger is from Maryland, a thirty-five-year-old mother of four with her own graphics business. She has been a firm believer in angels since a warning voice saved her from being horribly mutilated in an auto mishap:

It was August 11, 1977, and I had been on a date in Georgetown in Washington, D.C. We were driving back to my office in suburban Silver Spring, Maryland, so I could pick up some work I needed to finish.

We were on Colesville Road, a five-lane highway where the center lane changes direction according to time of day. At this time, about 11 P.M., three lanes were southbound, and we were traveling north in the second lane from the right, about to make a left turn.

I remember my date putting on his turn signal. We were in his Morgan, which is a British car with right-hand drive. It was a very warm night, as anyone who's been in the Washington area in August knows. So I had my arm hanging out the window of this very low sporty car.

As we began the turn, I heard a female voice say "Pull your arm in." I no sooner put my hand on my lap, when another car collided with us.

The initial impact was on the left rear of the car, but the other car slid up the left side where my arm had been dangling a few seconds before. There was a long gash in the side of the car. Unquestionably, I would have had my arm sheared off.

To this day I am convinced my arm, perhaps my life, was saved by the timely warning voice of my protective guardian angel.

I've thought about that incident more these days as public interest in the angel phenomenon has increased in recent times.

I'm glad to see that people are becoming more aware and interested in their angels. I'm sure these people are simply looking for answers that are otherwise unavailable in this crazy, fast-paced world we live in.

Hopefully, through angel contact, we will all find affirmation that there is more to it all than this life.

Her Father's Hands

Jeanne Zentner has no doubt she would have died a horrible death after she fell asleep at the wheel of her car if it had not been for the intervention of her guardian angel—in the friendly and familiar guise of her beloved dead father.

Jeanne, a sixty-nine-year-old art teacher from Algona, Iowa, was driving late at night after a long trip and she dozed off at the wheel and her car careened out of control toward the oncoming lane of traffic.

"I was dead tired, and my head kept nodding. I should have pulled over, but dumbly I tried to keep going on," recalls Jeanne, unaware that her car had ripped into a deep ditch in the grassy median separating the two lanes of highway and was in danger of toppling over into an oncoming lane.

Suddenly I heard a loud noise, and my eyes jerked open. I realized I was awakened by all the clatter under the car, and I was petrified to realize I was plunging down an embankment which divided the highway. My hands and feet were frozen in fear. I couldn't even think of slamming on the brakes. I was going 65 miles an hour with my foot still pressed on the accelerator. I was a split second from death, unable to react.

I was gripping the steering wheel with all my strength. Then, just as the car was about to roll, I felt two big strong hands on top of mine, guiding the wheel. I knew instantly who it was—it was my father, helping his little girl as he so often did before his death. The dash lights were bright enough for me to see my father's hands appear on top of mine.

Jeanne's father had died of a heart attack in 1974. But she is convinced:

> I was an only child, and my dad always saw that I felt loved and protected. I really loved him and he was the perfect father if ever there was one. And when I needed him that terrible night in 1992, he was there for me. With my guardian angel–father steering, my car angled back up to the highway.
>
> The car slowed down and was steered, at an angle, back onto my southbound freeway. I felt the wheel was again in my control. I was filled with a sense of peace as I finished the drive home."
>
> I haven't had any other experiences like that one at all, ever or since. It was rather shocking yet wonderful.
>
> I didn't see my father's face, no words were spoken, and as soon as my car was safe the hands vanished. But there was no mistake. They were my father's hands."

And I know now that there *are* guardian angels.

A Glimpse of Paradise

Young Mississippi artist Linda Johnston was involved in a nasty automobile accident—in which she was the "fatality"!

But after she was given a wonderful glimpse of paradise, her gentle and comforting guardian angel guided her back to the land of the living.

The forty-year-old mother's incredible encounter was triggered when her pickup truck was rear-ended on a busy highway. She was catapulted through the windshield, thrown through the air, and ricocheted off a heavy metal hospital sign, before bouncing and rolling across the concrete highway like a rag doll.

"It was while I was airborne that I died," says Linda,

a mother of two, whose multiple injuries included two broken legs, a shattered pelvis and right hip, and badly damaged vertebrae.

"I felt myself rise into the air, as if I was going through some kind of spinning tunnel. I was feeling nothing, but I did hear the last of my breath leave my body," says Linda. "I was told later that this was probably when I hit the pavement."

In any event, Linda said she vividly remembers continuing her journey into the spinning tunnel. "At the end of the tunnel, I saw a door with bright light and the sound of choral music coming from it. It seemed very warm and inviting. Then I saw my guardian angel!"

The angel was a familiar figure to Linda, whom she claims visited her twice before in her life—once when she was eight years old and was saved from walking into the path of a speeding car, and another time when she was twelve and undergoing an emergency appendectomy.

"When I first saw my guardian angel I wasn't sure what it was, only that it was four times larger than an ordinary human being, and I'd never seen anything as bright!" said Linda. "But there was nothing scary about it."

During her near-fatal crash, Linda was able to make out more details of her protector. She saw no wings, or halo, or anything like that, but the spirit's head was covered by a hood, so she couldn't make out whether it was male or female.

"A glow surrounded its entire body. It was a white light, flecked with blue and yellow," she recalled. "It was so bright you couldn't see eyes or the mouth of the angel, but you could make out hands and arms. Its voice was very calm, very distinct, very soothing, very reassuring."

The angel pointed and Linda's eyes followed the outstretched arm. She saw her own body lying lifeless on the tarmac. She was on her back in a pool of blood. Linda shuddered. The angel asked her, "Are you ready?"

"No! No!" she cried out desperately. "I've got my husband and two children. I've got so much to do. I've got to go back." The angel nodded its head very slowly before responding reassuringly, "Very well. It is not your time."

"Then came a period of blackness. I came to, and when I looked up, my husband and the paramedics were all around me calling my name. I was alive!" remembered Linda.

Ahead of her were fifty-eight grueling days in the hospital, followed by rehabilitation, as her shattered body slowly mended. Then there were five frustrating months in a wheelchair. These days, Linda walks with a cane and continues to improve.

But she was never in any doubt that she would come through the ordeal okay. Four days after the mishap, while her condition was still touch-and-go, her angel visited her in the hospital to reassure her she was destined to make a full recovery.

"The whole experience has changed me," says Linda, who now paints angel pictures, drawing on her knowledge from her own encounters. "I've learned to take one day at a time. My recovery from this has been a miracle—but, of course, I've always believed in miracles."

An Angelic Chauffeur

It was all Sister Mary Lucy Astuto could do to stop falling asleep as she drove home in the early hours one day in June 1991, after attending an all-night prayer vigil.

She was unable to fight off the drowsiness and, just two miles from her home, the Omaha, Nebraska nun dozed off at the wheel.

Sister Mary didn't come to her senses until a gentle nudge woke her from her slumber. Incredibly, she was sitting behind the wheel in front of her house. For that last two miles, an angel had been her pilot!

"I know I can't prove this scientifically, but I *know* an angel drove me home," says the former schoolteacher.

Today, Sister Mary has her own evangelical mission and loves sharing her angel story as she travels around the country. There is little skepticism. "I can assure you, as I travel the country, there is a growing devotion to angels," she says.

Jeremiah to the Rescue

When her children were little, caring Californian mom Barbara Poprac assigned each of them guardian angels.

She named son John's special angel Jeremiah—a maternal touch that was to pay dividends.

In 1993, twenty-nine-year-old John was driving with a friend in his jeep on a busy San Diego highway when the jeep overturned and skidded across four lanes in front of oncoming traffic.

Despite the congestion, no cars struck the out-of-control jeep and both young men escaped unscathed. "I guess Jeremiah was doing his job," said Barbara when she learned of their miraculous escape.

She had to explain to her puzzled son that Jeremiah was his guardian angel who had been looking after him since he was a baby.

John's companion, also unhurt, asked her, "Can you give me one too?" Barbara smiled and replied, "You must already have one."

Miracle in the Desert

Another life-saving intervention happened to motorist Daniel Kramer of Phoenix when he was stranded in a scorching Arizona desert in 1958.

A tire blew out, and Kramer found himself totally stranded with no jack, no water—and no air conditioning. He was thirsty and weak and there wasn't another vehicle to be seen along that desolate stretch of road.

That's when a tall, slender man with a soothing voice, dressed in dark pants and a dark shirt, appeared beside Kramer's car. On the gravel shoulder behind him, says Kramer, he saw an old Ford coupe, presumably the stranger's car, although he had not seen or heard another vehicle drive up.

As soon as he was told what was wrong, the stranger went to his own car and came back with a jack, and set to work changing the tire. "I tried chatting with him as he worked, but he didn't answer. When he finished I offered him two dollars, but he wouldn't take it," said Kramer.

"Instead, he told me, 'Just help somebody else one day when they're in need'. Then he drove away." Kramer pulled his car out behind the stranger's. Incredibly, the stranger's car—only one-hundred feet in front of him—mysteriously disappeared in the shimmering sunlight.

Says Kramer today, "At first I thought the stranger was just a gentle, kind soul who came along at the right time. But as I think about it more, there's no doubt in my mind that I was saved by my guardian angel."

An Angel on the Brake

An angelic hand on the emergency brake averted tragedy for Gail Buchanan of Wichita, Kansas late one evening in October 1982, as she was taking a shortcut home down an abandoned road:

I noticed a set of taillights ahead of me. It wasn't until I was ten feet from the car ahead that I noticed it wasn't moving—the driver had stopped to talk to someone in a car in the opposite lane.

The road was too narrow for me to swerve around either car. I was going to crash. I slammed on my brakes, gripped the steering wheel, and waited for death. I heard the tires squeal, then my car suddenly stopped short.

I had missed the other car by less than an inch. Looking around my car, I saw that the emergency brake was standing straight up. Someone had pulled it—but it wasn't me.

As I drove off, the words of Psalm 91 ran through my head: "For He will give His angels charge over you, to keep you in all your ways."

Encouraging Advice

Shirley Greene of Shalimar, Florida was in big trouble when she and her daughters had car trouble and were in despair until passing angels offered words of encouragement:

My two daughters and I had stopped in a deserted, dusty gas station parking lot, waiting for my car's over-heated engine to cool down. The water pump was leaking, but it was Sunday and no garages were open.

We were still nearly two hundred miles from our home in Fort Walton Beach, Florida, and the thought of being stranded along the side of the road with my children was frightening. I prayed that the water pump would hold out and that God would watch over us.

A minute later, I happened to look in the rear-view mirror and saw an old pickup truck pull into the lot. The next thing I knew, a man and a woman—who bore an amazing resemblance to my parents—were standing next to my car.

"Having car trouble?" the man asked. I said I was, and he replied, "Your water pump is going out. Hold it down to forty-five miles an hour, and you'll make it home fine."

They turned to leave. A second or two later, I looked up to say goodbye, but no one was there. The parking lot was empty, the dust undisturbed—and my car's engine was cool!

We drove the rest of they way home without having to stop again. The pump only gave out the next day as I pulled into a garage.

Something inside told me that I had met angels.

An Angel in Flannel

On her way to a party one Saturday afternoon in 1986, Judy Erkanat, then thirty-six and a customer-service supervisor for a Silicon Valley, California electronics corporation, ended up lost.

To make matters worse, a lightning storm struck. To shelter from howling winds and try to get her bearings in the maze of unfamiliar, hilly and curving country roads, Judy decided to pull up under a eucalyptus tree to consult her map before going any farther.

Standing near the tree she was surprised to see a bearded young man, dressed in brown corduroy pants and a gray-and-green flannel shirt. Where could he have come from? A few seconds ago, the road had been deserted.

Beaming a friendly smile, the man motioned for Judy to continue driving in the direction she was headed. "I assumed he was a friend from the party sent out to direct me to the house," says Judy. She continued driving—but soon found herself blocked in a dead-end street.

Frustrated and angry, she turned the car around and headed back in the direction of the young stranger. She was angry, wondering what kind of trick he had been playing on her.

What she saw made her abruptly slam her foot on the brake. Trembling, she pulled to the side of the road. She felt faint.

The eucalyptus under which she had planned to park two minutes earlier had crashed to the ground, blocking most of the street ahead!

"If I had parked under that tree, the way I intended to, I'd have been killed," says Judy. "That man saved my life. I wanted to thank him, but he was nowhere in sight. It was almost as if he knew that tree was going to fall."

When she finally arrived at the party, her friends saw she was pale and upset. Their concern turned to astonishment when she explained what had happened. Then they teased. "Everything's okay, Judy. You have a guardian angel—a guardian angel in a lumberjack shirt."

Judy forced herself to laugh, yet she wondered whether her friends might be right. She didn't believe in angels—or did she?

"There's simply no other way to explain what happened," she says. "The experience left me with a greater trust in a higher being. I later returned to organized religion, converting to Judaism, which, although many people don't realize it, also has a tradition of angels.

"I feel that somehow I am being watched over, that there was some reason my life was saved."

A Vision of Death?

Lying semiconscious in her overturned car after a nasty road accident, Phyllis Hurteau felt her spiritual self transported to a mountaintop, where she had a profound angel experience.

It happened to Phyllis, a Redington Beach, Florida resident, in 1957 outside of San Antonio, Texas, when she was on her way to Mexico.

Shortly before she was borne to the mountaintop, she was conscious of an intense bright light and a shrill ringing sound. From the peak, she could look down into a scenic valley.

Looking up, she saw a mysterious block letter "M" shimmering and quivering. For some inexplicable reason, Phyllis found herself reciting a phrase "Woman is kind, woman is true, woman is good . . ." over and over.

She felt if she completed the phrase, the letter "M" would stop shimmering, there would be no more suffering in the world, and we would all have perfect understanding. But, she says, "I couldn't complete it."

Then she felt an invisible power, as though a gentle hand was beckoning, saying, "Come back, little child, come back." At first, says Phyllis, she resisted, saying, "Not now, I have too much to do." The power seemed "amused" at her response, she remembers.

Then came other bizarre visions. Images of people, including herself, as descending autumn leaves, "as though falling through life." She also saw images of her mother and other friends.

"Then," recalls Phyllis, "I remember wishing I could tell the whole world what this experience was like, so they wouldn't be afraid to die . . . if that's what death is really like."

And that's when she returned to the land of the living, convinced she had visited the threshold of death.

Angel in White Tennis Shorts

Angelic Good Samaritans of the highway are true white knights of the road—they'll even change your flat tire!

It was an angel in white tennis shorts, says Barbara Anthony, who changed her flat tire when she was stuck outside the Harbor Tunnel, near her Seabrook, Maryland, home.

Totally stranded as other traffic whizzed past, Barbara was taken aback when the young man in white tennis shorts and a yellow shirt pulled over and got out of a late-model white station wagon.

Though she asked only to be driven to the next exit to call for a tow truck, the young man insisted on changing the flat tire. He could have been any college student heading for the beach that day, Mrs. Anthony remembered, except "the eyes were so blue. They were like hot ice."

He wasted no time changing the tire. But what was most remarkable about the incident, noticed Mrs. Anthony, was that—although he had sprawled on the dirty shoulder—when he stood up his clothes were still spotlessly clean!

Now convinced he was an angel, Mrs. Anthony says, "It was a surprise—but it wasn't. It's a task that they do."

A belief in angels has always been part of Barbara Anthony's Lutheran upbringing—but her 1986 encounter with the young tire-changer was her first angelic encounter.

"I don't think I've been chosen by God or anything," said Mrs. Anthony, a former English teacher and press office editor at the National Institutes of Health. Angels, she says, "are there for all of us, but we're just not always aware of them."

At a particularly low period in her life, beset by divorce and the death of her father, Mrs. Anthony became conscious of a man who looked amazingly like her father whom she saw regularly at the railway station as she commuted to work.

"I probably was feeling alone and unsupported at this point," she says. "And I think that this presence was sent to let me know I wasn't alone, that I didn't need to feel frightened. At first it was eerie. But after a time, it was comforting to know he was there."

Mrs. Anthony doesn't demand belief, only respect for these accounts of unexpected comfort in dire times. "These things are so personal you hate to cast your pearls before swine," she said.

An Angelic Trio

In 1974, an Alabama family reported being rescued by three mysterious angelic beings after their automobile crashed.

The angels in this case were three extremely fair, blond-haired men who appeared as if out of nowhere and pulled the family members from the wreck.

After checking to make sure they were not seriously injured, the three men mysteriously disappeared, as quickly as they had materialized.

Sign of the Rainbow

After Anne Nigh's daughter was involved in a serious auto accident in October 1994, she lay on a blanket awaiting an ambulance and told the people around her that she could see a rainbow.

Says Anne, of Glen Burnie, Maryland:

The people around my daughter did not appear to see the rainbow. Maybe it's because they were too busy, or thought she was babbling.

Later, we were devastated to find out that the woman who crossed in front of her on a major highway and was hit by my daughter had died at the scene.

But it was not a day for rainbows. There were hardly any clouds in the sky, and the weather was cool and brisk.

Both of us are convinced that my daughter was protected by a guardian angel and that the "rainbow" was a sign that the woman was given peace and will be with God.

Another Answered Prayer

"Angels, please, I need help. Please send someone to help me," prayed Carol Harmon after her car hit a large pothole, severely damaging a tire, as she was driving through the harsh California desert near Blythe.

"Someone sane," she added to her prayer as she nosed her disabled car to the shoulder of the road, recalling horror stories of stranded motorists who had been victimized by criminals posing as Good Samaritans.

Within minutes, a blue van packed with two young women and their children stopped nearby. They told Carol they lived just a few miles away and would fetch their husbands to help.

True to their word, the women arrived back at that desolate desert location with their husbands, who quickly changed the damaged tire. The men even gallantly escorted Carol to a service station in Blythe.

Carol, a resident of Scottsdale, Arizona, resumed her trip—but not before thanking the angels for hearing her prayer. "Angels follow us individually throughout our lives," says believer Carol. "If we are aware of them, we can call on them."

An Angel Sketch

Was it just a coincidence that artist Mary Cyphers drew a sketch of an angel hovering over a car the day her own car narrowly escaped being devastated by an eighteen-wheel truck.

Mary doesn't think so. "I know angels are looking out for me and my safety," says the Kettering, Ohio woman.

Earlier on the day of the accident, she had been busy drawing sketches for a painting she was planning. Without thinking, she sketched an angel hovering over a car. She thought it was ridiculous and tossed it out. Later that day, the big truck ran a red light and nearly hit her car.

Since the incident, Mary has been doing a lot more angel sketches. "Angels give me a lot of hope," she says. "I feel like I am really being watched over."

Invisible Hands

Powerful hands plucked eleven-year-old Rita Rizzo out of the path of a speeding car aimed directly at her.

Witnesses at the scene saw the frail girl soar into the air and over the car, as though propelled by a protective but unseen force.

Rita, one of six children from a broken home, was in a dejected mood the day her guardian angel stepped in to save her life. "I wasn't paying attention to where I was going," she recalls.

"I started to cross a busy street, then heard a woman's shrill scream behind me. As I turned to look back, I saw a car speeding directly toward me. I froze, expecting to die in the next second."

That's when the invisible strong hands grabbed her and lifted her high in the air. When she opened her eyes she was standing safely on the sidewalk. A bus driver who saw the incident said there was no earthly reason for Rita's miraculous escape.

The experience had a profound effect on young Rita. She grew up in the knowledge she was being protected and guided by an angel

When she reached adulthood, Rita entered a convent, changed her name to Angelica, and founded Our Lady of the Angels Monastery near Birmingham, Alabama.

Dodging a Bullet

Journalist and angel researcher Pierre Jovanovic says his angel research work was inspired by his own harrowing brush with death—and deliverance by an angel.

"I was with a friend driving along Highway 101 through Silicon Valley in California in July 1988," recalls Pierre.

"I wasn't behind the wheel, so I enjoyed myself by watching the colorful trucks on the road. Suddenly, without knowing why, I threw myself to the left. A fraction of a second later, a bullet whizzed through the windshield—right where my head had been!

"Later the Highway Patrol told us it was another of the sniper incidents that weren't uncommon there. I asked myself why I had jumped to the left just a moment before the bullet flew by!

Searching for an answer, Jovanovic began contacting people who'd had similar experiences—and concluded that his guardian angel had pushed him, sparing him from death.

A Christmas Story

One of the best-documented stories about Good Samaritans of the highway is oft told by angelogist–author Joan Wester Anderson, who became convinced angels watched over her family on Christmas Eve 1983, when a howling blizzard roared through the Midwest.

Her son, Tim, twenty-one, and a college roommate were en route home for the holidays. With snow blocking highways and a dangerous wind-chill factor of eighty below zero, travelers were warned to stay off the roads.

But the boys ignored the warnings and continued on their way—until their car sputtered and died on a desolate stretch of road with no other traffic in sight. A risky, life-threatening situation.

Miraculously, a tow truck appeared out of nowhere and the driver offered help. The driver, a man of few words, hooked the stalled car to his tow truck and drove the chilled students to a friend's home, where Tim borrowed money to pay the driver.

But when he went back outside there was no truck. Parked alone at the curb was Tim's car. And there was only one set of tire marks in the snow—and they belonged to Tim's car!

CHAPTER NINE

Angels: Suffer the Little Children

- A seven-week-old baby abducted from a city public health clinic was found a week later unharmed in a Chicago church, a couple of days before Christmas 1993

  Tiny Crystal Guerrero was found on the vestibule floor of the church shortly after a woman carrying the baby approached a priest about baptisms..

  The child was later reunited with her distraught mother. A woman was later taken into custody in connection with the incident, but no charges were filed.

  It's probably no accident that the name of the church where the infant was found unharmed was Queen of Angels Church.

- Nine-year-old Sam "died" from cardiac arrest and was guided, gently but forcefully, back to the living by an angel.

  "I didn't want to go back, but he made me," Sam told his doctors later, as he remembered in detail soaring upward, the earth rapidly vanishing beneath him, then passing through a dark tunnel where he was met by a band of "glowing, loving angels."

  Sam was told by his angels if he ventured beyond a fence into a heavenly, pastoral area he wouldn't be able to return to life. He wanted to continue, but he remembers one particular angel (his guardian?) telling him, gently but firmly, that he must return to his body. Reluctantly, he obeyed the angel.

- An eight-year-old girl was tumbling to certain death in a deep sewer when she suddenly stopped falling, just inches from the treacherous pit.

  She told her trembling parents, who had watched in horror, "Didn't you see the huge beautiful angel holding up her hands to keep me from falling in?"

These heartwarming stories are just a cross-section of thousands of similar stories that prove beyond any doubt that angels have a specially soft spot for children. Repeatedly, in the course of my research, I found that children, boys and girls alike, are particularly susceptible to angelic encounters and visions, most of them in near-death situations.

The wonder and innocence of a child seems to attract angels like a magnet. Innocent children, of course, have not yet been exposed to the greed, ambition, and materialism that enter our lives as we get older.

It seems these acquired, baser traits, accompanied by cynicism, skepticism, and distrust, tend to "angel-proof" grown-ups, making an angel encounter much more difficult, in some cases impossible.

Older people have better luck making angel contact, say researchers—probably because the older we get, the more spiritually aware we become, leaving us more susceptible to angel contact.

As James Nieder Geses, the Roman Catholic bishop of Nashville, says, "Angels have a special bond with children." He adds, "The first prayer I learned as a child was to my guardian angel. I still say it every day. How wonderful that angels are getting so much attention now!"

The Story of Daniel

One of the best-documented child encounter stories I came across is that of five-year-old Daniel Leary of Normal, Illinois, who "drowned" in a backyard swimming pool—but lived thanks to the intervention of a guardian angel.

Daniel, the youngest of Paul and Jodi Leary's three children, was swimming in an in-ground pool at the home of an aunt in Bloomington, Illinois, July 27, 1991, when he slipped beneath eight feet of water and remained submerged for three to four minutes.

The Learys, members of St. Patrick's Parish in Merna, Illinois, had brought Daniel and their other children, Michael, 7, and Katie, 8, to the swimming party to celebrate July birthdays in the family.

Before letting Daniel play in the shallow end of the pool with other young children at the party, his parents put plastic water wings around his arms. The boy had taken a series of swimming lessons earlier that summer and was not afraid of water, but he did not yet know how to swim.

"At some point he slipped off his water wings and ended up in the deep end," his mother Jodi said later. Moments later, she glanced at the pool and noticed a bright orange object—the color of Daniel's swimming trunks—at the bottom.

"In less than a split second I realized it was Daniel and I screamed 'Oh, God, it's Daniel!' " said Jodi. She jumped in after him but "just couldn't reach him because I was too hysterical. I jumped out of the water and screamed for help."

Her husband, meanwhile, had already dived into the pool and quickly pulled Daniel out—blue from lack of oxygen, completely limp, and showing no pulse, heartbeat, or any other signs of life. Paul breathed into the boy's nose and mouth while Tim Leary, Daniels' uncle, performed chest compressions.

"I was hysterical," Jodi said. "I was just begging God to give him back and not take him. Everybody was just praying." She refused to believe Daniel could be dead.

"I didn't cry because I felt God wouldn't do that to me," she said. "I really believe God doesn't give us what we can't handle and I couldn't handle it if he had died."

Daniel had already come to when the rescue squad arrived about three minutes later. When he arrived at St. Joseph Medical Center in Bloomington, he was still rather lethargic and dazed. And, when doctors asked him what had happened, he simply mumbled that he had "drowneded."

The lucky child spent the night in the hospital and was discharged the following day. His mother knew, however, he had something important on his mind. Here is an excerpt from the journal Jodi kept about the family's life-altering experience:

> Accident—7-27-91 (3:15 P.M.) Spent night in hospital. Admitted in serious condition—moved to fair condition that evening. Daniel was basically speechless during his time in the hospital. He answered some "yes" or "no" questions and said only that "I drownded." He remained awake for the rest of the afternoon and the early evening. But he just stared straight ahead. He didn't talk to any of the many relatives who stopped to see him.
>
> He slept so soundly and peacefully that night that the heart monitor kept going off. The nurse had to come in and lower the rate on the heart monitor every few minutes because the alarm kept going off. She finally ended up spending the rest of her shift on the floor next to the monitor and Daniel's bed. That night I still thought Daniel might really die. He just seemed to be slipping farther and farther away from us. His little body was there, but I didn't feel Daniel was totally with us.
>
> The next morning Daniel woke up totally normal again. He was perky, silly, smiling—happy. We got out of the hospital just in time to make it to the church to see my mom walking down the aisle during her wedding.

"At the wedding reception," Jodi Leary recalls, tears in her eyes, "Daniel looked very pensive. My husband asked him what he was thinking about. Daniel replied softly, said, 'Did you know there was an angel?' Daniel continued, 'I'm thinking about how beautiful God and Jesus and heaven was.' Then he said, 'Did you know I really did see a tunnel and a light with an angel in it?' "

After Daniel had repeated his story to his mother and other guests at the reception, a friend of the family gave him a St. Christopher medal as a gift. That's when he recognized "my angel." And when another relative asked him if that was the angel who helped him in the pool, he replied "Yes."

"I asked him, 'Was it scary or was it beautiful?' " said Jodi. "I emphasized the word 'scary' to see if he'd change his story. But he simply repeated, 'It was beautiful, Mommy.' And he has never wavered in his story of the tunnel, the light, and the angel.

"And I believe him with all my heart," says Jodi, even several years after the near-tragedy. The experience has "really strengthened" the family's faith in God and in heaven, she says.

"Even for someone who had a shadow of a doubt that there's something after this life, how could you doubt it now?" asks Jodi. The whole family is grateful "for the fact that God gave him back to us. It's one huge miracle—but there have been a whole lot of little miracles involved because of the incident."

She added that Daniel does not like to talk about his experience as much as he did at first, but still describes it very calmly and has no fear of going in the water again.

"I'm convinced God sent an angel to be with Daniel so he wouldn't be scared. It just makes me cry when I think about it. He's been real peaceful about it," she said. "He's still begging to go swimming again, although we haven't let him yet."

Before the incident, Daniel's parents had explained God's love and the concept of heaven to him in simple terms and often prayed with him at bedtime.

"We've talked a lot about how much God must love

us to let us have each other," Jodi said. "I'd also told him heaven is a nice, beautiful place where there's no pain and no worries anymore. We'd also told him that when you do go to heaven you don't come back—which might be somewhat confusing to him."

The family also attends Sunday Mass together, Jodi said, because "I like my children to be with me in church ... the times I feel most blessed and closest to God is when I'm with my kids."

Although Daniel doesn't remember much about the incident these days, the days and weeks after his rescue he spoke more and more about his experience. Jodi Leary jotted down all her child's comments about his angelic encounter. They make interesting reading. Here are a few of them, all made in the first three weeks after the experience:

- "Only some angels have wings."
- "Now I have angel ears ... I see and hear things more brighter."
- He said he met my dad "at the edge of heaven." Dad said, "Are you the little guy I've never seen?"
- Daniel said he "flew back from heaven." When asked if he had wings, he said, "No, I was a angel what didn't have wings."
- He said he saw "Lad and Sheba" (our dogs) his "grandpas and a whole bunch of people that I didn't know."
- His angel, who "helped me get to heaven and then back," had "white hair, a beard, and moustache, was wearing a white gown and carried a stick."
- "The light makes you start to float up ... when I got in the tunnel, I started to float really fast. It feels like I was flying really fast ... it was like a rollercoaster, only it went up. It feels like going down a hill on a rollercoaster, but up."
- "Everything just disappeared when Daddy got me out of the water."
- "The angel got to Heaven first; I followed him."
- "Heaven is where the light is."

"These are the last comments Daniel made about his experience. He started not wanting to talk about it anymore "because you always cry, Mommy."

Daniel's story bears remarkable similarities to the stories of other children who have had near-death by drowning experiences.

Another five-year-old who almost drowned said later: "When I went underwater, the next thing I remembered was passing down a long tunnel. The light went from being very harsh to so bright that I could feel it. Then I saw God on a throne. People—maybe angels—where below looking up at the throne.

"I sat on God's lap, and he told me that I had to go back. 'It's not your time,' he said. I wanted to stay but I came back."

Nine-year-old Katie wasn't given much hope of surviving after being found face down at the bottom of a YMCA pool. Emergency room physicians offered little hope for her survival even as they hooked her to an artificial lung machine.

Incredibly, Katie rallied and later astounded doctors with her memory of being admitted to the emergency treatment, details of the treatment she received, her recollections of visiting relatives—all while she was ostensibly comatose.

Katie's most vivid memory, however, was of going through a tunnel of light where she met "Elizabeth," her guardian angel. She also told of going to heaven and meeting God, and playing with two children called Andy and Mark—"souls waiting to be born."

Dr. Melvin Morse, a Renton, Washington pediatrician, has intensively researched near-death experiences of children at Seattle's Children's Hospital and Medical Center.

Dr. Morse's research team monitored 121 patients at Children's Hospital who were seriously ill, medicated, and under stress but who had not come close to dying. Not one of those children described anything resembling a near-death experience. "The only patients who had near-death experiences were the patients who were truly at the brink of death," Morse said.

Within the experimental group of true near-death survivors, however, eight out of twelve children described at least one of the classic features of the near-death experience—being out of their bodies, zooming up a tunnel, seeing a bright light, visiting with dead relatives, and, in some cases, deciding consciously to return to their bodies.

"At least to my satisfaction, we proved these experiences are not merely some kind of psychological defense mechanisms," concludes Dr. Morse.

Laying Fears to Rest

By the time she was five, Eileen Freeman was afraid of nearly everything—dogs, the phone, the vacuum cleaner.

When her grandmother died, Ms. Freeman trembled in fear that her grandmother's spirit would snatch her away, too.

But, says angelogist–author Freeman, her guardian angel laid her fears to rest. "My angel came and stood at the foot of my bed, and there was the most incredible light. He said not to be afraid. He said, 'Your grandmother is not in a cold, dark grave; she's in heaven with people she loves, and she's happy.'

"I remember the eyes especially because they were so brilliant and so compassionate and they looked right through me. I felt all the fear drain out of me the way water drains down a drain or infection drains from a wound. All the fears disappeared overnight and never came back. That's one of the reasons I know it really was an angel and not a dream or a childhood fantasy."

Her Angel Took Control

A guardian angel actually took over control of Debbie J.'s legs and helped her walk away from a situation that could have meant crippling or certain death. Now fully grown, Debbie, of Upper Arlington, a suburb of Columbus, Ohio, recalls the day she almost died:

This is my own private angel story, which I've never shared with anyone before.

I was about eight years old, attending a Girl Scout camp, where we got horseback riding lessons. I was quite confident, because I had ridden before. I loved horses. I was assigned a horse named Trixie.

The second day of riding lessons, we were still getting used to our horses. We were all riding around the ring at a walk that day when Trixie suddenly went down on her knees. I was surprised because I'd never had a horse do that before!

I pulled on the reins, but she wouldn't get up. I didn't know what to do! Was she hurt? Just tired? Lazy? I was a terribly shy little person, and didn't want to attract attention to myself—so I couldn't bring myself to yell to the riding instructor. I didn't have a clue what to do.

So there I was, sitting on this horse which had slumped to its knees. By this time I was scared to death. Then all of a sudden, I kind of went numb below the waist.

An unseen force seemed to take over control of my legs. My legs stood me up, walked me three big paces away from the horse, and turned me around to face Trixie. Then I felt the control come back over my legs.

It was an odd feeling, but for some reason I wasn't scared any more. My first thought was that there was something wrong with the horse. So I started to walk back to Trixie when the riding instructor looked over, sized up the situation, and yelled, "*Stay away from Trixie!*"

I backed up as Trixie suddenly rolled over on to her back, her legs kicking wildly in the air! I gasped. I realized it could have been me on the ground underneath the horse, being crushed under its heavy weight!

I could have been badly crushed or injured, or even killed. I am certain now that it was my guardian angel who took control of my legs that day and walked me to safety.

Plucked to Safety

Worried mom Michele Smith raced frantically to an accident scene after she learned her husband Chris and three-year-old daughter Kailey were involved.

She was horrified when she got to the scene and looked down a five-hundred foot cliff. Below her was her husband's mangled Ford Ranger. The backseat where her daughter had been was totally smashed in.

It was a devastating image. How could anyone survive that? she thought. But Chris and Kailey had survived, she was told by police. They had been rushed to the hospital.

Driving to the hospital, Michele braced herself for the worst of news. At the hospital, she was told both had survived, although Chris was badly injured. A compassionate doctor, who had treated both, eased some of her fears when he said her husband was expected to make a full recovery.

But what about Kailey? "You can see your daughter for yourself," the doctor grinned reassuringly.

Rushing to her daughter's bedside, Michele was both astounded and ecstatic to discover her daughter wide awake and all in one piece, nursing only a black eye and bruises. But it was little Kailey's version of what happened that really filled Michele with awe and brought the tears pouring from her eyes. "We were falling and then the angels pulled me out of the car and set me on a soft bush," Kailey told her mom matter-of-factly.

Michele didn't know what to think. To get a proper grasp of what happened, she spoke to police investigators who were early on the scene. Yes, they told her, Kailey and been found just as she described, sitting on a bush not far from the road.

They had no explanation as to how she could have freed herself from her securely fastened safety harness and made a safe exit backward out of the fast-tumbling jeep.

"We will never know exactly how she survived," police told her mother. But Michele knows: "Angels saved her."

Following the Light

Twelve-year-old Dolores was in her bedroom, choking and coughing from smoke, when a luminous figure beckoned to her: "Come, follow me. Everything will be all right."

Dolores followed the light as it led her down a passageway. She was gasping for air, crying, when a fireman reached through the patio doors of her home and lifted her to safety.

Her parents thought she was trapped in her room, and firefighters were puzzled as to how she could have escaped through the dense smoke.

Dolores believes she was saved by her guardian angel.

A Mother's Premonition

Overcome by a horrible feeling that her thirteen-year-old son was in danger, Elizabeth C. Steiner of St. Paul, Minnesota felt compelled to pray to an angel—a prayer that paid off.

She tells the story:

Many years ago, my son Jimmy went off on his bike

one day. As I watched him go, I was overcome by a horrible feeling that he was going to get hit by a car.

I was panic stricken—until the idea of praying to Jimmy's guardian angel popped into my head. I knelt down to do it, and I felt a calmness come over me. I knew my son would be safe.

After a while, I heard Jimmy coming through the back door. He had been hit by a car in the street, but suffered only a small scratch on his leg.

The driver of the car had said, "All I can say, son, is that your guardian angel must have been riding with you. When I hit you, you let go of the handlebars but never fell over. It was as though a pair of invisible hands controlled your bike."

To this day, I firmly believe that is exactly what happened.

A Long-distance Miracle

Mother of six Shirley Halliday began praying desperately for spiritual intervention as a vision flashed into her mind that her youngest daughter was in grave danger— fifteen-hundred miles away.

Shirley's premonition was 100 percent on target. As she prayed, her thirteen-year-old daughter Janie's life was indeed in grave danger—she was toppling down the steep slope of an Arizona canyon.

A mother's prayer was answered. For no apparent reason, Janie's fall was stopped after only fifty yards, as if an unseen hand had interrupted her topple to disaster.

The Halliday family drama took place in May 1976. Shirley Halliday, after raising six children, felt utterly alone. Her husband had died three months earlier and baby of the family Janie, the only child still living with her mother, was far from the family home in Hartland, Michigan, on vacation in Arizona with one of her older brothers.

Shirley, a nurse, had just got home after finishing working a night shift at the hospital. A strange icy-cold feeling swept over her and she began sobbing uncontrollably. She just knew—absolutely knew—that Janie was in danger.

Fifteen hundred miles away, at that very same moment, Janie was fascinated by the scenery of the Painted Desert, where she had gone on a tourist trip with her brother and sister-in-law. She had wandered away from them to the top of a ravine so deep she couldn't see the bottom.

As she stepped over a low guardrail to get a better look she lost her footing and began falling into the bottomless pit.

Frantically, she tried to stop or slow down her fall as she slithered down the sloping canyon walls, to no avail. The canyon wall was weathered and slippery, and loose sand only helped to accelerate her descent. She was headed for certain death.

At the family home in Michigan, Shirley called on the angels to save her daughter. Aloud, she read Psalm 91:11–12: "For He shall give His angels charge over you, to keep you in all your ways. They shall bear you up in their hands, lest you dash your foot against a stone."

Upon the recitation of that prayer—as the family later reconstructed the chain of events—Janie's fall was mysteriously halted. As she slithered to an abrupt stop, dazed, white-faced, and trembling, Janie remembers looking around to see who had halted her descent.

There was no one around. There was no bush, rock, or any other type of vegetation that might have interrupted her accelerating descent. It was as if an invisible hand from nowhere had reached across her path and caught her.

Slowly, Janie was able to inch herself back up the steep slope, pushing herself backward to the top, where her worried relatives would find her, bruised and covered in dirt and gravel—but otherwise unharmed.

Back home in Michigan, Shirley shuddered with relief as an overwhelming feeling of peace and safety swept over her entire body. As only a mother can feel, she knew her baby was safe. Today, Janie, now in her thirties and an interior designer, and Shirley, who has since remarried, are still awed by the miracle of the Painted Desert.

"From that moment on, I knew that the Lord watches over the widow and is father to the fatherless," says Shirley. "I had no more doubts or fear about raising my youngest child alone because I was confident that I had the help of God and his angels."

Mystery Man in a Multicolored Shirt

A four-year-old boy was saved from suffocating in his smoke-filled bedroom by a mysterious stranger in a multicolored shirt, who entered the boy's home and pulled him to safety.

Linda Gates of Sacramento, California will never forget the day that particular stranger paid a visit:

I was cleaning the kitchen one afternoon in 1977 when I suddenly heard one of my children, four-year-old Michael, running down the hall.

The front door then slammed shut with a bang—odd, because the door was warped and needed an adult's strength to close tightly. Going outside, I found Michael, his eyes wide. "A man got me out, Mama! A man got me out!" he cried.

Michael led me inside and showed me his smoke-filled bedroom, where a curtain was burning. (He had been playing with a box of matches he had hidden.) I called for help. Fortunately, the blaze was soon out, but one firefighter told me that the smoke could easily have killed my son.

Michael told me that a man with long blond hair and a "many-colored" shirt had appeared at his door and said, "Michael, come out of there." When my son said he wanted to look for his teddy bear, the man pulled him out of the room.

Our bedtime Bible story that evening happened to be about Daniel and the lion's den: "My God sent

His angel, and he shut the mouths of the lions. They have not hurt me, because I was found innocent in His sight." I knew then that God had mercifully sent his angel to rescue my son.

Walking on Water?

A former beach lifeguard herself, Susan Russell knew her six-year-old daughter Hilary was in big trouble when she got caught in a treacherous riptide far from shore—until a mysterious stranger who seemed to walk on water came to her rescue.

As Mrs. Russell, of Coconut Grove, Florida related her miraculous story to her local paper, the *Miami Herald*:

It was 1978 and my daughter Hilary was six years old. She loved the beach, so we tried to go there as often as possible. The wind was strong as we drove to old Miami Beach pier, where we had never been before.

Hilary's dad, Richard, immediately headed to the shoreline, chasing dog and child to water's edge, as I unloaded the blankets and toys from the car and paused on the dune to observe my family.

Hilary was in the water, already too far from shore. I screamed at Dick to get her in, my words lost in the wind. As a former lifeguard, I sensed great danger. Dropping everything, I tore for the water, all the while watching Hilary being pulled farther and farther out.

I tried to throw my weight to get through the water, but I couldn't make any headway. It was as though I were shackled. Nothing I did propelled me through the boiling riptide.

I knew it was impossible for me to save her. I was like an ant swimming upstream against a storm-filled drainage ditch.

There was no one around; it was too rough a day. Suddenly, I saw someone else in the water. It was a man. He seemed to be standing in the water next to Hilary, but that struck me as impossible. It was too deep, too wild. No one would be out there.

But he reached over and plucked Hilary from the water and effortlessly carried her the long way into our waiting arms. I released Hilary long enough to thank the stranger—and then he was gone.

Was he an angel? I think so, but it doesn't matter. The gift came from an unknown hand outstretched to meet a sudden need, something that countless strangers do for others every day.

Angel on the Tracks

Almost half a century ago, the powerful unseen hand of a guardian angel pushed fourteen-year-old Marilynn Webber to safety out of the path of a roaring express train.

The train was so near, Marilynn remembers to this day, that she could see the blue eyes and terrified, red face of the train's engineer as he blew his whistle, waved his arms, and screamed "Get off the tracks! Move! Quick! Get off!" to the young girl frozen to the spot in his path.

Now in her sixties, Marilynn still vividly remembers that warm Friday in the spring of 1946 when she was a high school freshman from Wheaton, Illinois.

She was coming home from her school in Chicago, thirty miles east. And while she usually looked forward to her weekend visits with her family, she was deeply depressed this particular day after learning her favorite Sunday-school teacher was dying of cancer.

Deeply grieved and hurt that bad things could happen to good people, she had got off the train at her station and was walking home, head bowed, nursing her deep grief, oblivious to what was happening around her.

Suddenly she heard the rumbling of the oncoming train. It was almost upon her. Above the roar she could hear the shouts of its engineer. She remembers his terrified face.

Literally paralyzed with fear, she knew the train couldn't stop in time. This train is going to hit me and send me to heaven, she thought. But I don't want to go—not yet.

Then, says Marilynn, "it was as if a giant pushed me from behind. I went flying off the tracks and fell down on the cinders just beyond."

Too grateful to worry about her scratched hands and legs, she jumped up, eager to see who had shoved her to safety. She looked in both directions. There was no one in sight.

"My guardian angel saved my life," says Marilynn. "Who else could it have been?"

This was a story Marilynn didn't tell many people over the years because she didn't want people to think her "strange." But today Marilynn, a mother of two and a retired schoolteacher, confesses, "This event changed my life. It made me want to do something worthwhile ... to be an earth angel."

Recently she opened a shop of angel collectibles in Riverside, California, where she has surrounded herself with visible symbols of her invisible protector—a collection of more than two thousand angels over the years, from figurines to postcards to the seven-foot tree in front of her house that she has pruned and sculpted into angel form.

Every November, Riverside's angel lady organizes an auction locally to raise money for abused children. "I'm combining my love of people with my love of angels," says Marilynn, "and I'm having so much fun doing it."

On the Titanic

Angels were on the decks of the ill-fated *Titanic* to give comfort and reassurance and lend a hand during its tragic sinking in 1912.

Before survivor Michael Joseph of Detroit died at age eighty-four, he often related the story of the unseen guardian angel that grabbed his hand when he was a lost five-year-old on the sinking ship's lower deck and whisked him to a lifeboat!

Recalls his grandson, Brian: "He didn't remember walking. He just felt picked up and put there. It's incredible. To the day he died, my grandfather never forgot the angel that saved his life."

CHAPTER TEN

How to Make Contact with Your Angel

Thousands of happy people are in daily touch with their guardian angels and have no problem making contact any time they want. Others are less fortunate and can spend a lifetime unaware that their greatest ally in life is as close as their own shoulders. Yet anyone can get in touch—actually see and talk with—their guardian angels.

There are a variety of ways of achieving this: During times of crisis, many people are conscious of an inner voice urging encouragement and advice. Some call it personal intuition, good judgement, perhaps just a hunch.

As far as true believers are concerned, you should listen carefully for that inner voice—for it is the voice of your guardian angel.

How many of us have been on a long, monotonous drive and found ourselves dangerously dropping off to sleep? Then, in the nick of time, a warning inner voice prods us awake, often averting a nasty accident.

"There are many incidents like that when we come to our senses and thank our lucky stars," says one researcher. "In reality, we should be thanking our guardian angel."

Saying the Right Thing

"My angel helps me say the right things at the right time. Words just pop into my mouth," says one young

woman, Debbie J., who credits the inner voice of her
angel companion with saving a friend's life.

In this case, the friend was another young woman who
was going through a depressing period in her life and
was contemplating suicide. Debbie reports:

> She called me and during the course of our conversa-
> tion, a thought popped into my mind—if that makes
> any sense. Anyway, before I could really even process
> the thought I found myself speaking it.
>
> Anyway, that thought (an expression of comfort,
> love and friendship) apparently really made her stop
> and think. She told me later that it saved her life.
> When she tried to thank me for saving her life, I told
> her not to thank me, that the thought was not really
> from me. It was from the divine part of myself. It was
> actually kind of cool.

Sensing the presence of an invisible angel in your vi-
cinity is no big deal, say experts. Their presence is signaled by a warm feeling of spiritual well-being and inner
contentment—a feeling of security and that everything
is right with the world.

Some subjects have even detected almost impercepti-
ble movements at the edge of their vision. Others know
their angels as a reassuring inner voice.

When these feelings are strongest it is possible to
make contact with our gentle guardians. Concentrate on
the presence—meditation or prayer techniques can help.
There are even self-massage techniques that can stimu-
late angel contact.

Verbalize your feelings—express out loud your gratitude for that timely warning or feeling of contentment.
There are countless examples of believers who have
done this and established a lifelong dialogue with angels.

Visions and apparitions are commonplace. But most
of us are programmed to react with fear. We have been
taught since childhood to fear the unknown, be it ghosts,
strange noises, or other unexplained phenomena.

Experts do not deny that some spirits can be unfriendly and should be ignored and banished from your mind. But they can easily be detected by a sense of foreboding.

The presence of a comforting angel, on the other hand, is accompanied by a warm spiritual feeling of happiness. In these cases, the entity can be encouraged to identify itself, if we initiate a welcoming dialogue.

Some happy angel believers report making contact with their guardian angels like this.

Many believers I spoke to report having delightful, enlightening conversations with their personal angels, sometimes accompanied by gentle, half-felt caresses round the face and head, neck and shoulders.

Angels also make themselves known to us in our dreams, particularly in twilight sleep when we are only half awake. This is a moment when we are enveloped in a feeling of utter contentment and security. We hear a soft, gentle voice whispering words of support and encouragement that we retain in our subconscious and carry into our waking lives.

Just Ask!

If you really want to find out more about your guardian—just ask! Seriously, try asking questions, out loud, a little bit at a time. Ask your guardian's name and see if you don't get an answer.

If you do—and a lot of people have—then ask more questions, one at a time. You might try forming a question in your mind, along with good thoughts about your guardian, when you go to bed.

Slow down, step back, and retreat from the rat race— these are the first steps for making angel contact, taught by the Rev. Stephen Valenta of Seaside Park, New Jersey, at the parish retreats he holds on the subject. The sixty-eight-year-old Franciscan priest advises members of his flock who are interested in making contact to slow down, relax, and be receptive. "If you've got a tense body, forget it—you can't get a communication," says Father Valenta.

If your angel seems to be elusive, perhaps you don't believe enough. Modern-day skepticism is one of the biggest roadblocks to angel contact.

And too often the strident sights and sounds of everyday life—including the cacophony of radio and television—overwhelms the silence and solitude necessary to open people to spiritual experiences. So make an effort to tune out these kind of distractions before you even try to initiate angel contact.

Go It Alone

Since making angel contact is a very personal experience, you really need to be alone and at peace with yourself to get in the proper frame of mind.

The trouble these days is that most of us fear being alone because we think it means nobody likes us or we're abandoning the people who care about us. But it's very important to your well-being to spend quiet moments by yourself. After all, you are *not* alone—your angel is only a meditative thought away.

People who know how to balance time alone with time spent with others are likely to be healthier mentally and physically. Being alone has gotten a bad rap over the years. People who like being alone are thought by some to be a little weird.

But the truth is that many people don't get enough time to be by themselves—and this can cause stress, irritability, and restlessness. Everyone needs time to be really alone—quality time by yourself without the background accompaniment of radio, television, or even a book.

Solitude will pay off for you if you're anxious to make angel contact. Being alone is the first step toward freeing your mind to focus on spiritual matters, or any other deeply personal subjects you don't think about normally.

That kind of solitude refreshes you. It also gives you a chance to shake off anger, develop a fresh point of view, and ask yourself those questions we all should ask ourselves once in awhile.

"Walks in the woods, along the beach, or anywhere in nature are wonderful ways to get this kind of aloneness. So is riding your bicycle, jogging, or swimming," recommends Dr. Jack Leedy, a psychiatrist at Brooklyn-Caledonia Hospital in New York. "Knitting, wood carving, needlepoint, painting, sewing or other handicrafts are good, too, because they give you something to do while allowing your thoughts to wander."

So start putting aside some quality time by yourself every day. If you work all day, shut yourself in the bathroom for half an hour before starting dinner and meditate in the bathtub. Or enjoy some meditative walking exercise after work. Or set aside some time after dinner to simply sit and gaze out of a window, or contemplate a favorite painting or objet d'art.

Stepping back from your life gives you a chance to have moments of inspiration and relaxation. It will also give you a chance to initiate a dialogue with that guardian angel who has been waiting patiently to hear from you for years.

Learn to Relax Properly

Many people I spoke to revealed that they made their first angel contact when relaxing in bed. Late at night or first thing in the morning, when you are in that warm twilight state, are the recommended times.

But first of all, you must be totally relaxed. Here are five simple stress-relieving exercises, which take just a minute to do, that ensure a proper relaxed frame of mind:

Leg Relaxer: Keep your head on your pillow and your legs extended straight. Bend your right knee into your chest, grasping it with both hands. Hold for a count of ten. Relax and repeat the exercise with your left leg.

Leg Refresher: With your head on your pillow, bring both knees to your chest, hugging them with your arms. Hold the position for a count of ten. Then slowly extend both legs overhead, toes pointing toward the ceiling.

Grasp the back of your thighs with your arms and flex your toes backward toward your body. Hold for a count of ten, then slowly rotate both feet clockwise ten times and counterclockwise ten times.

Bend knees again and bring them slowly toward your chest. Hug your knees for a count of ten and relax.

Full Body Soother: Extend your legs in front of you and stretch your arms toward the headboard, palms up. Now s-t-r-e-t-c-h from head to toe, trying to make yourself taller, for a count of ten.

Keeping your back flat, turn to the left at the waist and stretch both arms toward the headboard, keeping hips and legs still. Hold for a count of ten. Turn to the right and repeat.

Take a Breather: With a pillow under your knees, rest your hands on your stomach and close your eyes. Inhale deeply through your nose for count of three and exhale slowly through your mouth for a count of six. Repeat five times.

Tension Reliever: With a pillow under your head, place your arms by your sides, then point your toes for a count of three and release them for a count of three. Keeping your head on the pillow, raise your shoulders and chest for a count of three. Then relax and take a deep slow breath. Exhale forcefully.

You should be fully relaxed and stress free after these procedures and in the right frame of mind to initiate angel contact.

If you tire easily and tend to suffer from chronic fatigue, these exercises might not be enough. But no matter how worn out you are you can still conquer stress and fatigue by observing a few simple guidelines.

Dr. Susan Lark, author of *Chronic Fatigue and Tiredness*, suggests these stress-reducing steps:

Listen to soothing classical music. This can slow your pulse and heart rate, and lower blood pressure and stress hormones," said Dr. Lark, a Stanford Medical School lecturer. "Tapes of nature sounds, such as ocean waves and rainfall, also work. If you're feeling depressed, try gospel and pop music. Many people find this music improves their vitality."

Breathe deeply. Fatigued individuals often find their breathing becomes shallow and may get out of breath without realizing it, thus decreasing the oxygen in the body causing muscle tension and poor blood circulation.

To develop deep breathing, lie flat on your back with your knees pulled up and your feet slightly apart. Inhale through your nose as you breathe in. Allow your stomach to relax so the air flows to your abdomen. Picture your lungs filling with air as your chest swells.

Then breathe out through your nose. Let your stomach and chest collapse as you imagine the air being pushed out, first from your abdomen and then from your lungs. Repeat ten times.

Relax your muscles. Lie on your back in a comfortable position. Allow your arms to rest, palms down, on the surface next to you. Now clench your hands into fists and hold them tightly for fifteen seconds. Let your hands and body relax for thirty seconds.

Next, tense your face for fifteen seconds. Relax for thirty seconds. Then do your shoulders, followed in order by your back, stomach, pelvis, legs, feet, and toes. Each body part should tense for fifteen seconds and relax for thirty seconds.

Finish by shaking your hands as you imagine the remaining tension flowing out of your fingertips.

Take a warm bath. "It's a great way to unwind," says Dr. Lark. "The warm water loosens tight, constricted muscles and promotes better circulation to the muscles and skin."

And if you can use a hot tub with whirlpool jets, that's even better. "Hot tubs are particularly helpful for people who suffer from insomnia," adds Dr. Lark. "Heat appears to induce brain waves related to a deep and restful state of mind."

To achieve the stress-free state necessary for angel contact, you must make the effort to steer clear of stressful situations. And that includes hanging around with people who cause you stress!

Yes, stress is catching. Anxiety-filled people can easily pass on tension to those around them, warns Dr. Robert Amstadter, medical director of the Center for Psychological Growth and Development in Tustin, California. Fortunately you can ward off contagious stress by following a few of Dr. Amstadter's tips:

If possible, avoid the stress carrier. For example, if you're bumping into the person at the same time and place, like on a bus or at lunch, adjust your schedule to avoid meetings.

Don't allow yourself to get swept up in other people's stress. Remind yourself that their problems aren't yours, and tune them out mentally. You can do that by thinking of soothing images when the stressed-out individual is nearby. Imagine yourself in a relaxing setting, such as a tropical beach or a green pasture. It will set up a psychological barrier against the anxiety.

Try to make yourself laugh as soon as possible after contact with a tension-spreading individual. Keep a joke book handy, have a look at cartoons you find amusing. Laughter is a great stress buster.

Don't panic. When a stressful person mentions a problem that might affect you, check it out and take action if necessary. For example, if an anxious coworker warns you about possible layoffs, ask a supervisor if it's true. If it is, don't fret. Do positive things like updating your resume or going on job interviews.

Do some exercise to relax after dealing with a stress carrier. If you're at work, walk around the block at lunchtime.

Keep your home or office stress resistant with flowers, plants, posters, or pictures of soothing scenes. A relaxing setting will act like an inoculation against someone who's spreading stress.

Another problem that besets people with too much stress in their life is that they don't know the difference between relaxation and recreation. University of Texas psychology professor Paul Silver, explains: "If you ask a person what he does to relax, he may say, 'I go fishing' or 'I bowl.' But that's recreation—and not usually relaxation, although in some cases it can be. Relaxation is a state of mind and body. An activity such as bowling may or may not be relaxing, depending on your state of mind."

For example, if you set unrealistic bowling goals or blow up every time you fail to make a strike or spare, you're just going to stay tense. But you can use bowling—or another recreational activity—to relax if you stop worrying about your performance and instead concentrate on enjoying yourself. For instance, go bowling alone and practice rolling balls down the alley without putting any pressure on yourself.

Here are other ways you can relax, recommends Dr. Silver:

- Watch a sunset. Pick a good viewing spot and imagine all the tension and stress in your body disappearing with the sun.
- Listen to music you find peaceful but not too stimulating.
- Have someone give you a massage with baby oil. You can have soft music playing in the background or just enjoy the silence.
- Take a hot bath and make a production of it. Use bubble bath or bath oil, light the room with a candle, use a folded towel to cushion your head, turn on some soft music, and just stretch out in the tub.
- Calm yourself with visualization. First, block out distractions by taking the phone off the hook, telling your family not to disturb you and, if necessary, using earplugs to block out noise. Then sit or lie in a quiet place, close your eyes, and imagine your favorite scene in nature for twenty minutes. For example, if you prefer the beach, imagine the sound

of the waves on the shore, the wind rustling palm trees, and the cries of seagulls. Try and remember how relaxed you were the last time you went to a beach and you'll start to get that same feeling back again.

If you're uptight and want to loosen up fast, here are three little numbers that will help: 6–3–6. Those are the number of seconds in three steps of a breathing routine designed to relieve stress and relax you.

First inhale slowly through your nose for six seconds, gently hold your breath for three seconds, and then exhale for a count of six seconds. Repeat this several times, and your everyday worries should just melt away.

You might also want to try stretching your stress away. You can shuck off the physical and emotional aches of everyday tension by following these tips from stress experts:

Set the mood for relaxation. Put on soft music and turn the lights down low. Remember, stress reduction isn't just physical, it's also psychological.

Brush stress away all over your body with a soft, dry bath brush, always working in the direction of the heart. But don't brush your face and neck. The brushing will help improve circulation and the pampering will take your mind off the tension.

Breathe your tension away. Either sit or lie flat on your back. Put one hand on your abdomen just above your waist and the other on your upper chest near the shoulder. Breathe out, then in, and feel your lower hand rise as your abdomen swells. Hold your breath for a second, then let it out slowly. Do this five times. Now concentrate on your chest, filling your lungs with as much air as you can while you feel your upper hand rise. Do this five times.

Stretch stress away with one or more of these five exercises. Hold each stretch for ten to thirty seconds.

1. *Start with the calves.* Stand at arm's length from a wall, put your two palms on the wall for support

and put one foot in front of the other. Gradually shift your weight so you're putting more of it on the front foot while you keep your back heel down. Hold the stretch, then reverse your legs and do it again.

2. *Relax your hips.* Stand facing a wall with your arms stretched out to the wall. Keep one foot behind the other and shift your weight forward so it's mostly on your front foot. Put one hand in the small of your back, then flatten your back to get rid of the inward curve. Next, round your back so you have an outward curve.

3. *Relax your neck* by sitting and bringing your chin toward your chest slowly and very gently.

4. *Get rid of shoulder tension.* Stand with both hands clasped behind your back. Without leaning forward or backward, push your arms away from your buttocks as if you're moving them back toward a horizontal position. Most people won't get more than six inches from their buttocks, but every little bit will help you relieve tension.

5. *Stretch your lower back.* Lie on your back, bend your knees, hold both legs on the back of your thighs and bring them to your chest. Keep your shoulders on the ground.

Don't get carried away by trying to do all these stretching exercises at once. Save them for the day you want to completely unwind and prepare yourself mentally for making contact and beginning a dialogue with your angel. And, again, the best way to end your anti-stress workout is with a nice warm bath.

Loosening up your facial muscles can also help you banish stress from your life. Face muscles get involved in every emotion we feel, including stress. People tend to clench their jaws when they're tense. It becomes a habit and even if you're not feeling particularly stressed you will clench your jaw throughout the day, which leads to feelings of stress. And many people who clench their jaws develop tension headaches, the kind that feel like a vise or tight band around the head. This tension can go down into your neck and shoulders too, causing pain and fatigue.

You might want to try this simple three-step technique for relaxing your jaw: Pay attention to your jaw right now. Are you clenching it? Every so often throughout the day check to see if it's tight. If it is, follow these techniques which you can do while sitting at your desk, or in a rest room if you prefer that nobody sees you. You need only take twenty seconds or so for the first two steps, and as long as you like for the third step.

1. Put your lips lightly together and keep your teeth slightly apart. Your tongue should be gently touching the roof of your mouth.
2. Let your jaw drop comfortably. You want to feel your jaw hanging by its own weight.
3. Close your eyes and relax.

Stay Happy

If you are a sourpuss who doesn't find life enjoyable, then your negativity can be a stumbling block toward opening a dialogue with your personal angel. So don't feel guilty about savoring the enjoyable pursuits life has to offer. Pleasure not only makes your life enjoyable—it helps keep you healthy.

The pleasures we're talking about here can be as simple as a midday siesta, low-intensity exercise, good sex—even pleasant fragrances. There's a lot to be said for stopping and smelling the roses.

For example, there is clear evidence that married men and women live longer than single people, and that has a lot to do with their sex life. Good sex bonds men and women together and reduces the impact of certain stresses, thus contributing to good health and a longer, happier life.

Daytime naps or rest periods are also health-enhancing pleasures. Catnaps relax and clear the mind while they refresh the body. In any case, some experts are convinced our biological rhythms are programmed to accommodate a midday rest.

Pleasurable scents can work wonders for your health, as in aromatherapy. People with insomnia, anxiety, panic attacks, back pain, migraines, and food cravings are now being treated with aromatherapy.

For example, some patients with chronic pain are taught deep muscle relaxation while inhaling a peach fragrance. Later, when the pain comes back, the patient takes a whiff of peach—and is able to calm the pain.

Mild exercise is also conducive to a happier frame of mind. This can include simple gardening, such as hoeing, digging, and pulling weeds—which can improve all-around health by boosting the heart rate 25 percent.

Although the idea of napping, making love, taking a walk, or just playing catch with a child seems nonproductive to many in our bustling, materialistic world, they are simple pleasures that can contribute to our well-being and make us more angel-aware.

Other even simpler pleasures, like chewing gum or sucking on a lollipop, help you relax more deeply and quickly, say other experts.

"What works for infants works for adults," says psychiatrist Dr. Leo Wollman, former president of the American Society of Psychosomatic Dentistry and Medicine.

"Put a pacifier into the mouth of a wailing, tense infant and he'll stop crying and become completely relaxed in seconds. Oral gratification works almost as well for adults. Sucking or chewing on something—a lollipop, gum, gumdrop, celery stalk, carrot stick, pickle, or whatever—will help you wind down faster. Sucking or chewing is a natural way of discharging pent-up body tension."

Dr. Wollman conducted research involving 150 anxious men and women. All were told to relax—and half of them were given gum to chew or a lollipop to suck on. Those who received the gum or lollipop achieved a

10 percent deeper level of relaxation than the subjects who didn't, according to equipment that measured their level of relaxation.

What's more, they reached their deepest levels of relaxation 20 percent faster on average. "The bottom line is, if you don't have much time to relax, the best way to mellow out more quickly and efficiently is to chew or suck on something," Dr. Wollman added.

"Whatever leisure-time activity you're pursuing—TV viewing, reading, fishing, gardening, stamp collecting—you'll relax more completely and rapidly with something in your mouth."

So the next time you want to relax yourself to welcome angel contact you might want to keep a lollipop handy!

Keep Stress at Bay

Stress doesn't have to take over your life. You can keep it at bay by following these tips from the experts:

Limit your exposure to stressful situations. For example, if rush-hour commuting makes you a wreck, ask your boss to consider flexible hours. You could come in earlier and leave earlier, which would allow you to work a full day, but avoid rush hour traffic.

Don't make any unnecessary changes in your life. "When you find yourself under a lot of stress, try to keep to your normal routine," says one expert.

Slow down your hectic daily routine and you'll never have to meet stress head-on. The old fable of the tortoise beating the hare may also be true in real life. Being super-fast in your lifestyle has long been equated with efficiency. But that isn't necessarily so. More often than not, haste really does make waste.

When you rush through tasks, you complete them faster but you're also apt to make more mistakes—and when you don't do tasks correctly you're likely to come out a loser.

So slowing down whenever possible can cut down your mistakes and make life less stressful. By slowing down you'll be in better shape to deal with crises and less likely to develop stress-related illnesses.

Here's how to slow down whenever you feel that tension building up:

Check yourself three times during the day, at prearranged points such as noon and the middle of the afternoon. Ask yourself if you're going faster than needed. Are you making mistakes?

If you find that you are rushing, close your eyes and take several deep, deep breaths. Let them out slowly and completely. As you exhale each breath, imagine your stress leaving your body. Do this about five times.

Avoid coffee when you're feeling hurried. Instead, drink water or herbal tea that doesn't contain any stimulants. And don't gulp the beverage down—sip it, savor it, and imagine you're swallowing a little bit of relaxation with each swallow.

Take a short relaxation break. Don't worry about falling behind in your work—after the break you'll be ready to work more effectively and efficiently.

Talking to yourself is another simple, fun way to keep stress away. Simply reciting messages to yourself can help you relax and beat stress.

It's a very simple concept. You repeat to yourself a series of six instructions, explains psychologist and stress expert Martin Shaffer, author of *Life After Stress.*

As you say each instruction to yourself in a relaxed way, observe what is going on in your body. "To perform the process, sit in your favorite chair or lie down on a comfortable bed or couch, in a quiet room. Loosen any clothes that feel tight," instructs Dr. Shaffer.

"Close your eyes. Breathe deeply and evenly as you give yourself each instruction. Each one should take you about five seconds. After each instruction, exhale slowly, taking about five seconds to observe its effect. Repeat the instruction the number of times indicated."

The six instructions are:

1. My hands and arms are heavy and warm. (Repeat five times)
2. My feet and legs are heavy and warm. (Repeat five times)
3. My abdomen is warm and comfortable (Repeat five times)
4. My breathing is deep and even. (Repeat ten times)
5. My heartbeat is calm and regular. (Repeat ten times)
6. My forehead is cool. (Repeat five times)

Dr. Shaffer adds these further instructions:

After you've finished the six instructions, say to yourself, "When I open my eyes, I will remain relaxed and refreshed." Repeat this statement three times without opening your eyes. Before you open your eyes, slowly move your hands and arms about in a variety of directions for about ten seconds. Next, slowly move your feet and legs about for about ten seconds.

Rotate your head slowly, both clockwise and counter-clockwise, for about ten seconds. Finally, slowly open your eyes. The process should take about ten minutes. Practice the technique twice a day. Within a week, you'll experience feelings of heaviness, warmth or lightness as signs of relaxation.

You can use the technique almost anytime and in any quiet place. It is especially good for those who have trouble falling asleep, if they do it right before going to bed.

And it's yet another technique to be used as preparation to get you into an angel frame of mind.

You can also unwind and refresh yourself quickly during your valuable limited leisure moments by observing these tips:

Change your pace. For example, if you're in a highly competitive sales job, you'll feel renewed after a non-competitive activity like fishing or woodworking. If you're in a high-pressure decision-making job, you'll benefit more from "no-brain" activities such as watching television.

Free your mind from work-related concerns. Although worries can keep you from relaxing quickly and completely, here are two techniques that can help you control them:

First, set aside a specific time for worry and try to do it only at the designated time. Second, dump your problems in someone else's lap by sharing your concern with a friend or co-worker, then giving him time to come up with an answer.

Do things that suit you. It's hard to relax when you don't enjoy what you're doing. So join a friend or your spouse only for activities you both enjoy. For example, if you can't stand spectator sports, don't go just to please someone else.

Share leisure activities with upbeat people. It's difficult to completely relax when your golfing buddy is a complainer or your bridge partner is critical of your play. If your leisure time companion is a "downer," find someone else who can help lift your spirits.

Spend quiet time outdoors. At least once a week, find a peaceful spot to sit or lie for 15 minutes while thinking as little as possible. Smell the air, look far into the distance and listen to the sounds of nature.

This weekly outdoor refresher break will relax your body, help you achieve peace of mind—and put you in a susceptible state for angel contact.

Any time you feel as if you're living in a giant pressure cooker, you can melt away stress almost instantly by observing these other pleasurable techniques recommended by experts:

1. Do something with your hands. Performing a simple task, such as tinkering with a car or cleaning out a closet, relaxes you and also makes you feel good about yourself. Just don't take on something so challenging you wind up ever more tense and frustrated.

2. Eat a "comfort food." Choose a snack from a happy time in the past, such as meat loaf like Mom used to make. You'll feel calmer and happier.
3. Sing along with your favorite music when you're home or in your car.
4. Work up a sweat. Rake leaves, go dancing, take a brisk walk through the park. Physical activity is a great way to work stress out of your system.
5. Take a mental trip to a special spot. Close your eyes and imagine you're in the most peaceful place on earth—such as a balmy mountain meadow surrounded by snow-capped mountains.
6. Avoid life's minor hassles. If you're fuming from standing in a long bank line, come back when there are fewer customers—or use the automatic teller machine. If rush-hour traffic bugs you, window-shop until it thins out.
7. Set an 8 P.M. curfew on worrying. If you take a day's problems home with you, you'll wake up stressed—so read a good book, talk with a friend, or do something else to occupy your mind.
8. Recall a past compliment. Sit down in a quiet spot and think back to the nicest thing anyone ever said about you. Savor the wonderful memory for a full minute and you'll feel much calmer and have a renewed sense of vitality.

Okay, now that you're in a relaxed and contented frame of mind, you are likely to ask: Where do I find my angels?

The simple answer is: inside your mind. You are best equipped to open a dialogue with them when you are in this relaxed and meditative state of mind, open to possibility and willing to be taught a higher truth.

How you go about making contact with them is up to you. This can be accomplished through meditation, prayer, talking aloud, asking questions—whatever works best for you.

Remember, method is not as important as motive. Skeptics might want to try by yelling at the top of their voice, demanding a response (which they're not likely to get). Believers might achieve their goal with a sincere, whispered "Hi!"

Also remember, you are not always going to have some kind of dramatic experience. Don't expect a spirit figure with a halo and wings to appear out of a white cloud. Initial angel experience can be as simple as a soft, inner voice—that mysterious small, still voice inside that all of us hear at one time or another. You may not "see" the encounter, but you most certainly will feel it.

The most important first step toward making contact is to simply believe. Communication with angels starts by accepting wholeheartedly the concept that they exist and are all around us. Become quiet and go inside yourself. All you have to do is ask—then sit back and wait. It will come.

According to those regularly in touch with angels, they may appear in many forms far removed from the winged creatures with bright halos we see in paintings (although children and the elderly have sometimes reported seeing this version).

Angels may look like the guy next door, a sweet-faced child, a beloved relative who has passed on; a beautiful man or woman; a bright, unearthly light. Or the experience might be nothing more than a strong and overpowering feeling of love, peace, and contentment.

Frequently, the appearance of an angel is accompanied by a greatly heightened sense of brilliant colors, especially blues and greens—the hues commonly associated with angels.

St. Bartholomew once wrote that angels may appear "trailing wonderful fragrances in their wake." So the unexplained scent of roses or pines in the air—or other pleasurable scents—may be a clue that an angel is nearby.

Even the scents have special meaning. The smell of a rich pine forest is associated with angels on a healing mission, as is the fragrance of sandalwood. But the latter can also mean the arrival of angels with inspirational messages or instructions. Guardian angels are said to radiate a fragrance that is sweeter than a flower garden in bloom.

Angelogists point to three common ways to tell if angels have come calling:

1. If a feeling of calm and peaceful serenity sweeps over you even when nothing is visible.
2. Angels only bring good news, so if you are left with nagging or worrying doubts in your mind, your angel has not come through for you.
3. If you remember with pleasurable clarity what you've seen and felt, and feel that your life is changing for the better, then the odds are in your favor that you've had a genuine angelic encounter.

To help make contact, some angel experts suggest following these steps:

1. Study literature that contains mention of the angels. Familiarize yourself with all the known realizations about them.
2. Keep praying that you will be drawn into an association with one who sees and understands the great ones. Strive to live so that your teachers will seek to become your friends.
3. Once each year, take a pilgrimage into nature and practice sending the angels love, devotion, and receptivity.
4. Every day be eager to feel the guidance and the nearness of the "shining ones." Be grateful for the slightest token of their helpfulness.

Finally, just be aware that you are in the presence of angels and the angels may make their presence known.

CHAPTER ELEVEN

A History of Angels

To better understand the angel phenomenon, it is useful to digest what different angels mean to different people.

But it is nigh impossible, given the countless different interpretations and beliefs, to crystallize the role of today's guardian angels and what they should mean to you as an individual.

These are conclusions only you can reach, based on your faith, your personal experience, and the comforting relationship you have reached with your special angel.

Your own angel is your best counselor as you travel down life's spiritual path. You will, however, find it an interesting exercise to compare your experience with traditional teachings and the experience of others.

Here, for example, is an excerpt from a question-and-answer session at the conclusion of a "Calling All Angels" conference held recently in Orlando, Florida.

Remember, the answers and opinions of the guest speakers (who didn't agree with each other half the time) do not necessarily have to reflect your personal agenda. But you might identify with some of the opinions expressed:

Q: Can angels be seen?

A: Some people say they see angels. Some hear voices. Some see a white light. Some feel a comforting presence.

Q: Are angels former humans?

A: There are no theological accounts of angels as former humans. Most experts see them as separate entities entirely. But some believe that angels can appear as humans in times of need—say, to help lift a car off an accident victim or carry your baggage in a crowded airport.

Q: Does everyone have a guardian angel?

A: We all have a guardian angel assigned to us from birth. They stand directly behind us. Did you ever see something in the corner of your eye, but turn and find nothing there? It was a you-know-what.

Q: If we have guardian angels, why do bad things happen to us?

A: If there is something to be learned from misfortune, an angel will not intervene.

Q: What is the job of angels on Earth?

A: They are messengers who come to protect and love.

Q: Are there different kinds of angels?

A: Yes. There are seven archangels who serve specific functions, such as healing the sick and comforting the sad. There are guardian angels assigned to each human being. There also are cherubims—tiny angels with bows and arrows—whose job is to make us laugh. If you're laughing right now, you're probably being impaled by one.

Q: Can archangels be in two places at once?

A: Archangels have "armies of tens of thousands" that serve as helpers and perform the same functions. Comes in handy.

Q: What do angels want from us?

A: They want us to pray for the world.

Although there have been reports of Archangels in "armies of tens of thousands," guardian angels in today's context bear little resemblance to the warriorlike entities we read about in some parts of the Bible or in classical poetry and literature.

In the Old Testament, angel depictions can be quite fearsome and powerful. In Genesis, they guard the east gates of Eden with flashing swords; in Ezekiel they are four-headed, multi-winged, and many-eyed, overpowering the prophet with awesome visions; in Revelation they do battle with a dragon.

Fast-forwarding a few centuries to the New Testament, we find angels did little to improve their stern image. In even the most tender Nativity stories, we read how Gabriel strikes fear in Mary at the Annunciation and how at Jesus' birth, angels make the simple shepherds quake.

And major poets and writers focused on angels. Thomas Aquinas wrote extensively about them. In Italy, the great poet Dante Alighieri's *Divine Comedy* was filled with vivid images of angels, both good and bad.

The great English poet John Milton spent most of his life writing his masterpieces, *Paradise Lost* and *Paradise Regained*, which explored the mystery of fallen angels and their impact on human history. Milton wrote of a "flaming Seraph, fearless, though alone, encompassed round with foes."

Later, Emanuel Swedenborg, the renowned Swedish scientist, wrote about his celestial encounters that lasted until his death in 1772. Through these visions, he was able to accurately predict future events.

Swedenborg's writings on angels influenced other great thinkers of his time. One of these was the English mystic, poet, and painter William Blake. Poet William Blake's angels were equally stern and tough.

In the eighteenth century, Blake produced some of history's greatest angel art by illustrating Milton's *Paradise Lost* and Dante's *Divine Comedy.* Both the angels he painted and those in his poetry were based on angels he had seen since boyhood. He wrote that he awoke one morning to a vision of innumerable angels chanting, "Holy, holy, holy is Lord God Almighty!"

All the great Renaissance artists painted angels. Fra Angelico, the fifteenth-century Florentine artist, saw angels and then painted these personal encounters. Angelico, who believed his work was divinely inspired, is considered one of the greatest angel artists of all time.

Raphael the artist loved to paint the celestial kingdoms often occupied by Raphael the angel. And the works of Michelangelo overflow with spectacular images of angels. The beautiful ceiling of the Sistine Chapel is perhaps history's greatest example of Michelangelo's angel art.

And the imagination of artists Rembrandt and Botticelli gave us the plump, rosy-cheeked little cherubims.

Islam is one religion that takes its angels very seriously, says David Kerr, director of the Islamic Studies Center at the Hartford Seminary, observing that one of the reasons author Salman Rushdie incurred a death sentence from Islamic Mullahs was by disparaging an angel in his book, *The Satanic Verses.*

"It's difficult to conceive of Christians reacting that way," he says. Angels, Kerr says, seem to be more important in religions in which the god or gods themselves don't get down to Earth much.

The poet Rainer Maria Rilke wrote of the stern angels of Islam in his haunting "duino Elegies" as "distant awesome and terrifying." Rilke writes stirringly, "If the archangel now, perilous, from behind the stars took even one step down toward us, our own heart, beating higher and higher, would beat us to death." Every angel, he declared, "is terrifying."

Scary stuff, eh! Nothing like the gentle, protecting messengers reported in such large numbers today.

These early descriptions were of the strong, mysterious, vengeful, fierce angel figures who dominated the writings and textbooks of our forefathers. Little wonder the belief in angels of such ferocity began to go on the blink three or four centuries ago.

Yet these are the figures that appear time and time again in the sacred scriptures of Judaism, Christianity, and Islam. The same characters also found their way into much of Western literature and poetry.

They don't bear the remotest resemblance to the protective guardian angels reported today in such vast numbers; angels described by AngelWatch founder, author Eileen Elias Freeman as "givers, providers, facilitators—not generals, bosses, commanders."

But according to the Bible that's exactly what the prominent angels were—"generals, bosses, and commanders." The ancient Israelites believed angels to be loyal members of God's heavenly army, sworn to defend God's heaven on earth, who traveled around delivering powerful messages on behalf of the Creator—and spent their free time singing God's praises.

When their assignment was to deal with us common mortals, their judgments could be harsh and unbending, although they were also known to be fair and kind, and generally supportive, in what they deemed to be the right circumstances.

Whether their angel belief is rooted in biblical teachings, classical writings, or the New Age idea of spirit guides, everyone whose life has been touched by an angel will agree with the concept that angels are "messengers from God; beings of beauty, purity and kindness; or guardian spirits."

In the dictionary, an angel is defined as "a celestial attendant of God; one of a class of spiritual beings who, in medieval angelology, were the lowest of the nine celestial orders: seraphim, cherubim, thrones, dominions, virtues, powers, principalities, archangels and angels."

Who are the angels, and who does what? At the risk of complicating a simple, straightforward spiritual look at angels, it is only fair to take time to consider the angels of history, biblical and otherwise.

If the pecking order and their roles seem confusing, you are not alone. For years, religious traditions have been confused and conflicted on who was who and who did what.

For example, in some ancient writings there are two contenders for top angel—Michael and Metatron. Metatron? Personally I don't think Metatron (reportedly created out of the prophet Enoch) qualifies because of his reputed links with Satan. But more about Satan later.

Before you give yourself a headache further researching the role of Metatron in the angel hierarchy, spare a thought for the poor angelologists of the fourteenth century, who believed there were as many as 301,655,722 angels—give or take a few million.

Another Bible scholar in the Middle Ages, St. Albert the Great, figured there were 399,920,004 celestial beings. Jewish tradition puts the number of angels at forty-nine million. Others, including some followers of Martin Luther, put the angel population at around a staggering ten trillion!

An Angel Hierarchy

To simplify matters, here are the names of five popular angels you might want to familiarize yourself with—they're important because they are archangels and crop up most often in angel discussions. They are:

Michael: We know him best as the leader of the heavenly army, the guy who threw Satan out of heaven and the angel you would want on your side when the chips are down.

Michael, which means either "He Who Is Good" or "Who Is Like God," is usually depicted as the warrior angel. Michael was God's strong arm who defeated Lucifer in the heavenly battle, destroyed 185,000 soldiers in the Assyrian army to save Jerusalem, and saved Daniel from the lions' den.

In Jewish tradition, Michael is the guardian angel of Israel. And Islamic lore lauds Michael as the angel of the Last Judgment with "wings the color of green emerald . . . covered with saffron hairs."

Gabriel: Gabriel is God's main messenger, the angel who told Daniel of the coming of the Messiah and, in the New Testament, delivered the messages that Mary and Elizabeth would bear celebrated sons—Jesus and John the Baptist.

In the Islamic tradition, Gabriel is known as Djibril (or Jibril), the Arabic name for Gabriel. He is credited with appearing to Muhammad and dictating the Koran to him, verse by verse.

Some students of angel lore interpret Gabriel as being female—although all angels are depicted by most scholars as either genderless or male.

Raphael: He's a caring, protecting angel everyone

would like to have as a guardian. Raphael is associated with healing and with the general notion of guardian angels. He often is depicted as merry and lighthearted, and particularly caring towards children. Raphael, which can mean either "God heals" or "the shining one," is the angel who healed Abraham of the pain of circumcision and gave Noah medical advice after the flood.

Uriel: Uriel's role is hard to pin down. He's often associated with fire and light, and he's thought to preside over the underworld in some way. Some writers believe that he is the sort of angel from whom you are likely to get very, very tough love. He's very important, and don't make him mad.

Lucifer: Everyone is familiar with this entity, the prodigal angel who got himself turned out of heaven, some say for refusing to play second fiddle to man, God's new creature.

Whatever the reason he landed in God's bad graces, we do know he was expelled and went on to become Satan—or Iblis to the Muslims. Over the centuries, he has come to represent evil.

Incidentally, the -el ending found at the end of many angel names is an ancient root word that is found in several languages and translates as either "of God" or "from God" or simply "God." Other scholars say it can also mean "radiant one," "shining being," or something similar.

Ranking the Angels

As well as coming in all shapes and sizes with specific job functions, angels have a very distinct class system that was put together by the fifth century A.D. scholar Dionysus after extensive study of the Scriptures and other nonbiblical sources. He concluded there were nine classes or choirs of angels, divided into three different "spheres."

In the first sphere are the angels closest to God: seraphim, cherubim, and thrones. The second sphere includes dominions, virtues, and powers. The third sphere, which includes those closest to humans, includes principalities, archangels, and angels.

The *seraphim* are the angels who constantly sing God's praise and whose duty is to regulate the heavens. Lucifer—or Satan—was said to be a much-favored seraphim until he blotted his copybook and went on to become the head of the fallen angels.

The *cherubim*, when they were sent to guard the Gates of Eden, were originally depicted as God's charioteers, powerful beings with four wings and four faces. They have evolved to become those chubby little babies with cute wings.

The *thrones*, often represented as fiery wheels sent out to implement God's decisions, first appeared to Ezekiel in 580 B.C.

The *dominions*, lead the second sphere. Their job—much like the role of angelic bureaucrats—is to regulate the duties of other angels.

Virtues are the angels who manifest God's blessings on Earth, usually in the form of miracles. Also known as "the brilliant" or "the shining ones," they are also associated with acts of heroism and courage, as well as being the comforting entities who accompanied Christ on his ascension into heaven.

The *powers* prevent the fallen angels from taking over the world. Also known as the angels of birth and death, it is their duty to keep the universe in balance.

In the third sphere, *principalities* or *princes* are the guardian angels of cities, nations, and rulers. They guard against the invasion of evil angels.

Archangels, probably the best-known of all the angels, are entrusted with carrying god's most important messages to humans. They also command God's armies in the ongoing battles with the powers of darkness.

Angels, of course, are the celestial beings closest to humans, who act as intermediaries between the Almighty and mortals. It is from this class of caring angels that most people believe our guardian angels come from.

However, for most people today, an angel is an angel, regardless of rank.

And, thankfully, angels are no longer the stern, sometimes sinister apparitions conjured up by the artists and poets of yore. Their public image has softened as we enter the twentieth century.

Literary critic Harold Bloom of Yale University, who has authored a book on angels, *Memory and the Millennium*, says: "Everything that makes angels interesting—their sheer size, their otherness, their menace, their power and, above all, their ambivalence toward human beings—has been eliminated in the current crop of American books."

It's also no accident, then, that today's most important sources of angel lore are not the Bible, but lesser known Jewish, Christian, and gnostic texts written between 200 B.C. and A.D. 200, which take a softer, more cosmic approach to angelic activity.

But it is within these texts, however, that we also find the most vivid accounts of how Lucifer was transformed into Satan and the beginning of the endless conflict between good and bad angels.

Despite their current popularity, angels looked to be on the way out several centuries ago. Like sorcery and wizardry, they just didn't fit into an enlightened generation with a new scientific picture of the world.

"To the cultured elite of that time, believing in angels was like believing that all matter is composed of fire, water, earth, and sky," observes Kimberly Patton, a comparative and historical religion professor at Harvard University.

But deep within their collective psyche, the masses retained a soft spot for angels. So they didn't die out from cultures altogether. And throughout the centuries they gradually became more recognizable as benign messengers and personal protectors who could be called on to give hope in a troubled world.

"Although it is not always appropriate to call them angels, angel-like creatures are present in most of the world's religions," says Professor Patton. "The Koran, for example, says that every soul has a 'watcher' who acts as a compassionate protector and guide."

Reading about the benign role given angels in current Western literature, it is obvious why their popularity has increased in leaps and bounds. Whereas in biblical times, they were primarily relayers of God's messages. In modern times, their other role—that of "guardian angel"—has become fashionable.

"The main reason angels are here is to teach you why you are here," says English theologian Arnold Sprague. "They are here to offer advice, comfort, and wisdom. They are not here to serve some profound intellectual purpose. Their presence in increasing numbers today is all about understanding, to help us understand our inner selves. Their basic message is: You won't feel alone if you believe in angels."

Lest today's organized religions are perceived as trying to put a lock on angel belief, it should be noted that angel lore precedes biblical times, with earliest records dating back to 4000 B.C. in the city of Ur, a kingdom near Babylon. In those days, the role of the angels was as a courier, ferrying messages back and forth between the king and the gods.

Angels know no boundaries when it comes to race or religion. Encounters are just as valid in Christian America and Jewish Israel as they are in Muslim Iraq or Buddhist Tibet.

As Professor Marie Anne Mayeski, Ph.D., a theologian at Loyola Marymount University in Los Angeles, points out: All the major religions of the world—Christianity, Judaism, Islam, and so on—accept the existence of angels. She notes that today's "Angelmania is a sign of our hope that God's saving power is real."

Angels are universal. For centuries they have been crossing cultural and religious boundaries. While Christians, Jews, and Muslims may endlessly debate the significance of angels, adherents of all three religions, as well as Buddhists, Hindus an Zoroastrians, agree that they are real.

Angels were figures to be revered in the ancient cultures of Egypt and Assyria. Ancient Sumerian carvings and carvings in the tombs of the Pharaohs celebrate winged figures from the heavens.

Spirit Guides?

"Angels are reassurance that the supernatural and the realm of God are real," says Richard Woods, O.P., a Dominican priest and an author of books on angels and demons. "They are a reaffirmation of the traditional vision of a Christian world when that vision is under attack."

Retired rabbi, Morris Margolies, author of a book on angels in Judaism, agrees. "We're living in an era very similar to the Maccabean era for the Jews, where disaster confronts us on all sides. People are looking for simple answers."

Perhaps because of biblical references that sometimes depict angels as fearsome creatures wreaking the vengeance of a commanding God, many angel believers prefer to regard their mysterious benefactors on a strictly spiritual level—as spirit guides rather than God-sent umpires.

Even expert Joan Wester Anderson, author of *Where Angels Walk*, agrees that many people look to angels as a gateway to spirituality because they find the Judeo-Christian image of God too threatening.

But angels are not a spiritual end in themselves, qualifies Ms. Anderson. "They really should lead us to God eventually. They are messengers; they are not the message."

As previously mentioned, Anderson's own angel quest began ten years ago, when her college-age son and his friends were rescued from a Midwest snowstorm by a tow-truck driver who appeared out of nowhere.

After announcing his safe arrival, her son, Tim, ran back to pay the driver. The tow truck was nowhere in sight. There was only one set of tire tracks in the snow, Ms. Anderson said, and they belonged to Tim's car.

Skeptics often ask: Okay, if angels are such compassionate, caring entities, why do they not always come through for you? Why do they allow innocent children to perish? Where are they at the time of plane crashes or other disasters?

One simple answer to this is that angels are not here to change destiny, tamper with the course of history, or intervene in the will of a greater power. It's a harsh reality that some things are simply meant to be.

On the other hand, our guardian angels have the power to comfort, to heal, and to protect in certain situations that only they—the angels—deem appropriate. And in other situations we control our own fate—there is little that can be done for those who choose not to hear the wise counsel of that inner voice, which is probably your angel talking.

"Angels are not our bodyguards," ventures Ms. Freeman. "Angels are our spiritual guardians. It's not an angel's responsibility necessarily to stop evil in this world. Why don't *we* prevent those things?"

You, and you alone, have the power to make contact and converse with your own angel. Books like this, panels of experts, seminars, or surrounding yourself with angel artifacts can give you guidance and provide reassurances, but they're not going to lead you to the angel path.

Unfortunately, the current angel phenomenon has given rise to the appearance on the scene of a new breed of spiritual hucksters, New-Age carpetbaggers out for a fast buck who will try to convince you the only way to angel contact is via their commercial enterprises.

I've spoken to people who have actually had mail solicitations for angel dashboard ornaments that guarantee accident-free driving; foods that enable you to get in touch with your angel; and channeled messages from exotically named angels who can dramatically change your life.

Some opportunists have even spawned an "angel zodiac"—which you get for a price. If you were born in May, for example, you can now get your horoscope under the sign of "Gemini," or the angel assigned to that sign, "Ambrial."

Such developments have scandalized the orthodox. Because of this crass commercialism and pandering, not everyone is pleased with the rise of the "modern angel" in popular culture. It was because of this New-Age attitude that conservative Christian groups walked out of a recent World's Religions conference in Chicago. They were displeased that several so-called pagan groups wanted their spirit deities portrayed on an equal level with traditional angelic hosts.

While it is more reasonable to keep an open mind on the subject of angels in general, there is just cause for criticism of those who use guardian angels for everything from divining lottery numbers to selecting which TV shows to watch.

Because of this blatant commercialism, many old-style angel lovers are beginning to ask if the rise in guardian angels is just another fad, like mood rings and the Ouija Board. Of course, the almighty dollar is the root cause of this type of angel prostitution.

So beware. Being able to make contact with your guardian angel is one of the most treasured assets of your life—and it's 100 percent free of charge.

Be on guard too about the psychological effect a too-fervent attitude toward angels can have. Harvard religion professor Patton warns: "There's a fine line between the impression that a loving force is watching over you and the impression that you are controlled by these external forces. Taking it too far can lead to the loss of (personal) responsibility."

Angels Are for Everyone

There's a commonly held myth that you have to be Christian to believe in angels. This couldn't be further from the truth. Angels appear in Christianity, Judaism, Islam, and Zoroastrianism. In Hinduism, Buddhism, Taoism, and Native American religions, there are spiritual beings that are angels in almost everything but name.

For centuries our Native American religions have had their spirit guides, undoubtedly angelic in their ministry. And then there are the wingless angels of the Mormons, who also perform angel-like functions.

It was the angel Moroni who traveled to upstate New York in 1823 to guide Joseph Smith to the buried golden plates that, when translated into the Book of Mormon, became the foundation of the Church of Jesus Christ of Latter Day Saints.

Zoroastrianism, a Persian religion started in the sixth century B.C., also takes its angels seriously. Its supreme god, Ahura-Mazda, is often depicted as a winged being. In his eternal struggle against the forces of darkness, he has a coterie of six archangels and a bunch more angels.

Since most modern verses of the Bible carry approximately three hundred references to angels and most of us first learn about angels through those biblical stories, let's refresh our memories:

Angels and the Bible

THE OLD TESTAMENT

As early as the book of Genesis and the story of the Garden of Eden, we read about the angry angel with the flaming sword chasing Adam and Eve from Paradise, then standing guard at the gate so the recalcitrant pair cannot return.

Later an angel is sent to spearhead the exodus of the Israelites from Egypt, after God tells them, "Pay attention to him and listen to what he says, since my Name is in him" (Exodus 23:21).

We recognize an early mention of the existence of

guardian angels in Psalms 91:11: "For He will command his angel concerning you to guard you in all your ways."

And angels appear in the form of men to Abraham, the patriarch of both Jewish and Islamic religions, and to members of his family. It was an angel who told runaway slave woman Hagar to return to the home of Sarah and Abraham, where she would give birth to Ishmael, patriarch of the Arabic peoples.

When a jealous Sarah banished Hagar and Ishmael to the desert, the angel reappeared to Hagar as she and her son were dying of thirst, and directed them to a well of life-saving water.

A triumvirate of angels called on Abraham and Sarah, when the couple was in their nineties, to tell them they were going to have a child.

Another trio of angels warned Lot and his family of the pending destruction of Sodom and Gomorrah.

An angel, believed to be the Archangel Michael, intervened at the last second when Abraham was about to sacrifice his son, Isaac, as a test of his faith.

Jacob, Abraham's grandson, dreamed of countless angels ascending and descending a ladder to heaven. One came to him in the middle of the night and the two wrestled until dawn.

Angels appeared to many other biblical prophets. Two of the most profound encounters involved the prophets Ezekiel and Daniel, who lived almost a thousand years after the time of Jacob.

Ezekiel had a vision in which he saw the throne of God surrounded by cherubim with four faces. The sound made by their wings could be heard from one end of heaven to the other.

Daniel had a dreamlike vision of angels in which he saw "a thousand thousands that kept ministering to him, and ten thousand times ten thousand that kept standing right before him" (Daniel 7:10). And Daniel was the first to call two prominent angels by name—Michael and Gabriel. Daniel is saved in the lions' den by an angel who held the mouths of the lions closed. And Daniel's three friends, Shadrach, Meshach and Abednego, were rescued from the fiery furnace by an angel who appeared in the midst of the flames.

When King Sennacherib of Assyria invaded Judah, his mighty army camped outside the gates of Jerusalem, preparing to invade and destroy the Holy City the next day. But during the night, an angel went through the Assyrian camp and killed 185,000 of the invaders.

The many references to angels in the Old Testament demonstrates that the earliest Hebrews believed that angels were active in their daily lives. An awestruck Gideon proclaimed: "I have seen the Angel of the Lord face to face" (Judges 6:22).

THE NEW TESTAMENT

Angels are also important figures throughout the New Testament. Gabriel appeared to Zecharia to tell him that he and his elderly wife, Elizabeth, would have a son, John the Baptist, who would be the forerunner of the Messiah.

Gabriel also came to Mary to announce the birth of Jesus. An angel came to Joseph in the night and warned him to flee into Egypt with Mary and baby Jesus to escape the wrath of King Herod.

Following Jesus' ordeal in the desert, during which he resisted Satan's temptations, "the devil left him: and behold, angels came and ministered to him" (Matthew 4:11).

It was an angel that supposedly rolled aside the great stone who sealed Jesus' tomb and was waiting inside the empty chamber to inform his followers of Jesus' resurrection.

In Acts 5:19, after the apostles had been thrown in prison, "an angel of the Lord opened the doors of the prison and let them out."

Another time, when Peter was imprisoned by Herod, bound with chains and guarded by sentries, "an angel of the Lord stood beside him ... The chains dropped from his hands ... They passed through the first and second guard and came to the iron gate (that) opened to them of its own accord" (Acts 12:6–10).

In the Zoroastrian religion, there are the "Fravashis." If the Fravashis don't qualify as angels, what else can we call them? They are bona fide spirit guides whose role is that of guardian spirits who accompany a new-born soul to earth and remain to guide it through life's pitfalls. Sounds familiar?

Perhaps the closest parallels to the angels of Christianity, however, are in the two other great faiths of the Middle East—Judaism and Islam.

The Judeo-Christian cherubim is instantly recognizable as Islam's karubiyun. The Judaic angel of death has a counterpart in Islam's Azrail, "whose eyes and tongues equal the number of the living." If anyone shivers, say Islamic believers, Azrail must be staring at him.

According to the Talmud, the Jewish body of religious laws, every Jew has eleven thousand guardian angels. The Talmud is full of references to angels occupied with tasks both large and small—from leading nations in battle to exhorting blades of grass to grow. In Jewish mysticism, angels fashion wreaths from the words of prayers and adorn God with the crowns.

In Islam, every individual has two personal angels to make careful records of both good and bad deeds. More important, angels are bearers of revelation. It is Jibril (Arabic for Gabriel) who transmits the Koran to Muhammad, reciting it verse by verse. And in legends of his ascension through the seven heavens Muhammad meets exotic angels—one half fire and half snow and others with 4,900 tongues to praise Allah.

The Roman Catholic Church teaches that each of us is assigned a guardian angel at birth who remains always at our side. In the Islamic religion, everyone is said to have two angels—one to record good deeds, the other to keep track of bad deeds.

Angels shouldn't be looked on as ornaments sent to simply decorate our lives. In their essential role a biblical messengers, says Professor Daniel C. Matt of the Graduate Theological Union in Berkeley, California, "They provide a way to protect the pure transcendence of God, while carrying out the divine will."

Although, says Arthur Green, professor of Jewish thought at Brandeis University, "Angels do add color and richness to the spiritual life."

The Dark Side

Although it's not a subject angelogists care to dwell on, there *is* a dark side to the subject of angels.

We're not talking about ghosts here. Ghosts are a different kettle of fish. According to folklore, ghosts are restless human spirits. Dark angels, on the other hand, are corrupted celestial spirits—"fallen angels," if you like.

Hollywood—and the public, for that matter—has been fascinated by evil or "fallen" angels for years, as is evidenced by such popular movies as *Rosemary's Baby*, *The Omen*, and *The Seventh Seal*, all of which delve with relish into the dark side of the angel story.

But can these gentle creatures ever be capable of evil? "Reports of evil angels are legion," acknowledges Eileen Freeman, publisher of the newsletter "AngelWatch," but she says, "I refuse to give them any free publicity."

And no less an authority than St. Paul warned the faithful, in his second letter to the Corinthians, that Satan could be "transformed into an angel of light"— for Satan was once one of the most exalted angels!

Professor Kimberly Patton has also researched this dark side. "The oldest representations are demons. You notice how benign and how cloying some of these contemporary angels are? Well, angels are not always nice. Sometimes they're vengeful. That has been their appeal through the millennia. Remember it was the angel of death that took every firstborn of Egypt in one of the (Passover) Exodus accounts."

The vengeful, evil side of angels undoubtedly stems from the Christian mythology, which holds that demons are fallen angels who were cast out of heaven for defying God. While angels perform only good deeds, demons perform only evil. The most notorious of these is, of course, Satan, the prince of darkness and head of a devilish host.

Satan crops up throughout the Scriptures, but it is in the New Testament that we encounter his true villainy. The New Testament can be read as a war story between Jesus, representing the Kingdom of God, and Satan, as the leader of a Kingdom of Darkness. We read how Satan tempts Jesus. In turn, Jesus drives out devils from those they have possessed. And through his death on the cross, Jesus breaks Satan's hold over the world, but the Devil remains free to tempt the virtuous. And, to that end, Satan is still tempting us.

"In traditional theology, bad angels can take on any form they want," warns historian Jeffrey Burton Russell of the University of California, Santa Barbara, who has written three volumes on the origin and development of the devil.

So don't go around looking for an ugly guy with horns, clove feet, and a tail. Hopefully we should be able to resist and reject him by recognizing his evil intent and banishing him from our lives.

CHAPTER TWELVE

Honky Tonk and Other Celebrity Angels

Famous people through the ages have kept regular contact with angels—from historical greats like Joan of Arc, poet William Blake, Mormon Church founder Joseph Smith, to popular contemporary figures like evangelist Billy Graham, First Lady Hillary Clinton—even Dolly Parton and Elvis Presley.

White House Angels

First Lady Hillary Rodham Clinton has a tiny gold and silver angel-wing pin she wears on days she needs help. Angels are her allies in the White House, protectors and advisors even more important in their own way than her powerful husband.

"She's certain that the positive influence of her heavenly spirits will guide and protect her, Bill, and Chelsea through these difficult years in the White House," revealed a longtime aide. "She has a strong belief in the powers of angels."

A devout Methodist, the strong-minded First Lady often prays to higher powers to guide her. During the tough presidential campaign, recalled an aide, Hillary often found quiet moments to pray. One overheard prayer was, "Dear Lord, be good to me. The sea is wide and my boat is so small."

Says the aide, "I'm certain that this was a plea to her

angels to see her and her family safely through the troubled waters of what turned out to be a very vicious election campaign."

Once in the White House, Hillary continued to draw on her angels for strength as she and her beleaguered husband had to face sex scandal allegations, alleged financial misconduct in the "Whitewatergate" affair, and bitter criticisms of her health-reform plans.

In times of crisis, Hillary leans heavily on her spiritual beliefs, rooted in strong religious convictions she acquired while growing up in Park Ridge, Illinois. One of the powerful influences in her life back then was the Rev. Don Jones.

Now a sixty-one-year-old religion professor at New Jersey's Drew University, Jones led discussions with Hillary and her youth group when she attended Park Ridge's First Methodist Church. Spiritually fueled, she continued to study theology, as well as law, while in college.

It was no idle whim that prompted Hillary to make angels the theme of the White House Christmas tree the family's first year of residence.

Honky-tonk Angels

Call them honky-tonk angels if you like, but many of today's popular country stars are firm believers in the reassuring presence and power of guardian angels. Among them are Willie Nelson, Dolly Parton, Sammy Kershaw, Johnny Cash, and Becky Hobbs.

Down-to-earth Willie is seldom seen without an angel pin in his lapel; Dolly's childhood dreams were shared with her protecting angels; singer-songwriter Kershaw credits his guardians with saving his life at a low point in his life; Johnny Cash has spoken with heavenly messengers; and Becky Hobbs speaks publicly about many truly amazing encounters with her protectors.

HALO, DOLLY

The irrepressible Dolly's belief in angels runs so deep that she even volunteered to play one in an upcoming television series. In the Disney-produced CBS sitcom, "Heavens to Betsy," Dolly has to play a hell-raising Vegas lounge singer who, after a near-death experience, is given a second chance in life as an angel. Unfortunately, the series which was to debut in 1996, was cancelled due to production difficulties.

Angels are still very close to the petite singer's heart. Not only does she credit her personal angels with launching her career, she also reveals she underwent her own life-changing, out-of-body experience.

In her recent autobiography, *Dolly: My Life & Other Unfinished Business*, she recalls her childhood:

> Even if I was sure of my parentage, I still felt like I didn't belong. I was just different and I knew it. A person might think that a kid growing up with that many others would never be lonely, but I often was.
>
> Some kids make up imaginary friends, and I had my own version of that. I called them my angels. I would talk to my angels all the time. I felt safer because they were with me. They understood why I had to sing, why I had such dreams, why I wanted to climb on the wings of a butterfly and wing my way out of the Holler and into a world that I knew lay beyond what I could see.

She says she's been helped down her spiritual path by a circle of heavenly beings who guide her every move and protect her from disaster.

> I dance with them [she says]. They don't have faces, just forms of light, like a string of paper dolls. I do high fives with them, twirl and play tag. I love to shout at the light, rejoice and praise God.
>
> It's like the old shouting and rejoicing in the church back home. I just get overwhelmed by the spirit and the joy of it.

It was at the church she attended as a child that Dolly first discovered she was singled out for a special relationship with God. A local holy woman laid her hands on seven-year-old Dolly in church one day and declared in a loud, clear voice: "This child is very anointed."

> I asked Mama what she meant by that. "You have a mission," she said. "God has placed his hand on you to do some special things in this world, praise him and maybe help people." I took that to heart.

Dolly also claims she got a glimpse of heaven during a remarkable out-of-body experience—and now she can't wait to go back.

"I'm not afraid to die," says Dolly today. "I've seen the afterlife. It's a blissful place filled with peace, love, and light. I live life to the hilt, but I know how wonderful it is on the other side."

The never-forgotten experience happened when she was just thirteen years old. She got into her bed one night and closed her eyes. Suddenly, she saw her body rising above the bed and floating around in thin air.

"I began feeling as if I were rising," the country princess writes in her autobiography. "And it was wonderful. I saw bright lights. I got completely swept up in the peaceful, floating feeling."

Dolly's heavenly experience was so vivid and real that she was suddenly frightened out of her wits that she'd never return to Earth!

"I got scared," she admits. "I jumped up suddenly and I brushed myself off as if I had some spiritual dust on me. But the instant I got up and broke the spell, I was feeling very sorry."

Dolly has a belief in all things supernatural, even ghosts—although she accepts that ghosts are not to be confused with angels.

One ghostly experience in her life occurred when she was a child, shortly after her baby brother Larry died.

The entire Parton family had a ghostly visitation. "The house was locked up and all was still, until we heard someone come in the front door," she says. "Someone, or something, moved around our beds as we lay there listening. Our parents told us never to speak of it to anyone, because it was strange and people didn't believe in ghosts."

SAMMY'S SAVIOR

His guardian angel saved country star Sammy Kershaw from suicide at a particularly low point in his life, when his personal life was in a mess and his singing career was virtually nonexistent.

In fact, Sammy had quit singing altogether and gone into the dry-cleaning business. Then his second marriage landed on the rocks and his business foundered. He was broke and didn't know where to turn.

I went into the boiler room of my shop and put a shotgun to my head. I was going to end it all. Just then the bell went off, indicating a customer had come into my shop, so I went out front.

It was real wild because the woman customer told me, "I don't have any dry cleaning. I was just walking by the store and I felt I had to stop by to see you." And I didn't even know this person!

We talked for a while and then she left. I never saw her again. But she definitely was my guardian angel. I unloaded the gun and never thought about using it again. I owe that woman my life.

Within weeks, the Lafayette, Louisiana troubadour restarted his singing career. And he's never looked back.

COMFORT FOR CASH

Legendary country music star Johnny Cash is also no stranger to angels. The Man in Black is convinced that on three separate occasions in his life he was visited by angels who were sent to comfort him and to deliver messages that certain people he knew were soon to die.

Each message came with the comforting reassurance that the deaths were part of God's plan and that he should not grieve.

In his autobiography, *Man in White*, Johnny describes his first visit, which came when he was a child. A luminous figure, whom Johnny is now convinced was an angelic messenger, appeared to warn him that his beloved brother, Jack, would soon die. Two weeks later, Jack was killed in a freak accident.

"Another time I had the same forewarning of a close friend's death. I called his home the next day—and he had been killed in an auto accident the night before."

Certainly the most dramatic and memorable visitation was when his dead father appeared to him as an angel with words of comfort. The day after my dad died, I visited the funeral home with the family," Johnny recalled. "He looked so handsome in a fine blue suit and burgundy tie." Drained with grief, the singer went to bed early that night. As he slept, his father appeared to him in the guise of an angel.

I was standing in front of my parents' house. A long, bright car stopped at the curb. The car had no driver, but the left rear door opened and my father got out and started walking toward me.

His clear eyes sparkled. They were not covered with the dull film of age I was used to seeing. His teeth were like a young man's, and his hair was full and dark.

"I was waiting for you to come home," I said. I reached out my hand toward him to shake hands. His hand reached out toward mine, and we were only a few paces apart when suddenly a long row of light streamed up from the ground between us.

Then his father spoke: "Tell your mother that I couldn't come back. I'm so happy where I am. I just don't belong here anymore." The light grew in intensity as the vision of his father dematerialized.

The following day Johnny related the dream experience to his grieving mother. "She cried and then she laughed. And we both felt great peace that day," recalls Johnny.

BECKY SINGS FOR HER ANGEL

In Nashville—Music City USA, the heartland of country music—singer-songwriter Becky Hobbs is one honky-tonk angel who firmly believes in angels from an even higher plane.

Noted for her wild, hard-core country style, Becky was so moved by an angel who visited from heaven to save her life that she wrote a song about it that became a smash hit for the country group Alabama.

Becky's celestial encounter occurred on January 14, 1986, which, coincidentally, was her birthday. She recalls:

I'd been having premonitions about a car accident for several months. On my birthday, in the wee hours of the morning, something literally pulled me out into the front yard and told me to look up into the sky.

Then a voice told me, "This might be your last birthday. Be careful." It was the loudest, most booming voice my ears had ever heard. It was overwhelming, but I wasn't afraid of the voice. Somehow I knew this was connected to those premonitions of having a car accident.

The very next day me and my band were on our way back from a show in Alabama. We were at a four-way stop and I looked out to the left side of the van, and there was an eighteen-wheeler just barreling toward the intersection in the rain. At that moment, I knew. I felt the driver's foot go off the brake and I yelled, "Stop!" He didn't see the truck coming at all.

We were hit in the left side and the van was totaled. A split second later and we would have been broadsided; we would have all been killed. I know that 18-wheeler is what I'd been warned about. And I feel that my guardian angel saved my life that night.

Since then, Becky has met others who have had visits from angels, including a terminally ill little girl who says her angel has taken her flying.

Becky also began to write her song, "Angels Among Us," but didn't finish it until she teamed up with Don Goodman after hearing the Jessica Tandy character in the 1991 movie *Fried Green Tomatoes* say, "I believe there are angels among us." The country super-group Alabama selected the song for its 1993 Christmas album and issued it as a single.

When producers of the two-hour NBC special heard Becky's story, they invited her to sing her song and tell her story on the television special, "Angels: The Mysterious Messengers."

"At my shows, people really respond to it. And afterward, a lot of them come up to tell me about experiences with their angels, too," says Becky.

"I've gotten more mail on that song than any song I've ever written," she says, and that includes her Conway Twitty chart-topper, "I Want to Know You Before We Make Love."

Becky isn't involved in organized religion but believes that "everyone has a common thread, and we all have a connection with God. I do meditate. I do believe there are angels among us. And I feel closest to that force when I'm writing."

WILLIE'S ANGEL

Women problems, drug busts, IRS troubles, the tragic premature death of his oldest son and namesake, Willie, Jr.—country superstar Willie Nelson has had more than his fair share of life's problems.

But his belief in angels has kept him bouncing back. Willie is proud to have that guardian angel looking over him—that's why he always sports that small silver angel pin on the lapel of his trademark denim vest.

Willie has also paid tribute to the angel who has helped him through tough times by writing that quintessential Willie Nelson song, "Angels Flying Too Close to the Ground."

His sister Bobbie recently revealed that the angel Willie had in mind when he wrote that classic was his late mother, Myrle.

CHASING ANGELS WITH ELVIS

It's no secret that the late king of rock 'n' roll, Elvis Presley, was fascinated with the unknown. An avid reader, Elvis was continually exploring and studying all aspects of the paranormal and spirituality.

He had a consuming interest in all things esoteric and loved to read up on topics like the UFOs, the mystery of the Bermuda Triangle—and, yes, the existence of angels.

Elvis loved to make a game of searching for answers to these mysteries of life. On one memorable occasion, his former wife Priscilla remembers how he got an irresistible urge to go chasing after angels.

It was around 1966 and the Presleys and their entourage were living at their palatial home in Bel Air, Los Angeles. Priscilla and his other friends were bemused to find Elvis sitting alone in the backyard in the early-morning hours quietly contemplating the heavens, where he claimed he had seen "planets moving across the sky." Writes Priscilla:

> His imagination peaked later on when we were all standing in the yard, looking over at the Bel Air Country Club, which was being watered by a fanlike automatic sprinkler system.
>
> "Do you see them?" said Elvis, looking intently at the course.

"See what?" I asked, ready to hear anything.

"The angels, out there."

"Angels?" I asked, looking down at the sprinklers. I wanted to believe him, we all did and we went along with it.

As if in a trance, he continued staring at the water for a few minutes. Then he began moving toward them. "I have to go," he said. "You stay here. They're trying to tell me something." He wandered off toward the golf course in pursuit of his vision. The rest of us were left dumbfounded.

Hollywood Angels

THE DAY A MOVIE QUEEN MET A REAL LIVE ANGEL

The late screen legend Ginger Rogers was convinced she came face to face with a real-life angel, whose intervention miraculously saved the life of a dying friend.

The guardian angel took the form of a mysterious stranger who approached Ginger out of the blue at Rio de Janeiro airport in Brazil to tell her a young actress friend named Elaine Stewart was desperately ill and needed to talk to her.

A devout Christian Scientist, Ginger raced to her friend's sickbed in a Rio hospital and, thanks to the healing power of prayer, watched as her friend came out of a coma, rallied, and went on to make an amazing recovery.

At the time, Ginger assumed the mysterious messenger at the airport was a concerned family friend. But later the sick friend informed Ginger there never was such a messenger.

The deeply religious former Hollywood screen queen described her brush with the angel—and other miraculous healings she has witnessed—in absorbing detail in her autobiography, *Ginger—My Story*.

Her brush with the angel was like a scene from the

late Michael Landon's television series "Highway To Heaven." She had just landed in Rio de Janeiro when a mysterious young Brazilian approached her in the airline terminal.

"Miss Stewart is asking for you at the hospital," the young man told Ginger before disappearing into the crowd.

Without giving the messenger any more thought, a solicitous Ginger raced to the hospital, where her young actress friend, stricken with peritonitis, was deathly pale in a coma and fading fast.

At the young woman's bedside, Ginger put her lips close to her ear, quietly whispering prayers of healing as taught in the Christian Science doctrine. Her fear and anxiety lifted.

"I looked again at my friend. Though her eyes were still closed, her skin was radiant. Her pale, dry lips were now cherry red. She turned her head in my direction and slowly opened her eyes. 'When did you get here?' she asked in a faint little voice."

Totally recovered, Elaine Stewart visited Ginger in Los Angeles a few weeks later and told her she didn't send a messenger to the airport, convincing Ginger she had a brush with a heaven-sent angel.

Right up until her own tragic death, Ginger was convinced the mysterious stranger was a messenger from heaven—"a real live angel"—who had intervened to help save a friend's life.

"This man was indeed one of God's angels ... after all, the Bible says 'For He shall give his angels charge over thee, to keep thee in all thy ways,'" says the Oscar-winning actress.

Angels, combined with the healing power of prayer, have played important roles in Ginger's life on many occasions—at least twice involving ex-husbands.

When she was a war bride, her marine husband Jack Briggs was plagued with painful, bleeding warts on his feet. Ginger introduced him to a Christian Science minister and, after a few days of prayer and Bible study, the warts that had bothered him since childhood miraculously vanished.

Another ex-husband, French actor Jacques Bergerac, was stricken with a painful attack of boils on his leg and back. Ginger asked a Christian Science minister to pray for him, and the boils drained and vanished completely overnight.

LIFE IMITATES ART

Della Reese is convinced that angels are real—and it's not just because she plays one on television.

The multitalented singer-actress says that heavenly helpers have winged their way to her aid many times.

"I *know* angels exist," she declares. "They're my best friends and have rescued me from dire and dangerous situations many times. They guided me to Dr. Charles Drake in Canada when I needed a brain operation, and helped me survive fires and earthquakes."

Della, who has studied divinity and spiritualism and is a founder of Understanding Principles for Better Living in southern California, also credits her angels with rescuing her from death on several occasions—including the time she had an out-of-body experience as surgeons fought to save her life after she walked through a glass window in her home, and another occasion when she suffered a near-fatal ruptured blood vessel in her brain as she was taping "The Tonight Show."

Della is delighted with her heavenly role in the hot new show, "Touched by an Angel."

I was talking to *my* guardian angels long before the show [she explains]. Angels are God's helpers, sent here to watch over us.

Skeptics think that if they don't see wings, a white robe and a halo then there are no such things as angels.

But angels work in mysterious ways.

There have been countless stories about people who

were helped, rescued, or had their lives saved by mysterious strangers who suddenly disappeared after their good deed was done.

Those are angels.

Keep your eyes open for them, and never doubt their existence, because they are truly real.

DI'S ANGEL CONNECTION

Princess Di's step-grandmother, Barbara Cartland, the world's best-selling author, is firmly convinced there are angels around us—and has actually seen one.

When she was a teenager she was confronted by the vision of "a very masculine-looking angel . . . very much like a drawing of Michelangelo."

She was kneeling in prayer when her angel appeared to her. She describes the experience:

> On the wall in front of me I saw the huge outline of an angel.
>
> His head nearly touched the ceiling and his feet were only a few inches from the floor. He was outlined in light like a line drawing and only his wings had any substance.
>
> He did not move, and his face, which was very beautiful, was turned sideways. I knelt looking at him in amazement for about sixty seconds. Then, slowly, he faded away.

The vision left a vivid impression on the young English girl, now almost ninety, who says, "I can still see that angel just as clearly today."

HIS HIGHWAY TO HEAVEN

Television's all-time favorite angel, the late Michael Landon of "Highway to Heaven" fame, was another celebrity angel believer who had real-life experiences.

Landon spoke publicly how his father came back to reassure him while he grieved his death, even placing a firm hand on his shoulder.

For many years, his "Highway to Heaven" series was one of the most popular shows. In it, Michael played an angel named Jonathan Smith whose mission on Earth was to persuade people to love and help one another.

The idea for that hit series with its positive message was actually inspired by the angels themselves. Michael said the concept came to him after he was stuck in a traffic jam on a congested Malibu freeway one day and noticed the boiling anger of other motorists around him. He recalled:

> I was on my way to pick up my kids and I ran into bumper-to-bumper traffic. Everyone was honking their horns and cursing at each other. I thought it would be good to do a show where people could see how much better and healthier things would be if they decided to go through life being nice.
>
> I began to think what a better world this would be if people put all that energy into being kind to others, rather than into useless and destructive anger. Anger doesn't solve anything. I realized it was time to do a show about people being good to each other.
>
> I believe that people are hungry for kindness—that they want to build far more than they want to destroy.

Thus "Highway to Heaven" was born. Just as his other popular series, "Little House on the Prairie," portrayed the simple nineteenth-century ideal of family values as a cure for complex twentieth-century problems, the subtext of "Highway to Heaven" sought a similar kind of reassurance in a modern-day setting—if we lead a life of righteousness, some kind of divine presence will watch over us.

Angels even sat on creator Landon's shoulder as he

penned countless scripts for the series. "It's as if God is doing the writing, not me," he once said.

> Sometimes I haven't the slightest notion of remembrance that I had anything to do with the writing of them. All of a sudden, it's there. That's the miraculous part about this show to me. It's amazing. It just seems to come from some strange place within."

The show struck an emotional chord for millions of Americans, who inundated Michael Landon with thousands of letters praising the inspiring series. Michael once said of his show, "The show is about little miracles that love can bring about. And this can happen in real life too, not just on TV."

All his life, Michael Landon was a firm believer in the existence of angels and the reality of life after death. His belief was strengthened after his late father communicated with him on the day of his 1959 funeral. He says he also felt his father's comforting hand on his shoulder.

"Ever since I can remember, I've believed in life after death," said Michael. "But when I heard my father's voice it proved that belief in a strong way."

In 1991, as he lay on his own deathbed stricken with cancer, his strong beliefs in a life beyond the grave had not weakened. "As I've drifted in and out of consciousness, I've seen a great white light out there waiting to absorb me," he told a close friend. "I've been given a glimpse of the other side—and it looked wonderful. I know death is not the end—it is just the beginning of a great adventure."

A compassionate and caring father to his nine children, Michael came up with a heart-tugging way to explain to his younger kids why he could not be around much longer. A family friend explained:

> Michael had the little ones watch a few episodes of his "Highway to Heaven" series. Then he told them

God was so happy with the angel he played on TV that he wanted him to come to heaven and really be an angel.

And he told his children he would always be watching out for them. He said to them, "Just talk to me. I'll always be listening." And this seemed to calm them.

Liz's Lifesaving Vision of Light

An angelic light guided movie queen Elizabeth Taylor back from the dead as she lay critically ill with pneumonia in London Clinic more than thirty years ago.

The young superstar later confided to a director friend, Waris Hussein, "I died, Waris. Shall I tell you what it was like? Being down in a long dark tunnel and there was a small light at the end. I had to keep looking at that light. If I stopped, I died."

Elizabeth says that near-death, out-of-body experience has been a source of spiritual strength to her all her life. It's only in recent years that she has talked about it in any detail, explaining:

Nobody talked about these things thirty years ago, because you felt crazier than a bedbug if you did. But I did see the light and the tunnel. And there was somebody who was deceased who was making me go back.

It's extraordinary. So vivid. I wasn't drawing in any oxygen because my lungs were filled with garbage and blood, which I was coughing up. I knew that if I did go into unconsciousness I'd be dead.

So I was fighting to hang on to the brink of consciousness with all my life. Maybe it was just obstinacy, but I did not want to die. And I used every trick in the book to stay alive, to the point of consciously making myself stay awake to keep breathing. That was a deliberate, painful effort.

I suppose in a way it disciplined me. I've had sort of an uncanny ability all my life to be able to pull myself back from the avalanche just in time. I think I'm very realistic.

Elizabeth, who says she stopped breathing four times during that serious illness, also once described her experience at an intimate Hollywood gathering of luminaries, including the late Senator Robert Kennedy. She said:

> Dying, as I remember it, is many things—but most of all, it is wanting to live. Throughout many critical hours in the operating theater, it was as if every nerve, every muscle, as if my whole physical being, were being strained to the last ounce of my strength, to the last gasp of my breath.
>
> Gradually and inevitably that last ounce was drawn, and there was no more breath. I remember I had focused desperately on the hospital light hanging directly above me. It had become something I needed almost fanatically to continue to see, the vision of life itself.
>
> Slowly it faded and dimmed, like a well-done theatrical effect to blackness. I have never known, nor do I think there can be a greater loneliness. Then it happened.

VANNA'S VISION

Popular television "Wheel of Fortune" hostess Vanna White has been in contact with a vision of her dead grandmother—whom she claims appears to members of her family in troubled times. Says Vanna:

> I have had several psychic experiences—for example, knowing that someone close to you is in trouble, or sensing that someone who has died is still, in some way "with you."
>
> Once, when I was in my early teens, I suddenly sat up in bed in the middle of the night and looked across the hall and into the bathroom. There, to my shock, I saw Grandmama staring at me, just smiling. It was very comforting, but frightening.

Vanna is also in contact with the spirit of her dead mother, who died of cancer in 1980. She credits her mother's ghost with inspiring her career. As she told a friend:

> If it wasn't for my mother's ghost giving me advice and building up my confidence when I was scared, I would never have made it.
>
> Mom lives with me and I talk with her all the time. She helps me sort out my fears of failing, or saying the wrong thing. She says, "Don't worry, honey, I'll protect you."

A NEW LIFE FOR RICARDO

Angels have also been working overtime looking after actor Ricardo Montalban, the mysterious Mr. Roarke of "Fantasy Island," who was also selected to play an angel in the syndicated television series, "Heaven Help Us."

But when he turned seventy-two, the once-athletic matinée idol thought his career was all over when he suffered spinal hemorrhaging, which necessitated major surgery and left him without mobility or feeling in his legs.

"I almost wanted to tell the Lord: 'Take me! I don't want to live this way,'" said Ricardo.

He despaired of ever working again until "my own guardian angel"—producer Aaron Spelling—came along. Spelling persuaded the actor to return to the small screen in a new series, playing the part of Mr. Shepherd, a guardian angel guiding the lives of a young couple, played by John Schneider and Melinda Clarke.

At first, Ricardo, who relies on getting around with a walker or a wheelchair while undergoing a painful healing process, was only to play a disembodied voice, not be seen on screen. That way he could record his voice-overs at home while he was recuperating.

But producer Spelling suggested that he expand his role with on-screen appearances. The star's physician urged Ricardo, who had spent most of the year after surgery in bed, to agree. He thought it would help lift his depression.

"My doctor said, 'Do it. The more challenges you have, the better for your mentality.' So here I am," said television's newest angel.

CHAPTER THIRTEEN

Angels and the Near-Death Experience

As death approaches, angels often come to comfort and reassure both the living and the dying. Billy Graham believes that the role of comforter is one of their most important functions. "An angel will be there to comfort us, to give us peace and joy even at that most critical hour," he wrote.

A decade of research and writing on near-death experiences may have paved the way for a new look at angels. Many near-death chronicles, including Betty Eadie's best-seller, *Embraced by the Light*, refer to angel visions.

Cancer patients and their families are continually reporting seeing angels, said the Rev. Percy Randle, director of pastoral care at Seattle's Fred Hutchinson Cancer Research Center.

One family recently reported such an experience. "There was this presence," the Rev. Randle said, "and they looked over in the corner, and there was this angel standing there. Everyone I've talked with has seen it as something positive, not frightening. We all wonder about what's on the other side."

A Phoenix, Arizona woman, who declined to be named, tells the amazing story of an angel who accompanied her dead husband to her hospital room as she was recovering from injuries from the auto accident that claimed her husband's life.

The woman received her first words of assurance immediately after the crash. As she was being extricated from the mangled vehicle, a voice reassured her that everything would be fine.

Drifting in and out of consciousness in the hospital, the woman often saw her husband keeping vigil in the corner of her room. When she told her children that "Dad" had come to see her, they gently broke the news that he had been killed in the accident.

The last time her husband visited, he was accompanied by a splendid creature the woman perceived as an angel. "I think he wanted to see me one more time before the angel took him to heaven," she said.

One graphic example of a suicide victim ordered back to earth by her guardian angel involved Katrina, an overweight woman who became despondent when her husband divorced her. She took a bottle of pills and lost all vital signs.

But when she "died," Katrina found herself in a garden of incredible beauty, lush with tropical plants. A handsome, cloaked man, whom Katrina knew instinctively as her guardian angel, approached her and told Katrina she was going to be sent back to earth. He also told her she would lose the weight she used as an emotional defense mechanism.

"The next thing Katrina knew, she was in a hospital. From that day on she lived fully, losing weight and ending the habits that prevented her from enjoying life," reports writer Arvin S. Gibson, who researched the case.

An Awesome Light

Charmaine Burton says her heart stopped beating for several seconds one bright afternoon not too long ago as she lay in her bed at St. Petersburg, Florida's Edward White Hospital.

Suddenly, an "awesome" bright light appeared on the wall, brighter than the sunshine beaming into the room, yet so soft that it didn't hurt her eyes.

The fifty-seven-year-old woman recognized the face of her long-departed mother as a young woman enveloped in the light.

"It was a very beautiful face, and it smiled lovingly at me, yet it did not speak," said Mrs. Burton. Immediately after the vision of her mother, an angel with curly black shoulder-length hair appeared.

The message I got, even though there were no words, was that I was going to survive. I had no fear. It was such a peaceful, beautiful thing.

This was no delusion. It was a definite experience. I was awake at the time. I have always believed in God and have a desire to be closer to God, but I'm not a fanatic.

Choosing the Hour

Four radiant angels visited Jacquelin Gorman's cancer-stricken mother in the night as she lay dying—and their visitation was so reassuring and inspirational it gave the ailing woman a new lease on life.

Mrs. Gorman, of Manhattan Beach, California, says that when her mother first told about the four angels, she thought she meant her four daughters who had gathered at her bedside for what they were told would be the last twenty-four hours. "But Mother said no, they were real angels," says Mrs. Gorman.

Her mother told her, "Four angels came in the night, and each held one corner of the sheet a few inches above my stomach. They said that I must have faith because there is still some time left.

"It was not a dream. It was not even a vision. It happened, and they were here, as surely as you are standing here right now." Pointing to Danny, the family's golden retriever, she added, "Danny had to shove one of the angels aside last night before he could find a place to lie down. I watched him nudge an angel gently with his nose. The angels told me that God has chosen my time. But He is allowing me to choose the hour."

After the angel's visit, Mrs. Gorman's mother got out of bed. For the next six weeks she lived a full life, enjoying things she'd always wanted to do.

She hosted a dinner party, visited with her little granddaughter, and even went for a boat ride. She passed away six weeks later. Adds Mrs. Gorman:

My mother chose her hour. She was home, sleeping in her bed, holding my father's hand. I did not ask, but I am sure God was somewhere nearby.

And I am surer still, that even closer to her side were those special friends that only my mother and our dog had been granted the privilege to meet, returning once more to reclaim their precious charge.

Those angels were the one positive note in the experience of my mother's death. It made me feel much better about where my mother is, about her faith, and her having made peace with dying.

The White-Robed Priest

A mysterious priest in a long white robe with an embroidered image of Christ on his chest brought comfort to a Michigan woman as she lay near death in a hospital bed.

Edward Bird, of Roseville, Michigan will never forget the comforting stranger who brought inner peace to his stricken wife during one of his family's darkest moments. He recalls:

Last year my wife was rushed to a local hospital emergency room suffering from congestive heart failure. She was near death, and it looked as if only some kind of Supreme intervention could save her.

She was given medication about 8 P.M. that evening, and myself and the rest of the family waited anxiously outside her emergency room cubicle, praying that she would rally.

At around 11:30 P.M. I was told that she had improved and I could go in and see her. I was able to sit by her bedside, and this is what she told me: "Dad, did you see the priest? He was here earlier, and he was dressed in a long white robe and there was an embroidered image of Christ on his chest. He placed his palm on my forehead and told me to repeat a prayer—one that you remembered being taught as a child."

Then the priest told her to close her eyes and said softly, "You are going to be all right now."

As soon as my wife told me this, I asked one of the attending nurses who had called the priest. She and other nurses in that ward told me no one had seen or called a priest. And there were no other persons or doctors in or near the cubicle she was in.

When my wife described the priest and his distinctive robe to the duty nurses, they said they had never ever seen a priest or any other person dressed like that. And they said they would never, ever call in a priest unless the family so desired.

Please believe me. No one in our family saw this person and we were just outside that cubicle. Nor did anyone on the hospital staff that we spoke to.

One person, the admitting clerk whom I know to be a religious person, asked one question, "Who did you think it was?" I replied I believed it was her guardian angel. And she agreed.

Knowing my wife and the condition she was in, there was absolutely no reason she would fabricate that story. I believe she met her angel. A year later, she passed away peacefully—and I believe that she met her angel once again.

Meeting Dead Loved Ones

When she was confronted with a comforting vision of her dear departed grandparents during a near-death experience, a woman named Maureen was faced with a dilemma.

Her grandmother wanted her to stay, while her grandfather urged her to return to the land of the living.

At death's door after suffering a deadly reaction to medication, Maureen felt herself transported to a lovely faraway beach. There, her beloved grandparents approached her, unwrinkled and unbent.

With reluctance, her grandmother finally agreed her granddaughter should go back to this world. And Maureen awoke in the hospital, revived after mouth-to-mouth resuscitation—and comforted in the knowledge she would one day be reunited with her grandparents.

The Gift of Peace

Time magazine and a television documentary have both featured the remarkable story of Atlanta filmmaker Melissa Deal Forth who relates the touching story of how an angel brought peace and serenity to her husband, Chris Deal, in the hours before he died from leukemia.

Melissa had fallen asleep at her husband's hospital bedside during those final hours. At three in the morning she was awakened by a worried nurse. Chris's bed was empty, and he could not be found. After a frantic search, Melissa eventually found her husband sitting in the hospital chapel conversing quietly with a total stranger.

Chris smiled at Melissa and assured her he was fine. The stranger, who remained quiet, was dressed in a flannel shirt, Levis, and work boots.

He appeared to be ageless. "No wrinkles. Just this perfectly smooth and pale, white, white skin and ice-blue eyes. I've never seen that color blue on any human before. I'll never forget those eyes," remembers Melissa.

When Chris returned to his room, there was an incredible transformation. "He was lit up, just vibrant. Smiling.

He didn't have the air of a terminally ill and very weak man anymore," recalls Melissa.

When asked who the stranger was, he replied: "He was an angel. My guardian angel."

Says Melissa: "All I had to do was look at him to know something supernatural had happened. Chris told me his prayers had been answered ... It wasn't a cure, it was the blessing of peace of mind."

His fear and pain banished, and at peace with the world, Chris died.

In Glorious Company

The Rev. Hugh Hildesley, rector of the Episcopal Church of the Heavenly Rest in New York City, had a classic near-death experience when he was under the knife in hospital. He felt his soul rise out of his body and "a pulsing, flowing light of incredible brilliance wash over me. Around me was a community of spirits."

Says the Rev. Hildesley: "They had a message for me—that there is a spirit community and an afterlife. I believe I was in the glorious company of angels and archangels."

She Wasn't Needed

"Go back—we don't need you," Marie Santoro's brother and other angelic figures cried out to her as she floated from her body in a near-death experience during a hospital operation.

She heeded his counsel. The next thing she knew she was back in bed in a hospital bed, with a priest at her side, holding her hand. "You gave us a scare," the priest told her.

Mrs. Santoro's encounter with the beyond came during an emergency operation for a blood clot on the lung in a Pittsburgh hospital almost twenty years ago.

Now in her eighties and a resident of St. Petersburg, Florida, she still remembers the incident vividly. She recalls an eerie sensation of leaving her body and looking down on the surgeon and his assistant working on her.

Then she found herself peering through a tunnel toward a bright light, feeling an overwhelming sense of peace. Inside the light stood her younger brother, who had died nine years earlier. He looked as she had known him in life, except that his feet were hidden in a mist.

She yearned to join her brother and the other beings she could sense were present with him. But her brother turned her away. "You've got to go back!" her brother insisted.

A Pretty Lady Escort

Nine-year-old Nina underwent a near-death experience during surgery, and later recalled her vivid angel experience as doctors fought to revive her:

> I heard them say my heart had stopped, but I was up at the ceiling watching. I could see everything from up there.
>
> I was floating close to the ceiling, so when I saw my body I didn't know it was me. Then I knew because I recognized it. I went out in the hall and I saw my mother crying. I asked her why she was crying.
>
> A pretty lady came up and helped me because she knew I was scared. We went through a tunnel and went into heaven.
>
> I was with God and Jesus, but they said I had to go back to my mother because she was upset. So I went back and woke up.
>
> The tunnel I went through was long and dark. There was light at the end. When I saw the light I was very happy. I still want to go back to the light when I die.

A Visit to Vietnam

Leonor Reyes's near-death experience involved being guided by angels to a beautiful meadow where she was introduced to Jesus. And while she was in her other-worldly state, the angels took her to Vietnam, where her husband David was involved in combat, and there she saw his life being saved by a protective hand!

Her near-death experience began in a U.S. hospital where she was undergoing surgery to remove a growth on her neck.

While on the operating table, Leonor says, "I began rising. I could see my body lying on the table with my neck still open, and my head tilted way back. Then I entered a place where there was total light. Others seemed to be around me."

Then she realized she was in the presence of angels. They told her not to be afraid, that she was going to meet someone who was very special to her.

First they took her to a beautiful meadow where she was met by a figure dressed all in white whom she recognized as Jesus. He told her, "I know you have been tired, sick, and worried. Would you like to come and be with me now?"

Overcome by joy, Leonor wanted to stay at first, but a longing for her soldier husband held her back. She said she was given three choices: She could stay by herself; her husband could join her there; or both could return to the physical world together. The angels then took her to Vietnam and showed her David, who was lying in a bunker on a hill and engaged in combat.

Asked if she had made her choice, Leonor said she wished she and David could return home together. At that instant, she saw a hand reach down over a grenade that had landed next to David.

Suddenly, she was back in the hospital. The malignant growth had been removed and the operation was a success.

Much later, when David returned from overseas, one of the first questions Leonor asked him was if he was ever in a bunker on a hill with another soldier when a grenade fell near him.

"Only once," he replied. "But the grenade was a dud."

A Profound Experience

Dying didn't seem that big a deal to Mary A. as she lay at death's door in July of 1988 suffering from pneumonia and toxic shock.

In fact, she found her near-death experience altogether quite a peaceful and pleasant sensation. She did return to the land of the living, however, to tell her own remarkable story:

"First of all, I found myself outside my body looking at the medical personnel from a vantage point high in the room as they worked on my body. I remember wondering why they were taking my blood pressure. I really felt quite well."

Her disembodied self watched with curious detachment as she saw a nurse go into the hall to call her husband and a priest. Her husband wasn't home. The next thing she knew, she saw her husband eating in a restaurant several miles away. "That's when I said to myself, 'Gee, I must be dying. This isn't too bad at all.' What followed was a feeling of peace and calm—absolute total bliss. Ecstasy. There is no joy on earth like it."

After that, Mary felt herself leaving the earthly plane and found herself floating in a nice, warm, comforting, velvet, soft place. It was very dark, midnight blue, and not frightening. Then, wherever she was began to get brighter and brighter and brighter. She began to move toward the brightest light, but she never arrived at her destination.

"I never did reach the light. I was interrupted," says Mary. "I don't know by whom or what. It may have been my guardian angel or an angel. It was certainly a presence—a nonthreatening presence as diaphanous as a cloud."

She was conscious that she still had a body of her own, but it wasn't her human body. It was an ethereal, spiritual body:

> It was like I could walk through walls if I wanted to.
> I began to feel very aware of myself—but as a very separate individual. I was conscious of the uniqueness of my own being. I wasn't anybody's wife, mother, daughter or sister any more. I was me. I was part of everything else, although I don't think I lost anything of my distinct personality; my individuality.

Mary says she mentally found herself going through a review of her own life, episode by episode, including clear memories of several memorable character-forming episodes from her childhood.

> I wasn't being judged by anybody but myself. But I couldn't fool myself any more. I also gained, for the first time in my life, a total understanding of the universe. All of a sudden, you know what you know is the truth. There is no denial in you.

As she looks back on the experience now, Mary says her greatest impression was of "the tremendous power—the omnipotence" of a supreme being.

When she returned from her otherworldly voyage, she says,

> I actually felt imprisoned in my earthly body. When I was in the spiritual realm, I could be any place at any time.
> But the biggest problem was the impossibility of trying to explain in earthly terms my experiences and feelings about the other world. The profoundness, the depth, of what you experience on the other side totally changes your whole way of looking at things.

The Latest Research

The profound experience of Mary A. is a classic example among the literally millions of astonishing near-death experiences reported every year to professional researchers.

Research into NDEs—the professional shorthand for near-death experiences—has grown into a cottage industry over the last two decades since psychiatrist Dr. Raymond Moody opened the floodgates with his best-selling 1975 book, *Life After Life*.

Since then, the study of the death experience has been taken very seriously by scientists and researchers at some of the world's most prestigious institutions.

But the whole subject—including the role that angels play as guides and comforters in the death experience—is still very much one of countless unanswered questions. Among them:

- Why do near-death experiences sometimes occur when a person isn't near death?
- How much or how little do religious beliefs determine whether someone will have a near-death experience?
- Are NDEs solely a product of American culture, or do they occur worldwide?
- Could they be figments of people's imaginations—dreams, hallucinations, or the like?
- Could they perhaps be visions induced by trauma or drugs, explainable in purely scientific or psychological terms?
- Or are they genuinely transcendent experiences that suggest a fourth dimension of human spirituality that is invisible to the eye, unmeasurable by science, but real nonetheless?

"Worldwide, more and more people are accepting NDEs as a legitimate field of inquiry," says Nancy Evans

Bush, president of the International Association for Near-Death Studies in East Windsor Hill, Connecticut. "We're finding, for example, an increasing number of people in university faculties and graduate students who are really taking a look at different aspects of this."

Ms. Bush, who says she has experienced a near-death experience herself, laments the sensational treatment NDEs often receive from the media and a skeptical public.

"I find it very sad for all of those experiencers who genuinely need to know they are not crazy," says Bush, who is an active Church of Christ member with a master's degree in pastoral ministry and spirituality.

"Everything is culturally colored in some way," says Dr. Moody, explaining, "In India a soul may be greeted by a 'messenger,' while in America it may be by a 'guardian angel.' But because near-death experiences tend to be beyond description, it is little wonder that stories across cultures differ in details, he suggests.

Few researchers doubt that people with stories of near-death experiences are sincere. Clearly, they have experienced something unusual. But a glimpse of the hereafter?

Dr. Michael Sabom, an Atlanta cardiologist who has been conducting an extensive study of near-death experiences beginning in 1976, has examined the accuracy of patients' observations during NDEs and out-of-body experiences.

"I think my work at least brings up the possibility that the accuracy of these experiences in most instances has some validity to it—certainly that the out-of-body part is occurring as they say it is occurring," says Dr. Sabom who authored a book on the subject, *Recollections of Death.*

And what about the million-dollar question: Are NDEs the ultimate proof of a life hereafter? Can we now say with certainty that our souls live on into eternity?

No scientist will attempt a definitive answer to these questions, although Dr. Moody says that new research he is conducting is able to produce visible, audible and tactile images of departed people. And that evidence leaves him in no doubt that there is a plane of existence apart from the three-dimensional world of science and secularism.

Which still leaves the time-honored question, "Is there LIFE after death" in limbo.

As Dr. Sabom cautions, "Yes, we can say there are *near*-death experiences. These people were in the dying process but they didn't die, so they didn't come back from the dead."

Indeed, moments after the visions of tunnels, beings of light and departed loved ones, a person's awareness may be extinguished for eternity. Who is to know?

CHAPTER FOURTEEN

Angels to the Rescue

Dramatic Historical Cases

If you think contemporary angel encounter stories are dramatic and inspiring, consider the following accounts from the past that have found their way into angel folklore.

Throughout history, when the chips were down, you could always depend on angels to come to the rescue at the eleventh hour and save the day.

From the battlefields of Vietnam and both World Wars, back to the Civil War and early historical conflicts involving Joan of Arc and Attila the Hun, the angel presence made itself known.

Here are some of the most vivid and memorable accounts:

An Army in White

Angels played a dramatic role in the Vietnam conflict—in some cases providing a celestial army of bodyguards to protect innocent victims against Communist insurgents.

Dutch historian and scholar H. C. Moolenburgh, in his book *A Handbook of Angels*, relates this truly incredible account of how Vietcong soldiers preparing to attack a remote village sympathetic to the South Vietnam cause were routed by an angel army.

As the attack was preparing to be mounted, the villagers—who all happened to be practicing Christians—fled to a church and began to pray.

"For two days nothing happened," writes Moolen-burgh. "Then the Vietcong slowly went away. A Viet-cong prisoner taken at a later date told how they had not dared attack the village as it had been surrounded by 'a whole army of soldiers clad in white.'"

The Unseen Hand

American GIs were also under the protection of guardian angels.

In 1969 in Saigon, Army Sergeant Jerry Delaney, now a Baptist minister in Fort Thomas, Kentucky, was knocked senseless and thrown into deep swamp water after a grenade exploded next to him.

He remembers later standing at the edge of a brightly lit field covered with golden daisies. He prayed to return to life.

His fellow soldiers watched in disbelief as an unseen but obviously powerful hand swept Sergeant Delaney's unconscious body from the treacherous swamp to the safety of firm ground.

Flying Angels

In the dark, early days of World War II, when tiny Britain was under siege by the invading Nazi air menace, angels came to the aid of the beleaguered Royal Air Force. Angelic presences were even seen in the cockpits of RAF fighter planes, helping dead or wounded pilots continue flying and fighting.

This little-known Battle of Britain air-war story was confirmed by the RAF's Air Chief Marshal Sir Hugh Dowling, a deeply religious man, at a tribute to the heroic pilots in bomb-ravaged London just a few months after the end of hostilities.

At the memorial service, reports U.S. journalist Adela

Rogers St. John in her book *Tell No Man*, Air Chief Marshal Dowling stunned such auspicious guests as King George VI and Prime Minister Winston Churchill when he quietly told of the role angels played in the historic air battle.

For several months, the nation's pitifully small air force was sent to repel the German invaders in violent aerial dogfights over the English countryside and the English Channel. The fighting continued day and night and the British pilots hardly slept. They were losing valuable pilots at an alarming rate and the situation looked bleak.

Dowling told the amazing story how airmen on these dangerous missions were cut down by withering German fire—yet their planes miraculously kept flying and fighting.

Pilots in other planes, reported the air chief, could actually see shadowy figures still operating the controls, even after the pilot had been killed or severely wounded.

The only explanation? Dowling said he firmly believed angels had actually flown some of the planes whose pilots sat dead in their cockpits.

Retelling this incredible story, evangelist Billy Graham wrote:

> That angels piloted planes for dead men in the battle for Britain we cannot prove. But we have already seen from Scripture some of the things angels have certainly done, can do, and are yet going to do as history approaches its climax.
>
> The important question here for each of us is how angels can assist us in our lives here and now: How do they help us attain victory over the forces of evil? What is our continuing relationship to them?

The Mild-Mannered Bodyguard

The mere presence of an angel is enough to deter enemy invaders. The quiet, reassuring presence of a guardian angel protected a small Christian bookstore in Shanghai, China, being looted by invading Japanese soldiers in 1942.

Following the invasion, Japanese soldiers did the rounds of bookstores, confiscating books and literature they considered offensive. One of their targets was the small store stocked with religious books and tracts patronized regularly by U.S. Missionary, the late Dr. L. Nelson Bell, father-in-law of evangelist Billy Graham.

The Christian Chinese shop assistant cringed when a Japanese truck loaded with soldiers and confiscated books drew up outside the store one morning. He feared the worst. The enemy was going to seize and destroy the tiny shop's inventory.

But before the soldiers could burst into the shop, a neatly dressed Chinese gentleman, a total stranger to the shop assistant, entered the shop ahead of them.

For some inexplicable reason, the group of soldiers was unable to follow the well-dressed stranger into the store. For two hours, the soldiers loitered on the sidewalk outside, peering in the glass windows occasionally, but seemingly unable to enter. As they hung around outside, the mild-mannered stranger comforted the distraught sales assistant, praying with him and reassuring him that everything was going to be okay. Eventually the Japanese soldiers climbed back into their truck and drove off. The mysterious stranger then quietly departed the store without giving his name or explaining why he had been there in the first place.

When the shop owner, Mr. Christopher Lee, showed up later that day, the shop assistant told him what had happened and asked him breathlessly, "Mr. Lee, do you believe in angels?"

"I do," said the shop owner.

"So do I, Mr. Lee," said the shop assistant.

Observes evangelist Graham, "Could the stranger have been one of God's protecting angels? My father-in-law, Dr. Bell always thought so."

Death Camp Angels

Guardian angels can provide a protective shield of invisibility—as they did amid the terror and deprivation of a Nazi concentration camp for respected author Corrie ten Boom.

Corrie ten Boom has written extensively of her experiences at the hands of the Nazis at the infamous Ravensbruck prison camp. One of her most dramatic stories relates how angels protected her and others by providing them with a cloak of invisibility.

She tells of entering a camp initiation shed with fellow prisoners where they were stripped of all their possessions, ordered to strip naked—and even had their hair checked for any hidden valuables.

As the prisoners were stripping, Ms. Ten Boom asked one of the woman guards if she might use the toilet, which turned out to be nothing more than a hole in a shower-room floor.

Inside the tiny cubicle, Ms. Ten Boom and one of her fellow prisoners, a woman named Betsie, stripped off their precious woolen undergarments, rolled them up together, along with a little Bible, then concealed the bundle in a corner.

" 'I felt wonderfully relieved and happy," she recalled. "The Lord is busy answering our prayers, Betsie', I whispered. 'We shall not have to make the sacrifice of all our clothes.' "

After showering, the two women joined the other prisoners in the larger reception room, where they donned the shirts and shabby dresses offered to them.

But under her loose, shabby dress, Ms. ten Boom concealed their bundle of precious woolen underwear. It bulged conspicuously underneath her shabby smock, so she prayed, "Lord, cause now Thine angels to surround me; and let them not be transparent today, for the guards must not see me." After that, she felt perfectly at ease.

Calmly, she and her friend strolled past the watchful eyes of guards, who were checking every prisoner. No one was escaping scrutiny. A woman just in front of her had a woolen vest she had hidden under her dress taken from her.

But Ms. ten Boom, despite the obvious bulge, was allowed to pass through. Her friend Betsie, who was immediately behind her, was also stopped and checked.

She is convinced she escaped detection because her angels had provided her with a cloak of invisibility and the guards simply could not see her.

She reached a second checkpoint and again escaped the attention of the menacing and watchful guards. "I knew they would not see me, for the angels were still surrounding me," Ms. ten Boom says today.

"I was not even surprised when they passed me by. And within me rose the jubilant cry, 'O Lord, if Thou dost so answer prayer, I can face even Ravensbruck unafraid.'"

The Angelic Provider

Angels are providers as well as protectors—as U.S. evangelist Kenneth Ware and his wife Suzie found out when they were refugees fleeing the Nazis in war-torn Europe.

As a young man, Tennessee-born Kenneth Ware became an evangelist preacher in Paris, where he married Suzie, the daughter of an orthodox Jew.

After World War II broke out, the Wares sheltered persecuted French Jews fleeing the Nazi witch-hunts. To escape being arrested themselves, the family was eventually forced to escape to neutral Switzerland.

Without funds and stripped of all their possessions, they all but starved. Destitute and hungry, Suzie resorted to this desperate prayer:

God, I need five pounds of potatoes, two pounds of pastry flour, apples, pears, cauliflower, carrots veal cutlets for Saturday and beef for Sunday.

A couple of hours later a stranger came to their door to answer her prayer. Suzie describes him as being over six feet tall, with deep blue eyes and white-blond hair. He was carrying a basket of groceries and there was a glowing aura around him.

"I'm bringing you what you asked for," the man said, emptying his basket of goodies on the kitchen table. Stunned, Kenneth and Suzie looked over the items strewn on the table—incredibly every item was exactly what she'd prayed for, right down to her favorite brand of pastry flour.

As they stammered their thanks profusely to their mysterious benefactor, he just smiled and quietly left their house by the only door. Tears in their eyes, Kenneth and Suzie stood at their window to wave a last goodbye. But the mysterious stranger never appeared on the street!

The White Cavalry of Ypres

One of the most remarkable mass angel sightings is the incredible World War I story of "The White Cavalry of Ypres," a band of angels that came to the rescue of beleaguered British troops at the height of the bloody trench warfare.

As well as being documented in British and German war annals, the story has long been part of European angel lore and was comprehensively written up and translated from *A Handbook of Angels* by a Dutch scholar Moolenburgh.

After a tremendous bombardment offensive which took its toll on the British, a confident German phalanx started moving toward some British trenches to the southeast of the French town of Lille.

The weary British soldiers were bracing themselves for the worst when something peculiar happened. One moment there was the nonstop deafening roar of explosions from the persistent enemy artillery barrage. The next second there was total silence.

Bewildered observers in the British trenches reporting seeing German soldiers fleeing in total disorder. Writes Moolenburgh:

> The British immediately sent out patrols who took a number of German officers prisoner. These men had a bewildered look on their faces and told an incredible story of how, just as they were moving up under cover of their barrage, the Germans suddenly saw an army looming up on the British side, clad in white and riding white horses.
>
> The first reaction of the Germans was to think that new Moroccan troops had been sent in, and they started pumping shells and bullets from their cannons and machine guns into the oncoming force.
>
> Not a man fell from his horse, and then they clearly saw that in front of the army rode a great figure with gold-blond hair and a halo around his head. He too was seated on a white horse (the archangel Michael, perhaps?)
>
> Panic and fear gripped the Germans and they broke off their extremely dangerous offensive.

Amazingly, the army in white was not seen by any of the anxious British troops or their observers. It was only in the following days, when dozens of fresh prisoners were taken, that other accounts confirmed the incident.

Angels of Mons

After the bloody conflict of World War I, more astounding stories of angels at work in the battlefields of the Great War began to emerge.

Typical of these is the dramatic story of the "Angels of Mons," an amazing tale of angel intervention on that famous Belgian battlefield in the early days of the war, around August 27, 1914.

Overwhelmed by superior enemy firepower, the battered French and British troops were retreating—when, out of the smoke and mist that shrouded the muddy field of conflict, an angel came to their rescue.

Descriptions of the rescuing angel varied between British and French soldiers who eyewitnessed the events. But both agreed on one important point: It was a tall man wearing golden armor, riding a white horse, and brandishing a sword.

To the French eyewitnesses, it was either the archangel Saint Michael or Saint Joan of Arc to the rescue. To the British, it was the patron saint of England, the gallant Saint George, they saw, in golden armor, his yellow hair streaming in the wind and his sword held high, crying "Victory!"

Whatever the appearance, it had a desired effect on the enemy. The German offensive eased, giving the exhausted allies breathing space to facilitate their retreat.

To this day it's not clear exactly what effect these battlefield visions had on the enemy, although one post-war German report described the incident thus: "The men were absolutely powerless to proceed . . . their horses turned sharply and fled . . . nothing could stop them."

The stories soon spread swiftly behind the lines. In field hospitals, badly wounded soldiers, some of them dying, displayed a strange inner peace as they described to their nurses the strange events of the battlefield.

One dying soldier spoke of seeing an angel with outstretched wings like a giant luminous cloud appearing in no-man's-land in front of the advancing Germans.

Another spoke of seeing three separate figures, wearing robes of gold and bathed in a white light, appearing on the battlefield between him and the approaching enemy.

At first, these reports were discounted, believed to be the results of hallucinations brought on by battlefield fatigue.

But stories began to filter through from the German side about the same incident. The Kaiser's soldiers said they found themselves "absolutely powerless to proceed . . . and their horses turned around sharply and fled."

Just like the report of "The White Cavalry of Ypres" later in the war, the routed Germans claimed the Allied position was held by thousands of troops—though in fact there were only two regiments there.

Later, it was reported that a severe military reprimand was filed against the German soldiers who retreated for failing to follow through with its offensive at Mons.

Civil War Angels

America's bloody Civil War has produced numerous stories of battlefield angels—including the oft-told phantom army of Confederate soldiers who appeared on the horizon to scare off a superior enemy force about to overrun beleaguered comrades.

Then there's the story of the Angel of the Wilderness. In May of 1864, over a period of only two days, more than five thousand men lost their lives and fifteen thousand more were wounded in bitter fighting at this heavily wooded area, ten miles west of Fredericksburg, Pennsylvania. Union Generals Ulysses S. Grant and George Gordon Meade ordered an attack on the forces of Confederate General Richard Stoddert Ewell at the Wilderness.

Battle lines soon became confused in the brush and woods of the Wilderness. Soldiers found themselves firing on their own ranks, and regiments lost contact with each other in the maze of thick trees.

At the end of day one, little had been accomplished on either side. Both sides retreated for the night, grateful for the opportunity to get some rest. But the chance of sleep was dashed when a new enemy reared its ugly head—fire.

A series of small fires ignited by exploding muskets now erupted into a full-fledged forest fire. Wounded soldiers from both sides found themselves trapped in the wooded inferno, their screams piercing the pitch darkness.

A hasty truce was arranged so both sides could retrieve their trapped wounded. Volunteer squads from both armies met in no-man's-land to rescue the trapped wounded, regardless of the color of their uniforms.

As a young rebel soldier named Private Joshua Bates was tending to one of the wounded in the fiery woods, he heard a loud cracking sound and a tall tree crashed down nearby—trapping the wounded man, Private Bates, and three of his gallant comrades behind a fast-approaching wall of fire.

Escape seemed impossible. The rescuers and the wounded seemed doomed. Still kneeling beside the wounded soldier, Private Bates—a Baptist minister's son from Virginia—encouraged his fellow rescuers to join hands and pray.

"Oh, Lord, our task this night has been a mighty one. We have risked all to save our fellow man. Would you now reward us for showing compassion by committing us to this fiery furnace? We beseech you, Almighty God . . . come to our aid in this time of great need. In your name, we ask. Amen."

Private Bates's impassioned prayer was answered—by an angel. A lone figure appeared beyond the fire. It was a tall man and he wasn't wearing a uniform. He wore what appeared to be a white sackcloth robe.

The figure raised a hand and called to the men surrounded by the flames, "Come out. Hurry! Come this way and bring your wounded brother."

Because the soldiers seemed puzzled and reluctant, the tall figure in the robe again exhorted them to follow him. So Private Bates and his three companions lifted up the wounded soldier and moved toward the mysterious figure beyond the fire.

They hesitated as they neared the flames. Then, all of a sudden, a gust of wind swept up. The wall of fire seemed to split apart. Suddenly and inexplicably, there was a path of about twenty feet wide between the flames.

The five trapped men were able to make their way to freedom. But their white-robed rescuer was nowhere to be found. He had vanished into the fire-engulfed Wilderness!

The strange tale of the Angel of the Wilderness has never been forgotten. Young Private Bates survived the war to become a Baptist minister like his father.

For years the angel who walked through fire to save Joshua Bates and his companions was a subject of many sermons and many prayers.

Heavenly Visitations

There are many documented reports of compassionate angels appearing to distressed American families, some accounts going back 150 years.

In Utah in 1852, a tall bearded man, dressed all in white, knocked on the door of a poor family and begged for food. The elderly stranger was invited in and, although food was scarce, the compassionate family invited him to share their sparse meal—bread, onions, and water.

The stranger ate quickly, then asked the woman of the house how much he owed her. When she declined payment, he said in a powerful voice, "Well, if you charge me nothing for my dinner, bless you and peace be with you."

He strode from the house and miraculously vanished, after promising the family they'd never go hungry again. After he left, the family saw the food—which they had all watched him eat a few moments earlier—lying untouched on the kitchen table.

The angel was as good as his word. In ensuing years, the area where they lived faced great hardship. They lived through periods of great deprivation. But, miraculously, never once did they go hungry. They credited their good fortune to their visiting angel, who tested their love and compassion at a time when the family itself was in a state of need.

A similar incident was reported twenty-two years later, in 1874 in Wah Wah Springs, Utah. Once again, a mysterious stranger with a white beard came calling, this time at the home of the Edwin Squires family. This stranger, too, said he was hungry and asked if they could spare a meal.

The family was strapped for food and money, but kindly agreed to feed the stranger. As he ate, the stranger kept looking at Mrs. Squires, then asked if she was in poor health.

Yes, she said. She suffered from a painful lower shoulder. "Your liver is responsible for that, but it won't be bothering you any longer," the stranger told Mrs. Squires.

And as he rose to leave, he added, "God bless you, sister. You will always be blessed with plenty." He left the house.

True to his word, Mrs. Squires's painful shoulder never troubled her again, nor did the family suffer any more financial hardship. In fact, when Mrs. Squires died at the age of eighty-nine, she left a considerable fortune to her heirs.

In another miraculous, more recent angel visitation, a tall, blond-haired man in a glowing white robe came to a home where a six-month-old baby was dying and couldn't hold down food.

The mysterious stranger instructed the mother how to make baby formula, using milk, cream, and raw eggs.

The mother followed his instructions and, within a week, the baby had miraculously recovered. The family never heard from the life-saving stranger again.

Then there's the classic story of the distinguished Philadelphia neurologist who answered a knocking on his door late one evening to find a small girl, poorly clad and visibly upset, shivering on his doorstep.

She told him her mother was very ill and pleaded for him to accompany her to her mother. It was a chilly, snowy evening, but the good doctor agreed.

He followed the little girl to her home and he entered. The mother was indeed dangerously ill with pneumonia. After arranging for immediate medical treatment, the doctor spoke to the woman, praising the intelligence and initiative shown by her concerned daughter.

The mother looked at him strangely, and said, "But my daughter died about a month ago." The doctor stood stunned, and the mother urged him, "Look in the closet—you'll see her shoes and coat there."

Looking in the closet, the doctor found the shoes and coat. He touched the coat. It was warm and dry. It could not have been worn by anyone that snowy, wintry night.

Angel Saves a Queen

Queen Victoria was a passenger on the British express train from Scotland to London as it raced through the night toward certain disaster.

Peering through a gathering fog into the darkness ahead, the engineer was startled when he saw a mysterious figure in a black cloak caught in the beam of the train's powerful headlights, standing in the middle of the tracks and waving its arms.

The engineer instinctively grabbed for the brake, and sparks flew as the express train screeched to a grinding halt.

The engineer, other railway officials, and Royal bodyguards jumped from the train to see what was wrong. They saw no sign of the mysterious man in black.

But less than one hundred yards further up the track, they were horrified to find a bridge over a swollen river had been totally washed away. If it hadn't been for the timely warning, the train would have plummeted into a watery grave.

After the bridge and length of track was repaired and the train continued to its destination in London, a full investigation was launched. And, incredibly, the mystery of the mysterious figure in black was solved.

Plastered on the glass of the train's headlight was a huge dead moth. When the light was switched on, the dead moth appeared as a phantom figure in black, arms outstretched. This was the "mystery man" who raised the alarm, concluded investigators.

The moth must have flown into the train's headlight seconds before it was due to reach the washed-out bridge. In the darkness and fog, its image in the beam appeared to the engineer as a warning figure.

So the image the engineer saw in the headlight was not an angel. The express train had been saved by a fortuitous accident of nature.

But when Queen Victoria was told of the strange occurrence, she did not accept it as a lucky freak of nature. The venerable monarch remained convinced that their lives had been saved by angelic intervention. She was convinced the moth had been placed on the lamp by an unseen protective force.

"I'm sure this didn't come about by some accidental freak of nature—it had to be God's way of protecting us," said the wise queen.

Missionary Miracles

These two missionary stories of protective angels' intervention—from two different but equally reliable sources—show clearly the strength and scope of guardian angels.

A band of angels was responsible for a remarkable miracle in the heart of a Brazilian jungle, saving the lives of a missionary group about to be slaughtered by a group of hostile tribesmen.

The Rev. David Keller, an Episcopalian priest in Phoenix, Arizona, likes to tell the story of the Brazilian jungle angels, told to him by a close friend.

His friend was part of a missionary group that years ago ventured into a remote Brazilian jungle to convert a tribe that had already killed one religious team.

There was still a distinctly hostile atmosphere when the missionaries encountered tribesmen on a hillside, where it appeared the Christians would be slaughtered. After a few tense moments, however, the natives mysteriously retreated—obviously in fear. The tribe later converted to Christianity. Some time later, one of the first converts was asked why the missionaries had not been killed on the hillside that day.

"Why? Didn't you see them?" he replied incredulously. "They were everywhere!"

Nevertheless, the Anglican Church has no clear doctrine on the subject, says Rev. Keller. "You will find people within our fellowship who believe in angels in the literal sense, and those who do not," says the minister.

"My own personal belief is that guardian angels don't protect me, but my awareness of God's presence can protect me in the sense that, the more aware I am, the more of life I will see."

And evangelist Billy Graham likes to recount this eerily similar story involving Rev. John G. Paton, a pioneer U.S. missionary to the New Hebrides Islands.

Paton and his wife found themselves threatened by hostile natives who surrounded their mission headquarters one night. Unable to escape, the couple spent the whole night in the mission chapel. As dawn broke, they were both relieved and amazed to find the threatening tribesmen had dispersed. They credited their good luck to the power of prayer.

It was some time later that they discovered the true reason for their salvation. After a tribal chief had converted to Christianity, Rev. Paton quizzed him about the night of the threatened attack. Why, he asked, had the natives retreated?

"Because of the army protecting your home," said the chief without hesitation. Taken aback, Rev. Paton told the chief that only he and his wife had been present that night. No, the chief insisted. There were hundreds of big men in shining garments also present, standing guard with drawn swords protectively surrounding the mission!

Angels and Attila

Attila the Hun's fierce warriors were at the gates of Rome in 452 A.D. and it looked as if nothing was going to stop them from pillaging and sacking the Eternal City.

The Roman legions had capitulated and nothing stood between the Huns and the destruction of Rome. The night before they were due to make the final attack, Pope Leo went to Attila's camp, pleading with him to spare the city.

After Pope Leo's visit, for some strange reason Attila withdrew, and Rome was saved. Some historians have speculated that his mysterious retreat was due to a plague that unexpectedly swept through the Huns' camp, weakening Attila's men.

But other historians say the real reason Rome was saved is because Attila was scared to death of the "two shining beings with flaming swords" he reported seeing standing alongside Pope Leo during the Pontiff's last-minute mission of mercy.

Angels in Space

A band of seven winged angels, who appeared to be hundreds of feet tall with wingspans as wide as those of a jetliner, shocked a group of space scientists when they glided past their orbiting space laboratory.

Six cosmonauts aboard the former Soviet Union's Soyuz 7 space station witnessed the miraculous appearance of angels on two separate occasions.

The incredible sighting happened in the 1970s, but it wasn't made public until 1985, when one of the Soviet space scientists defected and revealed details of the miraculous encounter.

The sighting was so mind boggling that the so-called godless communists of the former Soviet Union kept the story under wraps for more than a decade. It bears witness that angels may appear to anyone regardless of religious background or beliefs. Russian cosmonauts Leonid Kizim, Vladimir Solevev, and Oleg Artkov had been orbiting Earth for 155 days when a band of angels miraculously appeared outside their spacecraft.

They were working on routine medical experiments when suddenly they were almost blinded by a brilliant orange light that appeared outside the orbiting space laboratory.

For a few seconds they could see nothing as their eyes adjusted to the blinding light. Then, according to the reporting scientist, they saw "seven giant figures in the form of humans, but with wings and mistlike halos as in the classic depiction of angels. They appeared to be hundreds of feet tall with a wingspan as great as a jetliner."

For about ten minutes, the group of smiling angels floated slowly alongside the Soyuz spacecraft as the three Soviet cosmonauts stared at them open mouthed. Then the angels—described later as round faced and cherublike—vanished.

Stunned and embarrassed, the three scientists could not believe their eyes. They convinced one another they had been hallucinating and decided to keep the amazing sighting to themselves. They decided not to tell their companions, or enter the incident in their official log.

Twelve days later, the same seven angels reappeared, again floating alongside the space lab, smiling at its stunned occupants.

This time round, three more cosmonauts witnessed the

incredible sight. One of them, cosmonaut Svetlana Savistskaya, reported later:

We were truly overwhelmed. There was a great orange light and through it we could see the figures of seven angels. They were smiling as though they shared a glorious secret.

CHAPTER FIFTEEN

More Tips for Making Contact
And Other Angel Miscellany

While eliminating stress and anxiety from your life is an important step toward achieving angel contact, once you have mastered these relaxation techniques you can develop other simple tricks to encourage an encounter.

Angel experts and a whole host of other believers have developed their own special methods, which I'd like to pass on. Here are a few for your consideration:

Try to Act Like an Angel

You don't have to be some kind of mystic or have special paranormal gifts to make contact with your angel. Being the best you can be is good enough.

On your journey through life, try and stop from time to time and think how your angel would behave in a given situation. For example, your angel would never be rude in a restaurant or impatient with a child. Nor would you expect to find your angel argumentative, bad tempered, or otherwise mean spirited.

Since angels sometimes choose to speak to us through our thoughts, isn't it a good idea to always be thinking good thoughts? So accentuate the positives in life and become more considerate in your thoughts, words, and actions. If you make a conscious attempt to clear your mind of negative emotional debris, you'll find it easier to access your personal angel.

That's not to say angels are unavailable for those among us with cluttered or troubled minds. Remember, angels are the most forgiving of entities. When they're most needed, they will always be there.

Look for the Unexpected

Angels could be relaying messages to you on a regular basis—but you might be too skeptical or too preoccupied to recognize the signs.

Wise words might pop into your mouth, profound thoughts might leap into your mind—and you think, "Hey, aren't I clever!" You could be taking credit for your angel's spontaneous wit and intelligence.

Angels can convey their messages in other ways. It could be a phrase you hear on television and radio that you can't get out of your mind, words from a song that keep running through your head—even headlines from a newspaper or a passage from a book.

Watch for these signs and try to analyze them. It could well be that someone is trying to get through to you, trying to tell you something.

Don't worry too much about getting crossed or wrong signals. If the messages or signs trouble you or cause you grief or worry, ignore them. You can rest assured they are *not* from an angel.

Phone a Friend

Many people say the best way to contact an angel is just to sit yourself down on a comfortable chair and make believe you are phoning one of your closest friends for a chat. Invariably, the angel line is open. And this is one person who will never hang up on you.

Angel expert Susan Scott, a lecturer for Astro Soul, an organization that presents workshops on how to get in touch with guardian angels, consults with her angels every day and compares making contact to a telephone call to a friend. She even consults her angel for help with shopping lists and figuring out the quickest way home from the supermarket.

"They speak to us all the time," says Susan, who says that clues to their nearness are often signaled by chills, tingles, or goosebumps. "That's angels trying to let you know something."

The Violet Light

Everyone has their own special method of making angel contact. A member of the Angel Encounters forum on Compuserve, Chris W. prefers to meditate. He describes what works for him:

> I know that we all have guardian angels that try to help and protect us at all times. I now meditate on a daily basis, and I openly communicate with what I believe is my own guardian angel.
>
> One of my biggest challenges has been to learn patience. I do not get all the answers that I want when I want them. And these answers never come as directly or boldly as I might prefer them to be. But eventually, and subtly, I do get answers.
>
> In my meditations I have learned to identify my guardian angel, and my own heightened state of relaxation, by the emergence of a pinpoint of violet light as I stare into the darkness of my closed eyelids. The light gets bigger and brighter as I become more and more relaxed. After a while, as the violet spot fills my whole inner horizon it begins to sway, pulsate, and flicker like a flame.
>
> It now happens the same way every time I meditate, only the rich and luminescent violet has most recently been accompanied by another spot of lime green. Sometimes the two colors pulsate like alternating stripes before my inner vision. When I get really deep

they begin to flicker and vibrate, and I feel like my whole body begins to vibrate too.

Sometimes in this state I can ask questions and get answers, other times I feel like all I can do is be in the moment. Most of the time I feel like I am being told to slow down, be patient, or to just be more observant in the passing moments of each day. Generally, I feel like I ask too many questions, and want to know too much too soon.

Nevertheless, I am grateful for being able to experience this—whether it is simply my higher self I have come in contact with, or if it is in fact my guardian angel (I prefer to believe the latter), I am a happier, warmer person for it.

The Pendulum

Psychologist Joe W. says a serious approach with good intent is essential for anyone setting out to make angel contact. He offers this advice:

I think that prayer is a good idea. Ask whoever guides you to assist you in your efforts. State what you want to do and mean it. State that you will only talk with forces that are of "God" or of "good," however you want to define the term.

I believe if you approach this type of thing seriously, with good intent, then you have no worries. I have used the technique with patients and college students for years and have had no problems.

There is also "the pendulum approach." Essentially, the idea is to take a piece of string (sewing thread will do) and tie a paper clip to one end. Hold the string with the thumb and forefinger of your hand.

Place the point of your elbow on a kitchen table with the paper clip hanging like a pendulum over a cross hair drawn on a piece of paper. Do not intentionally move the string and do not stop it from moving as it begins to swing.

Ask the pendulum questions as though it were another person or a guest in your home. First ask which way it will swing to answer "yes," then ask which way it will swing to answer "no."

"You will probably be surprised to find out that the paper clip seems to swing of its own accord, as though someone else were swinging it. The force that swings the string is probably another side of yourself.

If you interact with this side of yourself as though it were another person you will find that it can answer a great many questions. Some with truth, some with no truth.

If you asked me if we were all going to die tomorrow, I could give you an answer. That doesn't mean that I know what I am talking about. So too with the string.

From my perspective as a psychologist, I think that you will be talking with what we often refer to as the sub-conscious, unconscious, or subliminal self. In a very real sense, this "side" of you is protective and much like what people refer to as a guardian angel. Try it; you'll like it.

Be Open and Receptive

Antonia C. Palumbo also believes the most important rule when trying to access your guardian angel's energy and love is to be open and receptive—but, above all, state your intent. Says Tonia:

At first you may not get anything but if you keep trying, I guarantee it will happen.

Remember to be open and receptive to their love and energy. Also be open and receptive to any strange or weird thought or happening. (This may be difficult as we are so used to shutting out or ignoring all kinds of stimuli.) It takes practice to begin noticing your thoughts, but it can be done.

In many cases, you won't get an answer the way

you expected. It may come as some kind of sign, or symbol, even a thought or a coincidence. For example, you might be given the name of a book to read. Or a book might fall at your feet. Or you might reach for a book on impulse, or receive a brochure unexpectedly in the mail.

As for me, after my initial contact with my angels, I saw angels everywhere—advertisements, on television, in magazines, in songs with the word angel in them. I talk to my angel all the time these days. But the first contact I made happened in a dream state or while I was in a semiawake state. Now I communicate with him/her while meditating, while driving to work, and so on—it gets easier as you practice.

There are times you might feel it's just your imagination at work, that you are making up these answers or messages that you get. And that is okay, because a lot of times our angels talk to us through our imagination.

Another way I access my spiritual guides and/or angels is through automatic writing. Sit quietly with a pen and a piece of paper. Clear your mind and ask to communicate with them. And then just write down what comes. At first it may be gibberish—but you will be surprised at all the good information you will get.

This is also important—keep it fun and light, and don't get *too* serious. I find that when I am happy I am the most receptive.

Sometimes it is necessary to enter a deep meditation or to be able to go into an altered state of consciousness to make contact.

What this simply means to me is clearing one's mind of the chatter or thought debris that is constantly going on in most of our minds. Unless you are able to get quiet, you won't hear an angel speaking to you.

What I do is use a key word or phrase to get me in that clear, quiet state of mind, which I have kind of hypnotized myself into doing after much practice.

And when I need for my mind to be quiet, I simply

say that word or phrase, either aloud, if possible, or in my mind. Believe me, it works.

When I meditate, I simply sit in a comfortable position, sometimes with a crystal I like in my hand. I may light a candle. Then I find I can quiet my mind and I simply ask my guides/angels to communicate with me if they have something to tell me.

Or if I am meditating on a specific issue, I ask mental questions about the issue. One of my most favorite meditations is when I imagine getting into a cocoon of light shaped like an egg and I then fly to this beautiful temple that I call the temple of light, where my guides usually meet me.

I imagine the temple full of flowers, trees, a babbling brook, huge marble pillars. I either just float around taking all the beauty in, or I imagine my guides around me in a circle giving me loving energy or a big cosmic hug. This takes a little practice.

What you can also do is quieten your mind by playing soothing music. I have a cassette that I use called "Music for the Angels," which is wonderful.

Automatic Typing?

If you are not into automatic writing, why not try automatic typing? That's what angel believer Will Burns uses sometimes to make contact with his angels. Here's Will:

I do the automatic writing technique with my computer, although any word processing program will do. Just type. And type. Try to type faster than you can think. Don't worry about missed keys, and don't try to comprehend what you are writing, as this will only slow you down.

Just type and type. Then, when it slows down, go back and read it. I've done this many times to great amusement and, more importantly, great insight. Good luck.

Angels with Green Thumbs

Dorothy Maclean is one of the world's most offbeat gardeners—she talks to her plant's angels to find out what it takes for the plant to flourish and stay healthy.

Dorothy is a sort of psychic gardener who twenty years ago helped found the gardening community of Findhorn in a Scottish sandpit, and proceeded to make flowers and vegetables grow in a spot where experts said it was impossible.

Today she has a worldwide reputation as a gardening expert and lecturer. She's even written books on how she communicates with the spirits she calls angels or devas—a Sanskrit word meaning "shining one."

Basically, she enters into a meditative state, tunes into say a cabbage plant, and the cabbage plant's angel tells what she should be doing with the soil to make it grow.

3,600 Reminders

Los Angeles artist Jill D'Agnenica has won herself a reputation as kind of the Johnny Appleseed of angels.

For the last couple of years, Jill has been scattering angels all across the neighborhoods that were ravaged by the 1993 riots.

In April 1994, on the first anniversary of the turmoil, she distributed four twelve-inch-tall plaster magenta cherubs at a prominent African-American church.

And she has continued to set the brightly painted angels on street corners, at bus stops, on walls, in parks, atop trash piles and in empty lots, always ten to the square mile—1,000 in all so far, with 3,600 more to go.

"The experience of seeing an angel, or even more important, when word gets out, the act of looking for an angel, would remind each person of their place in the City of Angels," says Jill

Footprints

Here's a favorite poem among angel believers. It's been around a long time and no one seems to know its origin:

> One night a man had a dream. He dreamed he was walking along the beach with the LORD. Across the sky flashed scenes from his life. For each scene, he noticed two sets of footprints in the sand; one belonged to him, and the other to the Lord.

> When the last scene of his life flashed before him, he looked back at the footprints in the sand. He noticed that many times along the path of his life there was only one set of footprints. He also noticed that it happened at the very lowest and saddest times in his life.

> This really bothered him and he questioned the Lord about it. "Lord, you said that once I decided to follow you, you'd walk with me all the way. But I have noticed that during the most troublesome times in my life, there is only one set of footprints. I don't understand why when I needed you most you would leave me."

> The Lord replied, "My precious, precious child, I love you and would never leave you. During your times of trial and suffering, when you see only one set of footprints, it was then that I carried you."

Angels in Seattle?

One of the strangest angel encounter stories in recent times is the weird tale of the Angels in Seattle.

When I first heard the story in October of 1994, I was fascinated, determined to track down sources for more detail. I heard it from several reliable angel believers. It went thus:

Angels were being seen in and around the city of Seattle—as hitchhikers! And they were causing all kinds of consternation by telling motorists who picked them up that they had been sent to warn of an impending disaster in the area—a devastating earthquake, to be exact.

Hmmm, they didn't sound much like angels to me. More like prophets of doom. But since the reports were filled with such geographical detail, I decided to investigate further.

The first report was that angels were appearing to commuters "on the 520 floating bridge on Lake Washington and also on the 15 corridor coming into Seattle." And they were warning motorists to stay out of Seattle because an earthquake was going to occur.

A second report went as follows: "Some of these beings (who were posing as hitchhikers) have appeared and spoken with different officers of the Washington State Highway Patrol. All of the beings made the remark: "Get ready—the trumpet is at his lips." Then the beings completely disappeared without a trace.

By this time the strange case of Seattle's hitchhiking angels was being discussed feverishly on on-line computer services. It was also reported discussed on a Seattle talk radio show. And reports of other sightings in California and on the east coast started to come in.

I really began to smell a rat when one of my informants told me it had been the subject of a news bulletin on a local television newscast. This time the hitchhiker/angels were supposed to have warned that Mount Rainier was going to erupt, melting snow and ice, thus causing serious flooding.

Sources in Ohio, Texas, and Florida began to report the same alarming story—although this time the hitchhiking angels were in their state.

One message I got read, in part: "In all of these cases, the person (or angel to me) was hitchhiking and when picked up they would start chatting and suddenly say, 'The trumpet is to his lips' and then completely vanish. The drivers in all these reported cases started weaving in traffic because of astonishment. Some of them were stopped by the police, highway troopers, etc. because of erratic driving, or they went to a police station to make a report, whereupon they were told by the authorities that several people had already been in and reported the very same type incident, and that the person/angel had also said the same thing."

Then a West Coast on-line computer buff sent me this Associated Press clip from a local newspaper:

Drivers Say Angels Warning
Of Rainier Eruption

TACOMA (AP)—Angels have joined the lineup of other worldly phenomena offering wisdom, warnings, and mystery from the slopes of Mount Rainier. The latest spate of rumors has angels warning hikers— none of whom have come forward with first-person accounts—that a major Northwest earthquake and eruption of Rainier are imminent.

"It's one of the many rumors we have every year," said Glenn Baker, spokesman for Mount Rainier National Park. "We're a veritable haven for rumor-mongering."

The angel reports started in September, Baker said. The account has ten hikers on Mount Rainier encountering an angel who told them the 14,410 foot mountain would erupt Friday and urged them to warn people in surrounding lowlands, he said.

"We have no information that would lead us to believe Mount Rainier is going to have an eruption in the near future," said Anthony Qamar, state seismologist with the UW seismology lab.

Angels aren't the first alien beings to buttonhole people on the mountain. Here's a rundown on some of their predecessors:

- The first modern sighting of Unidentified Flying Objects, reported by private pilot Kenneth Arnold on June 24, 1947, occurred on a flight over Mount Rainier. The sightings spawned the term "flying saucers."

- Tracks of the sasquatch reportedly have been found on Mount Rainier. Major E. S. Ingraham, an early mountain explorer, wrote in 1895 of a non-verbal chat with a pointy-headed, human-like creature—subsequently dubbed the Old Man of the Crater—inside a cave on Mount Rainier.

- Angel stories, like the others, involve alien creatures, notes William R. Seaburg, a linguistic anthropologist and professor of American Indian studies at the UW.

- "It seems to me that for some people it's important to create a non-human entity," Seaburg said. "It's boundary setting. It helps define being human."

- "It sounds like urban legend," he said. "You can never quite track down an actual person approached by the angel."

Thus ends the strange story of the Angels in Seattle, which I include here to emphasize that angel research is by no means confined to the inspiring and relatively benign accounts found elsewhere in these pages.

So, sure there are some angel accounts that have no basis in fact. Suffice to say this is the only one I came across!

Seasonal Angel Thoughts

Here are excerpts from the Rev. Sean O'Sullivan's inspiring Christmas message as published in the *Miami Herald* on Christmas Eve, 1994. Father O'Sullivan is director of substance abuse prevention for Catholic Community Services of the Archdiocese of Miami:

SEE THE ANGELS AROUND US
There are not too many angels at this time of the year,

walking the streets of big cities such as Miami, New York, and Dublin. In fact, you could say that alienation and despair are prevalent along the highways and byways of our teaming metropolises.

It is a commonly known fact that some people hate Christmas. Maybe they remember times past, when they were happier, their families were intact, or they felt more loved and successful than today. Or maybe they feel like a neglected minority and cannot identify with the omnipresent, dominant cultural and religious symbols of the season.

In the classic movie *It's a Wonderful Life* (1946), which we enjoy each year at this time, Jimmy Stewart plays a marvelous role as the small-town hero, George Bailey, who is plunged into depression and a suicidal despair at Christmas. Life has turned to ashes. He no longer enjoys his family, his friends, and his quaint little town of Bedford Falls. He wanders the streets of the town with a heart as dark as the swirling black river that beckons to him.

It is with similar dark and surly thoughts that Ebenezer Scrooge faces his Christmas season as portrayed in Charles Dickens's famous story, *A Christmas Carol*. Scrooge's cynical view of humanity reflects the emptiness of his own soul. His hatred of the season with its lights, jingling bells, and joviality prompts him to coin the now-famous Christmas put-down: Bah, humbug!

However, Christmas is quintessentially a season for conversion. The Greeks used a beautiful word for this process, and they called it metanoia. It means that we are called to have a change of heart, to be more spiritual, to pray, to practice altruism. Christmas challenges us to put aside our animosities and hatreds, our deep-seated unhappiness at the hand that life has dealt us, our bigotry, our prejudices, our racism, our stinginess, and our grasping avarice, among other things.

This is the lesson that George Bailey learned, and old Ebenezer Scrooge, too. Both found liberation from their loneliness, fear, and despair by undergoing a metanoia, which led them back to the light, sanity, and joy that was their salvation.

But what is truly amazing to us, sophisticated and

skeptical people, is that the change of heart in these two famous characters was accomplished through the intervention and help of angels. George Bailey was helped to negotiate the torturous maze of his soul by Clarence, an angel; Ebenezer Scrooge, on the other hand, depended on scarier, more ghostly interventions to help him see reality as a spiritual phenomenon in which altruism is rewarded by joy and peace.

Angels obviously exist and are powerful beings, who come from on high when we are befuddled but only if we call out in prayer and ask for their help.

This is the message of Sophy Burnham's *A Book of Angels*. Jesus, Jacob, Moses, Abraham, and Mohammed were all ministered to by angels. And someday, perhaps, when one of us is ill or in deep pain in a hospital, a char-lady may enter the room at just exactly the right moment to help; she will become our angel.

The religious philosopher Joseph Campbell, in his book *The Power of Myth*, helps us to understand that angels are archetypes in the Jungian sense. They make us aware of how strongly interconnected we are, because of our spiritual nature and how we find our deepest roots in God.

Now, it is quite clear that Santa Claus and Kris Kringle are angels. This is the story of both versions of *Miracle on 34th Street*. These delightful movies point out the danger of the rampant commercialism, conspicuous consumerism, and the unbridled avarice emptying Christmas of its spiritual content. How can an empty shell of commercialism inspire anyone to virtue?

Plato, writing 2,500 years ago in *The Republic*, saw the value of myth in molding people, especially children, to pursue altruism, virtue, and respect for others. This is the real challenge of Christmas: to reach out to the stranger, to respect others' cultures, and to seek an appreciation of their sacred symbols.

Our communities would be happier places if we followed the true spirit of Christmas. Non-Christians would feel less culturally and religiously isolated if they could see their sacred symbols displayed in public places, too. Why not have these two great religious symbols of our faiths, the creche and the Menorah, stand side by side in public parks and shopping malls throughout this land during the Christmas season? Now, that would make the angels sing!

Dialogue with an Angel

Brother C. Patrick Gardner, F.S.C., who teaches at St. Joseph's Collegiate Institute in Buffalo, New York, shared this wonderful account of a dialogue he had with his guardian angel about the world's first Christmas with the *Buffalo News* on Christmas Eve, 1990:

> I was seated in my easy chair dozing just after dinner on Christmas Eve when the thought entered my mind. Of all the times it had never occurred to me to ask him, I resolved that at the next opportunity I would do so.
>
> Since we have been companions for many years, the opportunities to talk together have been innumerable. I must say that over the years I have availed myself of these quite regularly. Most of our conversation pieces have been about routine matters. He is and has been most concerned about my safety, health, physical and spiritual well-being in general. Several of these chats in particular I recall very well.
>
> Many years ago I chided him on his lack of vigilance in my regard. On that occasion, I was lifted off a fire hydrant on our street, over which I was draped, and taken to a nearby hospital with a broken arm. He argued that his vigilance had been circumvented and rendered useless by an extra long crotch in the overalls that I was wearing. In attempting to jump the hydrant, while playing a game of follow-the-leader, the crotch of my new overalls caught on the top of the hydrant. My arms swung wildly over the far side, the elbow of my right arm giving way upon contact with the hard

surface of the hydrant. Even to this day I believe he chuckles a little when he recalls the spectacle of an eleven-year-old impaled on a fire hydrant.

I have tangible proof he was at my side several years later when I was taken sick in the terrible postwar epidemic of flu. He kept a constant vigil beside my brother Willie, who cried at my bedside all through the crisis of my sickness. Though I didn't see him, I knew he was there. I was in a coma most of the time but I recovered. I have always been most grateful to him and my brother for their solicitude.

It would be difficult to repay him for all the help he gave with the realization of my vocation. There were some difficulties and obstacles to be overcome at the time I announced my intention of entering religion. The objections, mountainous and insurmountable, vanished as soon as he entered the picture. For all his help, I am eternally grateful to him.

But, here he is now. I'll put the question to him immediately. He'll wonder too, I suppose, that I never thought to ask him before this. "I have a belated question for you," I said as I returned his greeting with a wave of my arm.

"And just what is it?" he asked in his usual jubilant tone.

"On that first Christmas night, two-thousand years ago, were you with the angels that appeared on the hillside of Bethlehem and sang 'Glory to God' to the delight and consternation of the shepherds?" I asked.

"Surely," he said "I was one of the legion of angels that filled the hills of Bethlehem with joyous singing on that first great night."

Then he detailed for me the many happenings of that holy night. He told me how the angels accompanied Mary and Joseph from inn door to inn door. How they had to restrain themselves from appearing to the human eye when the gruff innkeepers refused to give them lodging. Had not God the father ordained otherwise, the angels would have appeared sooner and forced the innkeepers to admit Mary and Joseph. It was difficult for them, he said, to hold back rejoicing and singing until the time determined by the Father.

It was shocking to see the indifference and callousness of men.

His radiance and brilliance seemed to increase and sparkle when he began to tell how they appeared on the hillside of Bethlehem to the simple shepherds. All of us, he said, burst the stillness of the quiet night with our exulting song of praise. The shepherds were startled and fearful at first. When they realized the import of our message, they hurried over the hills to the stable at Bethlehem. Some delayed but a minute to pick up a gift of food, clothing, or linen. As husbands hurried in quick pursuit of the angels, housewives hastily wrapped bread, dainties, and warm coverings and prized cloths into portable bundles.

My Guardian Angel told how he turned and saw a small boy hurrying after the rushing crowd. The lad's short legs were not equal to the strides of his elders. He fell repeatedly and was crying bitterly lest he be left behind. My angel swooped down, took hold of the lad by the collar and placed him in the front rank near the crib of Our Savior. The angel described the amazement of the child's mother when she beheld him at the crib before all others. The excitement kept her from asking him how he ever got there at all. My angel is of the opinion that this little lad grew up to be the Zacheus we read of in the New Testament, the man of low stature who climbed a tree to see Our Savior passing by. He wasn't too sure of this, however.

"Yes! What is it?" I asked as I woke, startled by some strange noise.

"Brother Superior," said Brother John, who had just entered my room, "the brothers and boys are all in the chapel ready for Midnight Mass."

"I must have dozed and slept," I answered. "Tell the brothers, boys, and the good angels I'll be there for Midnight Mass immediately."

Becoming One with the Angels

As a footnote, here's a message from New Age researcher Patricia Jepsen Chuse that makes a lot of sense to me:

As we include the angelic kingdom in our conscious awareness, we will begin to understand what miracles are all about. This means we are not separate. We are not to see ourselves living separately from the angelic kingdom, but one with.

It would not surprise me if we saw a broken leg restored, a misshapened hip straightened. Not because we are going to do anything, but because we have included the angelic consciousness, their gifts and their faculties within our own consciousness.

This is something new. It is the presence of angels *in our own consciousness* transferring their gifts through us! The angels live in grace. They are grace. And we are invited into that land *as one being.*"

Reprinted by kind permission of Crystal (Patricia Jepsen Chuse) of the University of Melchizedek/World Mother Center, 1994.

Bibliography

Books

Graham, Billy, *Angels: God's Secret Agents*
Moolenburgh, H. C., *A Handbook of Angels*
Parton, Dolly, *Dolly: My Life & Other Unfinished Business*
Presley, Priscilla, *Elvis & Me*
Pruitt, James, *Angels Beside You*
Ramer, Andrew, *Ask Your Angels*
Rogers, Ginger, *Ginger—My Story*

Newspapers & Magazines

Akron Beacon Journal, Oct. 10, 1992, Oct. 9, 1993
Albany Times Union, Sept. 19, 1992, April 24, 1993, June 25, 1994
Arizona Republic, April 12, 1989, Nov. 18, 1992, Jan. 2, 1994, Sept. 3, 1994
Anchorage Daily News, May 15, 1994
Atlanta Constitution, Feb. 5, 1994, Oct. 21, 1994
Baltimore Sun, April 19, 1992, Nov. 25, 1993
Boston Globe, July 7, 1991
Buffalo News, Aug. 21, 1994
Chicago Tribune, June 6, 1993
Dayton Daily News, Oct. 1, 1994
Enquirer, Jan. 12, 1988, Feb. 23, 1988, March 29, 1988, April 19, 1988, May 24, 1988, Sept. 13, 1988, Jan. 10, 1989, May 30, 1989, June 6, 1989, Aug. 22, 1989, June 19, 1990, July 3, 1990, Jan. 22, 1991, Feb. 19, 1991, Nov. 5, 1991, March 31, 1992, Jan. 26, 1993, Feb. 28,

1993, Dec. 28, 1993, April 21, 1992, June 16, 1992, Sept. 1, 1992, Oct. 11, 1992, June 14, 1994, June 25, 1994

Examiner, June 2, 1992, Feb. 3, 1993, June 28, 1994, Dec. 6, 1994

Ft. Lauderdale Sun Sen, Jan. 5, 1992, Nov. 11, 1994

Hartford Courant, 1994

Kentucky Post, March 18, 1992

Ladies' Home Journal, Dec. 1992, Dec. 1993

McCalls, Dec. 1990

Miami Herald, Dec. 16, 1994, Dec. 17, 1994, Dec. 23, 1994, Dec. 24, 1994, Dec. 25, 1994

Newsweek, Dec. 27, 1993

New York Daily News, Nov. 15, 1994

Orlando Sentinel, Aug. 26, 1989, June 7, 1992, Dec. 24, 1993, Jan. 14, 1994

Palm Beach Post, Oct. 23, 1992

People, April 11, 1994, May 17, 1993

Phoenix Gazette, July 1, 1988

Redbook, Dec. 1992

Seattle Post-Intelligencer, Oct. 2, 1990, June 2, 1991

St. Petersburg Times, July 3, 1994

Tennessean, May 24, 1994, Nov. 24, 1994

Time, Dec. 27, 1993

USA Today, April 11, 1990

Wall St. Journal, March 12, 1992

Washington Post, July 7, 1981, Aug. 21, 1993

Weekly World News, Aug. 17, 1993